DIALOGUES
WITH
KOHELET

Other books by T. A. Perry:

Art and Meaning in Berceo's "Vida de Santa Oria"

Léon Hébreu, *Dialogues d'amour:* Edition and Commentary

Erotic Spirituality: The Integrative Tradition from Leone Ebreo to John Donne

Santob de Carrión, *Proverbios morales: A Critical Edition*

The Moral Proverbs of Santob de Carrión: Jewish Wisdom in Christian Spain

Wisdom Literature and the Structure of Proverbs

T. A. Perry

DIALOGUES WITH KOHELET

The Book
of
Ecclesiastes

Translation and Commentary

The Pennsylvania State University Press
University Park, Pennsylvania

0257880074

Library of Congress Cataloging-in-Publication Data

Perry, T. Anthony (Theodore Anthony), 1938–
    Dialogues with Kohelet : the book of Ecclesiastes : translation
and commentary / T.A. Perry.

    p.   cm.
    Includes bibliographical references and index.
    ISBN 0-271-00882-2 (alk. paper)
    1. Bible. O.T. Ecclesiastes—Commentaries.   2. Bible. O.T.
Ecclesiastes—Language, style.   I. Bible. O.T. Ecclesiastes.
English. Perry. 1993.   II. Title.
BS1475.3.P47   1993
223'.8077—dc20   92-16256
                                                                              CIP

Printed in the United States of America

Published by The Pennsylvania State University Press,
Suite C, Barbara Building, University Park, PA 16802-1003

It is the policy of The Pennsylvania State University Press to use acid-free paper for
the first printing of all clothbound books. Publications on uncoated stock satisfy the
minimum requirements of American National Standard for Information Sciences—
Permanence of Paper for Printed Library Materials, ANSI Z39.48–1984.

To Joshua,
who at age thirteen coined the term "interactive prophesy"
and studies it with passion,
these dialogues are interactively and lovingly dedicated.

Contents

Preface

For two and a half years the House of Shammai and the House of Hillel argued over whether it is good for man to have been created. The former maintained that it would have been better if man had not been created and the latter held that it is better that man has been created. They finally decided that it would indeed have been better if man had not been created, but that since he has been created it would be best for him to scrutinize his deeds.

—BT Erubin 13b

The purpose of this translation, with its accompanying introduction and commentary, is to suggest that the Book of Ecclesiastes—in Hebrew "Kohelet"[1]—is structured as a transcript of a debate such as the one reported to have occurred between the Houses of Hillel and Shammai. Whether the contenders in this debate can be precisely identified is, strictly speaking, a historical rather than a literary matter, and given the dearth of such information one may prefer, rather than the historical Houses of Hillel and Shammai and the "rescued speech" of their meetings,[2] to read the alternation of sharp opinions as teaching techniques between teacher and student, or as a literary dialogue on the Platonic model, or even to imagine the text as an interior dialogue.[3] The reader's task in any case is to identify and sort out the ever-shifting and conflicting voices or points of view that constitute the entire text of Kohelet.

Such a dialogic reading of Kohelet has good accreditation, for "already in the patristic period different 'voices' in the book were heard: for example, Gregory the Great saw Solomon dialoguing with a fool or a knave."[4] Indeed, there are those who insist that the title "Kohelet" means "Collector" (Cohellector!), referring to his activity of gathering

1. I reserve this title for the literary work and designate as "K" the persona of this work often referred to as "Kohelet."
2. Fishbane (1979), paraphrasing Plato's *Phaedrus* (275c–d), has expressed the view that the Bible records the "rescued speech" of the meetings between God and man (xi).
3. This seems to be what Crenshaw (1987) calls a monologue: "Although Qohelet does describe an opponent's views, which he proceeds to alter in some way or to expose in toto, the book represents a monologue rather than a dialogue. Qohelet exposes the debate within his own mind" (29). Ibn Ezra had already noted this technique (on 9:8, referring to the change of narrative voice to the "you" in Koh 9:7–10): "This is the speech of one's heart, as if he is talking with himself."
4. Murphy 1990b:263. For partial approaches to a dialogic reading of Kohelet, see below, page 189, note 6.

and bringing into contact many different wisdoms and opinions and thus, as is quite possible, views dissenting from his own.[5] In the same spirit one can view the so-called pious Presenter, K's admiring antagonist in the debate, as yet another collector, that is to say, as the one who both assembled K's original sayings and attached his own critical commentary, in imitation of K's own method (cf. 12:10). The image of canon that emerges would thus be rather different from the rigid and monolithic one usually assumed: the sages *and their interpreters* would then both constitute the final or received text.

The enormous difficulties involved in the interpretation of Kohelet are obvious upon reading current translations of the work. The main obstacles are not philological or conceptual—although these are formidable enough—but literary. Such problems are not unique and certainly not peculiar to Kohelet: the Mishnah offers a reasonable parallel. In both works straight reading is impossible, and the student is soon entangled in the shift and interplay of argument, constantly asking: Who is speaking now? Which previous point does this agree with or contradict? In his recent translation of the Mishnah, Jacob Neusner presented a brilliant solution to the literary condensation of his text by typographically separating out the different voices of the argument so as to make them distinct and to clarify the sequences. I have attempted a similar solution for Kohelet. As previously mentioned, critics have long acknowledged various voices of dissent—termed "contradictions"—throughout the text, but such perceptions have never been applied methodically to the work's literary structure and genre. By identifying the main voices and with the help of typography, I have tried to sort out the dialectic of the text and to charter its main arguments. In my reading, the two voices that explicitly open and close the text, those of P the Presenter and K or Kohelet, conduct a sharp debate from start to finish, emerging as fully fleshed-out characters: K as the man of experience and P as the man of faith.

It is best to admit one's prejudices at the outset. Mine are literary, and though it is no longer necessary to justify literary approaches to Scripture, it is good to be as clear as possible about specific problems and methods. The most resistant obstacle in the interpretation of Kohelet involves contradictions, the clearest example being the "pious" conclusion on fearing God and keeping His commandments (12:13), which

5. Crenshaw (1987, 34) wonders whether the word "Kohelet" could also apply to the gathering of objects, in which case the name might designate a "collector of proverbs." In somewhat the same spirit, Ibn Ezra (on 7:2) cites the opinion (which he rejects) of "one of the commentators" according to whom "the work was written by Kohelet's students, each of whom spoke according to his own understanding." Thus, according to this commentator, Kohelet would represent a collection of limited but differing opinions.

seems out of step with K's call to pleasure and his complaints on the vanity of creation. Such contradictions have come to be seen as embarrassments, especially when the goal of interpretation is a smooth text, one devoid of contradiction and having a fixed meaning—what Barthes calls a purely classical text.[6] According to such a method, one is encouraged to explain away as many semantic dissonances as possible—by calling them, for example and with scant justification, quotations or redactional glosses—and then to perform surgery on the recalcitrant remainder.[7] Even more radically, one may rewrite or "paraphrase" the received text in harmony with one's own theological bias.[8] In my view, however, wisdom texts such as Kohelet have as their goal not the occlusion but rather the promotion of sharp or strong (thought-provoking, contradictory) readings, and their upshot can be seen in their practice of whatever makes the text truly plural, again in Barthes's sense: midrashic reading (already "authorized" by tradition and applicable even to the Torah and Prophets), a high sense of literariness (irony, wordplay), and especially the binary and dialectical mode of the wisdom statement, which seeks, often through the oppositional structures of proverbs, to *increase* contradiction as much as possible.[9] Whether this approach is pleasing to philologists and theologians will be a matter of record. I at any rate have tried to benefit as much as possible from their observations while insisting that philology and theology must not displace or postpone considerations of Kohelet as a highly sophisticated, enjoyable, and dialectical (in the Socratic sense) literary text. One corollary of this approach is to consider Kohelet's contradictions as opportunities rather than embarrassments, to view them as motivated, indeed, as forming the literary basis of the entire book. From this perspective the move is not to reduce but rather to seek and acknowledge and exploit and even expand the strong reading whenever possible.

This way of reading also makes certain claims about the generic substance of our text, what is currently known as "wisdom literature": it questions the assumption that the goal of Kohelet, inappropriately called the Preacher (dialogue is not preached, it is practiced), is indoctrination and preaching wisdom through the recitation of traditional formulas,

6. See the opening remarks of his *S/Z* (1970).

7. According to this method, one is asked to "recognize redactional glosses" (Crenshaw 1987, 37). What is imagined here is that "because editorial glosses touch up many books of the Bible, in all likelihood Ecclesiastes also has such redactional comments, for the radical nature of Qohelet's thoughts invited editorial softening."

8. Gregory Thaumaturgos (third century), author of the earliest extant systematic Christian treatment of Kohelet, is a remarkable example of such theological rewriting (Jarick 1990, 3).

9. I discuss the oppositional structure of proverbs and the contestatory purposes of wisdom literature in my forthcoming study, *Wisdom Literature and the Structure of Proverbs* (1993a).

and it considers the possibility that wisdom is a style of reflection on
one's existence, in particular a method of using language against itself in
order not to succumb to its enticements and limitations. One thinks of
Henry James's *The American,* whose hero wondered whether he could
learn French:

"It's a splendid language [says his friend]. You can say all sorts of
bright things in it."

"But I suppose [the American replies] that you must be bright to
begin with."

"Not a bit; that's just the beauty of it."

Like the French to be taught to our American, wisdom writing was in
danger of letting formulaic patterns do the job of thinking; to prevent
this, the author of Kohelet used wisdom formulas against one another:
through debate, contradiction, wordplay and, of course, humor. To
miss this point is to succumb to the *impression* of wisdom's profundity
and miss its substance. I propose that Kohelet is, in its literary and
spiritual specificity, an open debate to which each reader is invited to
contribute. As such, it appears to me as a most valuable pedagogic tool;
whereas other ancient dialogues (Plato's being the most accomplished)
are generically set in their ways, so to speak, Kohelet represents the
method of lived and live debate.

I would even argue that the burden of proof is on the side of the cynics
(not the skeptics). Indeed, how can one skirt the issue of the book's
canonicity? To urge that Kohelet is completely pessimistic but that it was
saved merely by the addition of a few lines here and there (e.g., Koh
8:12) and a pious conclusion stretches the bounds of credulity; one
would like to ask whether there is at least one other biblical book that
got away with so much—with Job as the possible exception. But even if
that were the case, one would still have to account for Kohelet's negativ-
istic theology: while put-downs do characterize later theologies and
inquisitions, the biblical text in this instance seems a bit more plastic and
inquiring.

At any rate, our most usual contact with Kohelet nowadays occurs
through the experience of reading, and in the current rage for commentary—which seems for the moment to have replaced theological
assertion—one simple literary prerequisite remains on the endangered
species list, and that is the naive and linear or sequential reading of the text
itself. I am not claiming that such a reading is entirely possible or even
desirable, since we all bring to a new text our own experiences and presup-
positions, and most of us fall into the trap of reading in terms of what is
coming up on the next page. But what does one gain by knowing or being
told beforehand what the text means, either by commentary or even by

editorial manipulation of the original text? Such procedures are like reading an introduction first rather than last, or like learning Shakespeare by reading the manuals, or like beginning a novel by first reading the last page. I assert that the uncluttered experience of reading the text must precede the use of commentary and that, while exegetical experience is a blessing, it is one best practiced in disguise. I am suggesting that, in our ever-renewed reading of biblical texts, Moshe Greenberg's (1983) directives be constantly before our mind:

> There is only one way that gives any hope of eliciting the innate conventions and literary formations of a piece of ancient literature, and that is by listening to it patiently and humbly. The critic must curb all temptations to impose his antecedent judgments on the text; he must immerse himself in it again and again, with all his sensors alert to catch every possible stimulus . . . , until its features begin to stand out and their native shape and patterning emerge. (21)

When the text before us is Kohelet or, indeed, any other book of the Hebrew Bible, then the "text" to which one must constantly revert is the received text in its pure state, before even those editorial and interpretative conventions are applied that are often taken as normal: punctuation, capitalization, formatting, Massoretic cantilation or trope signs and vocalization, and chapter and verse divisions.

In our pursuit of what is specifically literary in Scripture, I would argue for one further requirement, what Leslie Brisman (1990, xiii) has called the "need to hypothesize authorial voices, with personality and intention." The search for the "original author" is indeed a noble one, but even if that were possible, we would still want to know what plurality, what points of view, are being argued, and these are to be learned not from commentary or theology but from the text itself.

Of course, commentary can address many levels, depending on the audience and place where reading occurs. The one that interests me is the intelligent layperson, ordinarily sitting in the classroom or the parlor, tempted by the Bible but properly skeptical of the claims often made on its behalf. Kohelet is by far the biblical book least likely to irritate such sensitivities, and dialogue is the best mode of access. As to other levels of commentary, especially those addicted to large doses of philology and homily and thus too technical or irrelevant for my educated general reader (I refer mainly to the guild and the churches/synagogues), I have tried to respect these interests as well, but by limiting philological discussion to the elucidation of specific arguments, on the one hand, and by removing most homiletic expansion to a separate and later section of commentary (Part Three, Additional Notes). Finally, larger literary matters vital to the dialogic conception of Kohelet but not directed to specific verses of the text have been collected in a further supplemental section (Excursus) entitled "Dialogue and Its Methods."

Abbreviations

*	refers to Additional Notes
Abot	Pirkei Abot [Ethics of the Fathers]
BDB	Brown, Driver, and Briggs, *Hebrew and English Lexicon*
BT	Babylonian Talmud
E	English, where numbering differs from MT
GKC	Gesenius–Kautzsch–Cowley, *Hebrew Grammar*
JSOT	*Journal for the Study of the Old Testament*
K	Kohelet, the literary character
Koh	Kohelet (Ecclesiastes)
Kohelet	the Book of Ecclesiastes, the work as opposed to K
MT	Massoretic Text (the standard Hebrew version)
n.	note in the Commentary (nn. = notes)
NJV	*Tanakh,* the new JPS translation of the Hebrew Bible
P	the literary character who functions as the Presenter
RSV	Revised Standard Version of the Bible
v.	verse (vv. = verses)
VT	*Vetus Testamentum*
ZAW	*Zeitschrift für die alttestamentliche Wissenschaft*

Biblical books are abbreviated according to guidelines published in the *Journal of Biblical Literature* 107, no. 3 (September 1988): 579–96, except that Ecclesiastes is Koh and Ecclesiasticus or (The Wisdom of) Ben Sira(ch) is Sirach. All references to the Bible and to classical texts give chapter followed by verse or appropriate subdivision. Thus, Abot 5:12 refers to Pirkei Abot, chapter 5, mishnah 12. I cite Hebrew Scripture according to the chapter and verse of the MT and give the English, when different, except for Kohelet, where I cite only MT. My translations of the Hebrew Bible always consider the standard versions such as RSV and NJV. All other translations are mine unless otherwise noted. The classical Jewish commentaries such as Rashi, Sforno, Ibn Ezra, Kimhi, Abrabanel, and Malbim are usually untranslated into English but can be found in traditional Hebrew editions of the MT with commentaries called *Miqra'ot Gedolot*.

For the transliteration of Hebrew, since in all cases the goal is less to reproduce the exact spelling of MT than to recall the shape of the Hebrew words, vowels are transliterated as they would sound in an English reading. Consonants are transliterated as follows: ' b g d h w z ḥ t y k l m n s ' p ts q r s sh t.

Part One

Introduction[1]

1. Portions of this Introduction, here greatly revised, were previously published (Perry 1990). Permission to use this material is gratefully acknowledged.

1

The Problem: Pessimism and the Canon

Human affairs are not worthy of much seriousness, and yet one must take them seriously.
—Plato, *Laws* 803b

The Book of Ecclesiastes or Kohelet is known in world literature for its pessimism, a message proclaimed at both the start and conclusion of the book: *habel habalim,* Vanity of Vanities. K's pessimism is a correct commonplace, and one should resist attempts to sugarcoat the bitter pill, even in order to save the book for religion or consistency, by speculations that maybe "vanity" does not really mean utter emptiness but something less threatening like "enigmatic and mysterious" (Ogden 1987, 22). However, the term was traditional:

> A human is like a breath [*hebel,* vanity],
> his days like a passing shadow.
>
> (Ps 144:4)

and it is unlikely that such a substantial semantic heredity could be circumvented, especially for a poet who inscribes himself into that very tradition:

> . . . good will not come to the wicked nor, like a shadow, will he
> live long . . . (Koh 8:13)

Indeed, K's shopping list of the dirty tricks visited upon mankind is clear and forceful: divine and human injustice, forgetfulness and death, the fruitlessness of our labor, the monotony of human history, and the repetitiveness of natural events. He concludes that everything is as empty and valueless and fleeting and insubstantial and devoid of seriousness as a wind or vapor, and he repeats this conviction from start to finish.

If this message of pessimism were not vital, it would warrant exclusion; but if this were the entire message of Kohelet, the book itself would have been barred from Holy Scripture. This dilemma has been faced in a number of ways, the most popular being the assumption of a pious redactor in the book's closing remarks (he who speaks last speaks best!), who refocuses the message and sets it within a frame of ortho-doxy by pooh-poohing all this pessimistic talk and bringing the kiddies back to Sunday school with the threat that they had better grow up ("for this is the all of man") and be respectful ("Fear God!") or else. Such an explanation is strangely similar to the tactics of eighteenth-century erotic novels which, in order to avoid censorship, had to include arguments in favor of knowing sin "in order to avoid it." But it just seems impossible to confine the burden of rejection to the fringes of the work, for this not only makes the "religious" intervention laughable (why go to all the bother, simply leave the book out of Scripture, as some of the Rabbis argued!)[2] but also prevents our seeing the major religious import of the pessimism itself.

Another attempt to palliate K's radical condemnation of creation is to hold that the troublesome passages are quotations that Kohelet cites in order to contradict. What then are "quotations"? According to Robert Gordis, they are "words which do not reflect the present sentiments of the author of the literary composition in which they are found, but have been introduced by the author to convey the standpoint of another person or situation."[3] Now, this is fine for sanitizing such statements as "Keep the king's command" or even "It is better to go to the house of mourning than the banquet hall." But what about the more extreme "All is vanity"? Is this also another's point of view? If it is, then there goes the view of K as the archpessimist.

But if this view is indeed K's own, we still have to ask whether the work provides any leeway to this conviction. We might begin by asking whether the englobing "*All* is vanity" is meant as a necessary conclusion or, as I argue, as a debatable opinion. The first is usually assumed, and with disastrous consequences for the reading of Kohelet; it imposes a rigidity on the book that such a subtle and various text cannot possibly satisfy. By reducing a discussion and debate to a lament, it leads to the perception that the entire book is filtered through a "single brooding consciousness" (Fox 1989, 159). Why readers have succumbed to the enticing violence of the pseudoconclusion is worthy of reflection, but first it may be helpful to develop an alternative perspective. I like to compare the situation to a scene with my youngest daughter returning from school on Monday.

2. "This is why the sages of Israel (may their memory be for a blessing!) said: 'The Sages sought to withdraw the Book of Kohelet because of its many contradictions' " (Ibn Ezra on Koh 7:3).

3. Gordis (1968, 96); one can also consult Savran (1988).

"How's it going, Danya?"

"Awful!"

"What's the matter?"

"Everything!"

At this point the parent, if at all sympathetic, helpful, human, is required to slouch into a general despondency and provide the expected "I know what you mean." But Danya knows my thinking habits:

"What do you mean, *everything*?"

At which point the residual thumbsucker becomes human again:

"I got a C on that English paper."

My daughter had expected to be in good company: everybody loves generalizations, especially directed against "the system." She should also know, however, that these were taken very seriously by the sages. The person who spits toward the sky because rain has ruined an outing may get it back in the face, as the proverb goes. But, worse still, out of brooding anger he or she may come to question the way things function in general and formulate complaints against the One who has made them this way. If Job's lamentations prove anything, it is that complaints are as irksome to theologians as contradictions are to philologists and rhetoricians.

2

The Literary Genre of Kohelet

(2a) Essay, Collection, Debate

One of the outstanding successes of Kohelet is to have developed a perspective wherein the Pessimist's ranting and ravings can be viewed as limited and also valid. Since this is the achievement of a truly innovative approach to literary genre and structure, it seems important to reflect on this point. At the end of the first chapter something wonderful happens. K speaks in the first person, "I, Kohelet," marking the beginning of a new literary genre. Here the reflective voice of the ESSAY rises out of the rapid give-and-take of the dense first chapter and brings its competing voices to some level of resolution. K's autobiographical statement affirms that his past is an integral part of his present, that his critical method is based on an accounting of his experience; and, since his experience has been a search, competing and contradictory points of view are not excluded but rather honored and recorded, collected and possibly anthologized.

For a long time it has thus seemed to me that Kohelet is best conceived as a special kind of essay. One of the endearing qualities of the book is its modesty, its refusal to take the leap of faith, its persistent clinging to the limitations and integrity of human experience. In the same way, the author pictures himself as a purely natural man, reduced to his own experience and to conclusions based on experimentation, empirical observation, and personal reflection. There is a sense, too, that such conclusions are tentative, subject to further evaluation, analysis, and comparison with other formulations and values. Whatever else this wisdom Anthology is, when it is presented through an integrating personal voice, it is already an essay—Montaigne's early "Essais" provide a suitable parallel.

It is worth noticing other ways in which this literary environment brings contradictions and differences of opinion into contact—the kind of hospitality accorded them by the wisdom genre in which Kohelet is correctly classified. Let us call a basic unit of wisdom literature a "wisdom saying," which is an open-ended proverb, one that through its form and especially its context provokes a response. Just as biblical parallelism is often binary, a statement that requires another to complete it, often by contradiction (as in so-called antithetical parallelism), similarly a saying seems incomplete without a reply. The collection or anthology is the literary genre where this may occur. While it has been pointed out that proverbs are limited in what they can say, such shortcomings are transcended, or at least recognized as such, in the wisdom environment such as the Collection, which is an open form that entertains a symphony of points of view and attempts to bring them into meaningful contact. In wisdom collections this occurs in very precise ways: the development is typically local, monolinear, binary, each new saying arising out of the previous through comment and challenge. R. B. Y. Scott has posited that the proverb refers to a literary form wherein the teacher speaks the first line and the pupil responds with an appropriate second line. What Scott saw as a possible life-setting of wisdom sayings can in fact be applied to a generic and decisive feature: their "sharpness" or ability to provoke reply, as James L. Kugel has put it (basing himself on Koh 12:11).[4] It would be interesting to pursue the similarities with the stichomythic techniques of the classical theater, but even more pertinent is the discovery by recent proverb research of legal debates conducted entirely in proverbs in a number of non-Western societies (see Excursus 2d). Many of the exchanges between K and P have the characteristics of such debates, especially the rapid exchange of contradictory proverbs in such series as 1:1–11, 3:1–8, and 7:1–12.

What Kohelet did with the traditional wisdom genre was to personalize it, to develop further its ability to reflect upon individual experience through a method both empirical and literary. But the shakiness of method is more than compensated by a wonderful openness and pluralism and nonauthoritarian manner, a willingness to experiment and a need to share the findings with colleagues, a need for dialogue. The book's second achievement, therefore, was, much like Job's, the devising of a literary form that could render differences of human experience and value and bring them into confrontation, indeed, that could pit individual experience and judgment against the authority of more traditional methods and conclusions. The resulting literary dialogue has implications far beyond surface form: it implies a radical intellectual and spiritual approach, a dialogic view of truth and reality based on a willingness to consider human experience (as opposed to both revelation and tradition) as a valid basis for religious truth. At the critical level the problem may be refocused by recalling those well-known opposite views of the book: Heine's, according to which Kohelet is the quintessence of skepticism, and Delitzsch's, that it is the quintessence of piety.[5] I

---

4. Scott (1965, 9) sees a glimpse of this method in Isa 28:9–10: "Whom will he teach knowledge? . . . precept upon precept, line upon line"; see also Kugel (1981, 9–12).
    5. Both are cited in Ogden (1987, 9).

propose that both are valid, that Kohelet is the literary battlefield where piety has its day in court with skepticism, and vice versa.[6]

(2b) Dialogue and Its Alternatives in Kohelet

It might be helpful to preview the dialogic approach by comparison with more traditional readings. Take, for example, K's opening observations on the nature of the physical universe as rendered by the RSV:

> 1:4 A generation goes, and a generation comes,
>   but the earth remains for ever.
> 5 The sun rises and the sun goes down,
>   and hastens to the place where it rises.
> 6 The wind blows to the south,
>   and goes round to the north;
>   round and round goes the wind,
>   and on its circuits the wind returns.
> 7 All streams run to the sea,
>   but the sea is not full;
>   to the place where the streams flow,
>   there they flow again.

The accepted view, with which I agree, is that these verses form a single sequence, joined by poetic rhythm and especially by the inclusive thematic argument of the four primary elements of earth, fire (sun), air, and water. For the interpretation, however, it is customary to reach beyond the sequence, either above or below:

> 1:3 What does man gain by all the toil
>   at which he toils under the sun?

> 1:8 All things are full of weariness . . .
> 1:9 What has been is what will be . . . ,
>   and there is nothing new under the sun.

---

6. Whybray (1989, 23) transmits with approval the description of Kohelet as "a running dialogue with a hypothetical 'wise man' representing the conventional wisdom that has prevailed up to that time." This stunning and, to my way of thinking, correct view prompts two observations. The first is that such a view of the work's structure cannot be held simply as an impression, as it has far-reaching implications for all aspects of our understanding, including translation. For example, one needs a more appropriate response than fragmentariness to the (correct) perception of our book's way of arguing: "opposite opinions are juxtaposed and the thought appears to flow first in one direction and then back again" (Whybray 1989, 25). The second observation is that in Kohelet it is not Kohelet that has a dialogue with the sage but rather the opposite: it is the sage-narrator (P) who is pictured as introducing and provoking and questioning and nevertheless transmitting K's wisdom, *cum commento,* of course, since that was the traditional method.

The problem with this interpretation is that these introductory and concluding passages, even when taken together, fail sufficiently to explain what is new and interesting in the nature passage, nor do they account for all elements in that passage.

In the first instance, leaning too heavily on 1:3 assumes that a negative answer is implied: "What gain from toil? None at all!" Clearly, however, the question may be put simply as a topic of debate, leading to a consideration of *opposing* or at least different points of view, rather than a foregone conclusion. Also, the opening question focuses on humans, whereas the following sequence deals only with nature, so that the nature sequence would then have to be seen as mere analogy rather than direct argument. Finally, if the intent is to prove that everything is vanity and fleeting and nothing substantial remains, then the first point, in this very translation, is contradicted in a most stunning way:

> 1:4 A generation goes, and a generation comes,
> *but* the earth remains forever.

If one then goes on to argue, as does Rashbam (see 1:4–7n), that the intent here is to assert the *opposition* of nature to humans, then either the analogical thrust of the passage must be abandoned or the translation must be adjusted so that *all* the contradictions become patent: (humans) but not the earth, but not the sun, but not the wind, but not the rivers.

If, however, the nature sequence is read according to what follows (1:8–9), then other problems emerge. First of all, one notes a shift in argument, from the opening complaint on the passing of all things, to the admission that things in fact do not pass at all but rather persist with incredible sameness and repetitiveness. But if this is the case, then one would still want to ask why even these natural elements "pant" or seek or desire such a condition (see below, 3a).

There are problems with the usual, nondialogic reading even at the textual level. Returning to my daughter, what would we think of her complaint if it were to conclude as follows: "I got a C *but* the teacher changed it to an A"? In a similar way, consider the contradictions already mentioned: "A generation arises only to die *but* the earth is forever peopled. . . . The sun rises only to set *but* it returns to its place to try again."[7] Is it in the interest of the archpessimist of all of literature to introduce opposite evidence, and in the same breath?

---

7. I am in obvious disagreement with the RSV translation of these verses; see my Commentary and also below, Introduction 3a. Ogden (1987, 31), by acknowledging the presence of *two* arguments in this brief verse, makes an excellent case for a dialogic reading: "Whether this movement [of the sun] is wearying or bears a sense of eagerness and longing is not a question to be settled unequivocally. . . . Unfortunately our text leaves us without clear guidance as to

In order to deal more faithfully with the situation, let us recall that the Hebrew scroll of Kohelet has neither punctuation nor chapters nor verse-markers nor any of the other editorializing that we have become used to, and let us repunctuate the opening scene and posit *two* voices, locked in debate. The first is K the Pessimist and the second is the Presenter or Antagonist or, as some have suggested, the Arguer. Here is how their dialogue would sound:

1:4 **A generation goes forth, only to die!**
But the earth endures forever.

5 **The sun rises, only to set!**
Yet it pants to return to its starting point, where it rises
6 *again. Moreover, it goes southward but returns northward.*

The wind goes forth around and around!
Yet it can reverse its direction.
7 **All rivers flow to the sea!**
But the sea is not filled. And the rivers must return to
their source, since they continue to flow to their
destination.

Here the contradictory *but* ("but the earth . . ."), which frequently translates the *waw* connective, especially in proverbs, is generalized so as to apply to all four members of the analogical argument. Moreover, the nature sequence need not be referred to an introductory or closing formula for its interpretation; its argument is self-contained and sequential in its dialectical development, each statement—normally each verse—of the prologue having not one but two voices, related by an oppositional parallelism of sorts and differentiated by tone and style. The first, K the Pessimist, tends to poetic assertion, uses the enchantments of rhythm and generalization to support an otherwise weak argument, namely that everything in nature dies and therefore humans have no hope. By contrast, the Presenter's reply is cool, deliberately prosaic, unwilling to skip to hasty conclusions, and perhaps joyously contradictory. To configure this scene as a dialogue not only makes perfect sense but is consistent with the dialogic nature of both the wisdom genre and the essay, as noted above.[8] And what if this were the case for the rest of the book as well?

---

which view approximates Qohelet's. Only for those who, for other reasons, adopt the view that Qohelet's basic position is a pessimistic one, is it clear that the sun grows weary of this constant round."

8. For further remarks on the dialogic nature of wisdom sayings, see Perry (1993a).

Even at this early point in the book, of course, we have become unwilling to read dialogically because of accustomed ways of reading the book's preface:

> [These are] the sayings of Kohelet, son of David, King in Jerusalem: "VANITY OF VANITIES."

At this point there has arisen a widespread tendency to submit and be lulled to sleep. There is, first of all, the ascription to the "son of David," typically read as a call to authority, forgetting that not all of David's sons were in fact wise and that if Solomon was intended, then he might have been mentioned by name, as in Canticles and Proverbs—not that Solomon always acted wisely! Then there are those theological barriers, notably the view that would like to base support for a hatred of this life in a dogmatic and unassailable doctrine of human existence. Then, too, there is the generic view of the book as a monologic lament, a kind of reasoned Book of Lamentations, reinforced at the very start by reading the repetition ("vanity of vanities, vanity of vanities, all is vanity") as an incantation of reinforcement.

While all agree on the sages' pedagogic importance, this is usually referred to the content of their teaching, while the method is bypassed. Strange, since all of us have notions of the "Socratic method," even without the vaguest recollection of what the arguments actually were. But, again, what method can be ascribed to a pessimist, once we have decided that the entire content of the book is a relentless and monotonous complaint? However, what if the text were quite different from all that? What if we withheld our habitual agreement with a point of view that could only be advanced "for the sake of argument," namely that "all is vanity." Note that the first voice we hear is not "Kohelet" but rather an introducer, whom we name according to his function: the Presenter or P for short. This voice will develop its own personality, but at this crucial point and instead of following K down his mirthless path, we must allow our mind to kick in and try to hear P's exclamation, which I imagine as respectful but incredulous:

> Kohelet *too* has spoken a vanity of vanities!
> Is *every*thing vanity?

This announces not only the natural and human reaction to such pretentious "wisdom" but also the pedagogical intent and method never to be lulled to sleep and to examine everything. And what if K intended this all along and led off with an outrageous generalization only to provoke such a response?

This does not mean, of course, that negativity is to be excluded from our reading of the nature sequence; only that it is not the exclusive voice, that another point of view, excluded only by our ingrained and monological habits of reading, constantly surfaces and places the lament into a dialectical focus. We now begin to see why the dialogic method of reading is apt to be bypassed: what makes the opening passage of Kohelet so compelling, to the point of distracting the reader from any competing voice, is that the vehement, monologic assertion of the metaphysical All-argument ("All is vanity") is reinforced by K's persuasive poetic diction. We are tempted to compare Kohelet and Job; like the fairy-tale "Prologue in Heaven" of Job 1, the opening verses of Kohelet seek to localize the book's action within a global context, a paradigm of being and values according to which the entire universe is said to function and beyond which no further conclusions seem allowed. An appropriate title for K's opening effort might be "Prologue on the Nature of Things," and the totalizing "vanity of vanities" is meant to include man, whose effort is pictured as controlled and overwhelmed by the destined rise and fall of all natural things.

The text includes its own rebuttal, however, and in order to bring this into clearer focus we must take a closer look at P's counterargument and especially at the underlying thematics of the work that sponsor *both* points of view.

3

The Themes of Kohelet

Since my approach is based on an analysis of the main contradictions in Kohelet, it may be helpful to recall that many such listings have been attempted by other exegetes.[9] I propose, however, that there exists a more paradigmatic contradiction in Hebrew Scripture, which is introduced in the creation story of Genesis and receives important elaboration in Kohelet. It has to do with the way religious consciousness distinguishes itself from more empirical or experiential modes of viewing human life.[10] In the study of Kohelet this involves the nature of its theological theme as opposed to its local arguments, although, to be

9. For the sake of comparison, here is Ibn Ezra's (on Koh 7:3):
1. "Anger is better than laughter" (7:3), and "anger abides in the bosom of fools" (7:9).
2. "for in much wisdom is much angry frustration" (1:18), and "Remove anger [and therefore wisdom!] from your heart" (11:10).
3. "it is good and proper to eat and drink" (5:17; Ibn Ezra apparently also was thinking of the stronger assertion "there is nothing better for man under the sun than to eat and drink" in 8:15); and "it is better to go to the house of mourning [than to the banquet hall]" (7:2).
4. "I recommend contentedness [simḥah]" (8:15), and "And as for enjoyment [simḥah]: 'What does it do?' "
5. "how is the sage better than the fool" (6:8), and "wisdom has an edge [over foolishness]" (2:13).
6. "I should praise the dead" (4:2), and "a live dog is better [than a dead lion]" (9:4).
7. "in the grave . . . there is neither deed nor thought nor knowledge nor wisdom" (9:10), and "there is an appropriate time for every matter [and in the grave upon every deed]" (3:17).
8. "good will not come to the wicked nor . . . will he live long because he does not fear God" (8:13), and "the wicked lives a long life for all his wickedness" (7:15).
9. "it will be good to the God-fearing [who constantly fear Him]" (8:13), and "the wicked are rewarded as the righteous" (8:14).
Ibn Ezra adds that "he who looks carefully will find more [contradictions] like this." For a somewhat different summary see Crenshaw (1987, 46–47). The matter seems so important to Fox (1989) as to figure in the title of his work, *Qohelet and His Contradictions*.

10. By this I do not mean to exclude empiricism from the religious quest, although it may be an exaggeration to state that "experientialism, or empiricism, is the single most pervasive and persistent of the methods used by human beings to attain religious faith" (Gilman 1990, 109). To present Judaism as the possible exception, one would have to study closely such texts as Deut 1:8: "Behold, I have set the land before you . . . ." The Hebrew for "behold" is *re'eh*, "see," and Sifre Deuteronomy (7:33) stresses the empirical emphasis of the word, which is also one of Kohelet's favorites: "Moses said to them, 'I say this to you not on the basis of an estimate or a vague rumor but from that which you can see with your own eyes.' "

sure, the latter must somehow reflect the former. But we must first recognize those pervasive patterns of thought of Hebrew Scripture that saturate our individual text, what may be called the work's thematic substructure that sponsors the individual arguments or "topics."[11]

(3a) The Way of Nature and the Human Way

I would like to begin by offering two epigraphs. My purpose is to describe a paradigmatic opposition that pervades Hebrew Scripture and receives important elaboration in Kohelet. It has to do with the way religious consciousness distinguishes itself from more empirical or experiential modes of viewing time and human life. The first is an adaptation of Mishnah Ma'aserot 1:4.

> There are two kinds of almond trees: the one produces sweet fruit, which then turns bitter; the other produces bitter fruit, which then turns sweet.

I shall suggest that the first kind of fruit symbolizes the way of the world of nature; the second, the way of humans.

> And there was evening and there was morning, one day. (Gen 1:5)

These two epigraphs state my theme; they describe a substructure of meaning that saturates Kohelet and sponsors many of its most important arguments. In the Genesis version of the world's creation, the most obvious structural feature is the division into days. Note that, in its summary of the works of each day, the text does not state that the opposing components are essences or fixed states (night and day, light and darkness) but rather views them as moments, directions, points of transition or change: evening and morning, setting and dawning (Fishbane 1979, 4), one day. The order of progression is crucial. Here a movement from light to darkness (a setting) is followed by a movement from darkness to light, a dawning. It is thus not a matter of indifference whether we go from light into darkness or the reverse. It is true that this question is one of emphasis or point of view rather than of substance, for whether one conceives of one's day as starting in the evening or in the morning hardly affects the light and darkness themselves. Yet the per-

---

11. Ibn Ezra's conceptual approach is closely tied to the words of the text, thus basically topical. However, we must first approach the matter at another level, that of the theological theme to which Kohelet contributes. For the distinction between a work's thematic substructure and its argument, see A. Parker (1968, 59).

spective radically affects the way one lives and conceives the direction of one's life. It can lead one to say, for example, that a bad situation will turn out okay, or that, as the adage goes, "even this too is good."

(I) THE PROLOGUE ON THE NATURE OF THINGS (KOH 1:4–7)

The sharp debate of the Prologue of Kohelet analyzed above helps focus on the thematics at the center of the book: man's relation with nature (and Nature *sive Deus* . . .). The first position, held by K the Pessimist, is that man is a part and only a part of nature and thus entirely subject to its causality. K's view, as accurately described by Sforno (on Koh 1:15), is that "all perishable things infallibly rise to their peak of growth, whereupon the direction of their movement veers to its decline, so that it cannot be repaired and returned to its original line of growth and progress." Its motto is the German adage "Morgen rot Abend tot" and its precise argument: nature first "goes" forth and then "comes" back or in, *always in the same sequence;* everything is born only to die or, in terms of the language of Genesis, day always goes into night. This argument is supported by reference to all the elements of nature—there are four, according to Aristotelian physics (see Ibn Ezra on Koh 1:4):

1. The earth produces generations of people, who first "go" forth (*holek*) and then "come" (*ba'*).[12]
2. The sun "shines forth" (*zarah*) and then "sets" (*ba'*).
3. The wind "goes forth" (*holek*) here and there, around and around, and then "returns" (*shab*) to its returning.
4. The waters (rivers) "go" (*holkim*) into the sea, where they die without being able to fill it, but "return" (*shabim*) to try again.

The elements all repeat the basic pattern of *holek* and/or *ba'* set as a paradigm at the outset, and K sees each element as a member in an analogical series in which the qualities of each reverberate upon all the others (cf. Whybray 1989, 42, quoted below, 1:4n *goes forth* . . .). Thus, the initial action of each is to go forth and then to arrive[13] and spend itself. The point is that, despite the positive initial movement, there is absolutely no progress. Furthermore, and this is the main point, the direction is irreversible: decline always follows rise, life always ends in

12. I obviously disagree with the opposite interpretation of this verse; namely, that *halak* means "dying" (it does, however, in several texts; see Crenshaw 1987, 62) and *ba'* would then mean precisely the contrary of what it means in the very next verse ("sets, dies")! Such an interpretive move also upsets the rigorous analogical pattern of the series, as explained below.

13. As in Ruth 2:3: "She set forth and arrived (RSV: "went")" (*wa-telek wa-tabo'*); also 1 Sam 22:5: "So David departed and arrived at (*wa-yelek dawid wa-yabo'*) (RSV: "and went into") the forest of Hereth." I am in obvious disagreement with RSV.

death. This point is summarized by the first of two nuances of *hebel:* ephemerality (Crenshaw 1987, 57).

However, Kohelet also introduces an alternative to natural determinism and pessimism. In this initial Prologue the binary motion of natural rise and fall is neutralized by the concept of cyclicality. Thus, following each death or decline there is a starting again:

1. despite death there is a perpetual rebirth of people;
2. despite its previous setting, the sun always rises again;
3. the wind always "returns" (*shab*) to its returning;
4. the waters (rivers) always "return" (*shabim*) to try again.

In this way the voice of the Pessimist is neutralized, and the argument from natural analogies remains inconclusive since even in the natural realm the evidence can be read in two opposing ways. I summarize my first point by referring to what has become a fashionable characterization of Kohelet as a former-day *homme absurde* as portrayed by Camus: "not unlike the punishment imposed upon Sisyphus, who was condemned to an eternity of rolling a boulder to the top of a hill only to have it return to the starting place over and over again" (Crenshaw 1987, 64). Yet, though he knows that the rock will roll back down the hill, Sisyphus renews his task each day; and in his meditations on this myth Camus (168) provided an appropriate rejoinder: "Sisyphus must be imagined as being happy." This is to say, the assessment of Kohelet's (or Sisyphus's) endless repetition as negative is not a foregone conclusion, even according to those existentialist positions favored by such a reading. The Pessimist's argument of ephemerality is thus countered by the notion of cyclicality, which can be viewed as either positive, the chance to try again, or negative because futile, in the sense that each cycle is the same and there is nothing new. The argument will be continued (I would like to say renewed) in chapter 3 by focusing not on the perspective one takes on movement (whether it is binary or trinary/cyclical), but on the sequence and direction of the elements.

(II) THE CATALOGUE OF THE TIMES (KOH 3:2–8)

In Mishnah Abot 3:3 the Rabbis distinguished humans from their physical environment on the basis of place and time: "There is no man who does not have his time; there is no thing that does not have its place." This distinction is descriptive of the two major debates that occur in Kohelet in chapters 1 and 3 and the progression from one to the other. In the opening Prologue on the Nature of Things, the four elements are said to seek their natural place (1:5, 1:7), but even in the natural world the text remains ambiguous as to whether the *maqom* or place of each element is the place to which they strive and where they die, or whether this *maqom* is the place of their renewed beginning and striving. The suggestion is that place may be an appropriate concept for the physical universe but not for an analogical extension to things human.

Chapter 3 ("The Catalogue of the Times") then considers human action uniquely from the perspective of time. Again, the debate focuses on whether all is preordained (cf. 9:1), or whether the wise can discern the proper time of things, if not to decide what to do, at least to know how to do it and also to adopt the appropriate attitude (e.g., fear of God). In chapter 3 (vv. 2–8), without doubt the best-known passage in Kohelet, the two contenders return to the fray, and the form of the debate must surely be the most sustained chiasmus in all of literature. K renews his argument without the help of nature analogies and with examples of natural causality taken directly from human life, but now P introduces a more positive concept, arguing the biblically sanctioned possibility that man may act independently of natural causality.

Recent research, notably that of Loader (1979, 1986), has quite satisfactorily and even remarkably explained the rhetorical structure of Koh 3:2–8, which turns out to be much more than a mere listing or "catalogue of the times." But interpretation has been content with simple rhetorical and structural explanation and has not proceeded to the next level of understanding, has not advanced from seeing figures of speech as figures of thought. In order to understand the arguments, let us use a simple type of value analysis used elsewhere in the study of wisdom texts: Let us describe the Pessimist's way of nature as the decline from a life-enhancing "plus" to its "minus" or opposite, and the human possibility offered by the Presenter as the reversal of this order.

(A) NATURAL PATTERNS:	(B) HUMAN PATTERNS:
+ > –	– > +
Kohelet's position	Presenter's position

1.	born and die (3:2)	3.	kill and heal (3:3)
2.	plant and uproot (3:2)	4.	wreck and build (3:3)
7.	have intercourse and abstain (3:5)	5.	weep and laugh (3:4)
8.	embrace and hold from embraces (3:5)	6.	mourn and dance (3:4)
9.	seek and give up (3:6)	11.	tear and repair (3:7)
10.	keep and cast off (3:6)	12.	be silent and speak (3:7)
13.	love and hate (3:8)	14.	make war and peace (3:8)

The rigid chiasmus of supporting examples is 2–4–4–2 (1–2; 3–6; 7–10; 11–12), the only break occurring at the end, presumably as the reverse parallel of the opening "born and die" and also because it is better to end a series on a positive note.[14] By natural-versus-human pattern I do not mean that the first series (K's) refers only to nature's activities, since both series can refer to the human sphere. But in the first, man's activities conform to natural patterns and the succession from $(+)$ to $(-)$ is thus irreversible: pleasure always ends up in pain, rise always leads to fall, life is relentlessly destroyed and nothing (i.e., vanity) remains. The second or human series, by contrast, illustrates the paradox that "the end of a thing is better than its beginning" (7:8).[15]

The grand opening passage of chapter 3 can now be read as yet another round in the ongoing debate. Departure from the usual, literal translation is the only way to bring out the passage's clear chiastic design and especially the ideological debate in progress over the *two* possible directions that human life can take:

3:2 **There is an appointed time to be born inevitably followed by death!**
   Whatever is planted is eventually uprooted!

3   *There is an appropriate time to kill but also a time to heal,*
   A time to destroy but also a time to build up,
4   *A time to weep but also a time to be happy,*
   A time to mourn but also a time to dance.
5   **A time to disseminate your stones**
   but a longer time to hold them in!
   A time to embrace but always followed by separation!
6   **What is pursued is inevitably lost!**
   What is retained is inevitably scattered!

7   *But what we tear we can also sew up.*
   He who is silent will have his time to talk.

8   **What we love we end up hating!**
   There is indeed a time for war, but also a time for peace.

The usual, relentlessly pessimistic reading of this grand passage can be clearly exposed for what it is, for example, by reference to Gregory

---

14. This point is beautifully illustrated in the Massoretic text of Kohelet by the repetition of the uplifting 12:13 after the more somber 12:14.

15. Here two possibilities seem implied: (1) present misfortune and unhappiness may lead to relief; and (2) it is only through the first that one can arrive at the second.

Thaumaturgos's notorious rewrite, wherein he simply changed the order of all the sequences so as to harmonize them with his pessimism: $+ > -$. But one could as easily change them all to the opposite order so as to yield a message that is entirely optimistic. In truth, however, both messages are conveyed by the text, and this alone is highly optimistic.

We can now look back to the Prologue on the Nature of Things and also notice how in other books Scripture adapts nature's very semantics to celebrate the triumph over nature and express the deepest hopes. For example, the utter overthrow of the movement of nature is beautifully rendered by Isaiah through use of the familiar metaphor: when Israel is righteous (60:21), "your sun shall no more set" (60:20), signifying that natural determinism has permanently been transcended. These semantics receive particular stress in Ps 126, referring to the ingathering after the exile: "He that goes forth (*halok yelek;* literally, "going, goes forth") weeping . . . shall come home (*bo' yabo';* literally, "will, returning, return") with shouts of joy." Kimhi views such an event as contrary to the ways of nature and, like the presence of watercourses in the dry Negev, will constitute something new (*hidush gadol*), as if in response to the Pessimist's complaint that nothing is new (1:9). In other words, when the going forth of *holek* is reversed or balanced by negativity such as weeping, then the normal properties of *bo'* or return are likewise compensated and the decline is joyous because it is a fullness, bearing its sheaves.

At other times the words are different but the patterns are similar. At the start of 1 Samuel, for example, these structures are placed in clear counterpoint: on the one hand, the decline of the Priestly house of Eli ($+ > -$), on the other, Hannah's move from barrenness and despair to newness and, behind and beyond, Israel's "waiting that moves from trouble to well-being" ($- > +$), both violations of our reason and our reasonableness, as Walter Brueggemann (1990, 11–12) has finely put it.

Kohelet, more skeptical and doctrinally modest, is disinclined to overt optimism, and hope is expressed by innuendo: in the suggestion that a harsh face will make the heart better (7:3), through the use of chiasmus in our passage, or in the prohibition to assert the opposite possibility:

> Don't say: "how can it be that the old days were better than these?" For such questions do not arise from wisdom. (Koh 7:10)

This mode of teaching should be carefully noted, for here wisdom does not dogmatically assert that time progresses but rather advises not to foreclose on such a possibility.[16] But our text is not always so reticent on this important matter, especially in chapter 7: "A good name is better

16. See 11:8n, *all that dies.*

than precious ointment; and the day of death than the day of birth" (7:1); or in the assertion that "the end of a thing is better than its beginning" (7:8). Such possibilities raise insurmountable problems for the pessimistic reading of Kohelet.[17]

Before leaving this well-known passage, however, it is best to conclude. Many have seen in it the constant theme of the wisdom tradition, that good and bad depend on what is appropriate, since God has made every thing beautiful in its proper time (3:11). That theme is indeed constant, but the argument here is rather time's direction, which way people are headed. The argument can be encapsulated by one final illustration, a Hassidic tale about a clock belonging to the "Seer" of Lublin (Lamm 1987, 12):

> Every other clock, when it strikes the hour, has its own peculiar and characteristic message. The chime calls out, "One hour closer to death." But the clock of the Seer of Lublin has a message different from any other clock in the world. Its chimes sing out, "One hour closer to redemption."

Thus, the old characterization of the pessimist and optimist is overcome, for in such a view the glass is neither half-full nor half-empty but rather on its way to being (ful)filled.

On the crucial matter of time, therefore, it is not at all a question of "when?" or even "how fast?" or even of our wise understanding of the right time to act but rather of something much more accessible: In what direction are we headed? To answer this question we need only two points of comparison. For it does matter whether we view our lives as going from Sunday to Wednesday or from Wednesday to the Sabbath, whether the day is seen as going from day to night or from night to day, whether we end up with bitter or sweet fruit.

To what can the matter be compared, as the sages liked to say. To the two ways of kindling the Hanukkah lights (BT Shabbat 21b): the School of Shammai argued that on the first night all eight lights are kindled and one is removed on each successive night until, on the final night, there remains but a single light. But the School of Hillel, whose opinion is universally accepted, maintained that on the first night a single light is

17. The more positive possibility is of course but an instance of a pervasive theme of Scripture and of wisdom literature: that a person's happiness is to be judged by his or her end:

In the day of prosperity, adversity is forgotten, and in the day of adversity, prosperity is not remembered . . .

Call no one happy before his death; a man will be known by his latter end [*aḥarito*]. (Sirach 11:25, 28. RSV misconstrues the Hebrew *aḥarito* and translates: "a man will be known through his children.")

kindled and one is added on each successive night until, on the final night, eight lights are kindled. The difference between the two views is not in the number of lights, since both agree on the total number. The difference is one of direction, whether to begin in fullness and gradually diminish or to begin in paucity and gradually increase. In both views a single question is appropriate and it is asked at the moment of kindling the daily light: Do we add one or subtract one? Which way are we headed?

We are left, then, with two directions, two kinds of cyclical movement (cf. also ★1:4–7) and action: that of the sun and all natural creatures, which rises and then sets; and that of God, who first kills and then gives life (1 Sam 2:6), a patent absurdity (how can you kill what does not yet have life?!) that stresses the crucial paradox. Humans, as natural creatures, fatally gravitate to the first and yet are able to act according to the second.

(3b) Fullness and Growth

> Ripeness is all. (Shakespeare, *King Lear*)

But, in K's argument, the "all" is not ripe. Fullness is that goal, forever evasive, that all beings try to achieve through their endless cycle of activities and desires:

> . . . but the sea is not filled. (Koh 1:7)

> . . . but the eye is never sated with things to see. Or the ear filled with things to hear. (Koh 1:8)

Here man is but part of the totality:

> All man's toil is for his own sustenance.
> And this is why his appetite is never filled.
> (Koh 6:7)

This condition of existence is related to man's "goings and comings," and Naomi's exit from the Land of Israel and into exile is paradigmatic of the direction of man's profane or natural existence, the one shared with the strivings of nature:

> I went forth full [*mele'ah halakti,* RSV: "went away"] and God has brought me back [*heshibani: shab*] empty. (Ruth 1:21)

It is related, too, to the final return of all physical nature to its humble origins after its initial rise:

> Naked I came forth from my mother's womb, and naked I shall return. (Job 1:21)

Ruth's return to the point of departure is thus perceived as the very culmination of disaster.

Ruth's return, however, also becomes the point of a new departure, one toward a more permanent fullness. This hopefulness is hinted, first of all, in the circumstance that Naomi's return coincided with the beginning of the barley harvest (1:22) and also, even more tellingly, in Ruth's good fortune to have "happened" into the field of Boaz (2:3). Although such hopefulness is presented in a more positive, even providential, mode in Ruth, the same idea appears in Kohelet, for in both works the universal desire for fullness is reinterpreted: no longer the mere goal of striving, fullness comes to be viewed as a projection arising from the emptiness and darkness and vanity and ignorance which are its preconditions:

> Just as you do not know the ways of the wind, like the powers hidden in the pregnant womb . . . (Koh 11:5)

This radical unknowability at the origins of growth and renewal is directly related in Kohelet to an unpredictable God and thus constitutes not only a form of skepticism or pessimism but the very basis of trust and confident action toward the future. This is the point, I think, of the juxtaposition of two important verses:

> . . . you cannot know the workings of God, Who does everything.
> In the morning sow your seeds . . .
>
> (Koh 11:5–6)

The image of inner growth in Koh 11:5 is related to a level of imagery that traverses Scripture and that is distinct from the sheer strength of the purely physical universe as set forth in the Prologue. In that passage all of nature is depicted in its most elemental form—not its most savage form, as in the whirlwind of Job, but still as contrary to human hope for improvement. But there is another metaphoric system, one that focuses on God as the Creator of organic nature. Here growth is continuous, and the end of a thing can indicate its highest point of development:

> The righteous shall flourish like a palm-tree,
> he shall grow [tall] like a cedar in Lebanon. . . .
> They shall still bear fruit in ripe old age,
> they shall be full of sap and green.
>
> (Ps 92:13–15 E12–14)

Such continuous growth is reflected in Bildad's claim to Job:

> Although your beginnings are small,
> your end will grow great.
>
> (Job 8:7)

Such passages are put forth as paradoxes, deliberate challenges to the way of nature and the common sense that is its spokesman:

> . . .Better the day of death than the day of birth. Better to go to the house of mourning than to go to the house of mirth. (Koh 7:1–2)

Of course, these are propounded as true only if the end is viewed as the high-point of a continuous rise, as in the acquisition of a good name (7:1). In such situations, the end is paradoxically not an end, since, as in the present example, a good name lives long after death (see Cant 1:3). In the case of Ruth, the results will also be a "name" (4:11) in the form of the Davidic line.

In a deep sense, in Kohelet the end is in the beginning. Let us return to the characterization of the "all" as rising and falling. In fact and as we have seen, the process is not binary but trinary, since, after the fall or decline or return, there is a repositioning, a second start of the process:

> A generation is born [RSV: "goes"] and a generation dies [RSV: "comes"], but the earth remains forever (le 'olam). (Koh 1:4)

James G. Williams (1976:389 n. 46), after noting God's special concern for the earth, since it is He who made everything (11:5), suggests that "'olam and what pertains to 'olam must be the basic meaning of 'the earth' (ha-'arets)." The 'olam (e.g., in 3:11) is therefore "not the opposite of earthly being but its fullness." An equally fruitful suggestion was made by Rashi (on Koh 1:4):

> And who are those who survive [forever]? The humble and the lowly, those who lower themselves to the earth, as it is said:

"And the humble will inherit the earth" (Ps 37:11; RSV: "and the meek shall possess the land"). And the Midrash Tanhumah says: "All the righteous of Israel are called earth" (see Mal 3:12).

This attempts to bring Kohelet into the theological line of a text such as Ps 19:10 E9: "The fear of the Lord is pure, enduring forever (*'omedet la'ad*)." But it also attempts to fathom how it is that the lowly and suffering parts of humanity will triumph. The Torah boldly prophesied this in God's own assertion: "For all the 'earth' is Mine" (Exod 19:5). More modestly, the Presenter projects that lesson, or perhaps sees it reflected, in the physical universe itself, in both its "lowly" status and its eternal return, "to try again."

(3c) Kohelet as an Anti-Genesis

It has become fashionable (and correct) to point out the linguistic parallels between the creation story in Genesis and the Book of Kohelet, but one would like, in addition, suggestions as to why this borrowing occurs. Specifically, one should avoid the view that this is a purely formal and mechanical technique, that "esthetic categories have replaced theological ones" (Crenshaw 1987, 25). Quite the opposite: Kohelet presents a frontal attack against the grounding of creation theology, the notion of the goodness of God's creation; against the statement that "ALL is good" it counters that "ALL is vanity."[18]

Like Job, K is a complainer, but a scientific one. Job suffered in his flesh, howled with pain, justified himself against accusations of sin, and suggested that God had done him dirt. K's outrage is less personally felt, but as deeply. His search goes to the groundings of the whole project of creation and cannot avoid raising doubts about the intentions of the Architect. The truth is that K's pessimism is rooted in the Prologue in yet another way, as the Rabbis sensed when they pointed out that the seven "vanities" of 1:1 (vanity [1] of vanities [2] + vanity [1] of vanities [2] + all is vanity [1] = 7) refer to the seven days of creation and that K's complaint is therefore directed against the entire creation and, by extension, the goodness theology that the Genesis narrative supports.

K makes this point in a number of subtle ways. For example, the Genesis account (especially 2:2–3) stressed the totality of God's works:

18. A recent example of this is Arian Verheij, which includes the valuable observation that Kohelet's building of a personal estate in Koh 2:4–6 parallels God's own creation of the Garden of Eden in Genesis. But if indeed the literary point is being made that Kohelet is "posing as God," then shouldn't his vanity judgment be interpreted as a critique not only of his own purely personal experiment but of God's creation as well?

"ALL His work which He had done." K takes the matter head-on by claiming that they are ALL vanity or bad. Again, the argument that "two are better than one" (4:9) may seem rather abstract, but it is possible to appreciate the Presenter's strenuous opposition (4:7–8) to the book's antifeminist perspective. From Gen 2:18 ("It is not good that the man should be alone") one indeed infers that "two are better than one" and that marriage is a blessing. Not so, says the Pessimist in a violent diatribe (7:26–28), implying that God was therefore wrong in creating the Other, woman. Third, if Adam, man, is condemned to labor (cf. Job 5:7), why should he not be able to enjoy the fruits of his labor; why are they all vanity? Fourth, K's long diatribe against wisdom may also be considered as a covert assault against a creation theology such as Proverbs 8:22–31. Fifth, the Pessimist's suggestion that wisdom's superiority over folly may be compared to light's supremacy over darkness (2:13; cf. Gen 1:4–5) results in a devaluation of the former by the quip that one fate overtakes them all. Finally, it may even be that K's model of the universe as made up of four elements can be viewed as a deliberate subversion of the "days" of creation model.

There are even hints, in an astonishing verse, at a more radical attack on creation theology:

> What will be has already been, and every action is doomed to be repeated. (Koh 1:9)

P correctly interprets this argument as asserting that "there is nothing new under the sun." (Koh 1:9) Nothing new! But that is precisely the injunction, to "make yourselves a new heart and a new spirit" (Ez 18:31), and one must "sing to the Lord a new song" (Isa 42:10; Ps 33:3, 96:1, 98:1, 149:1). Here the observation is framed almost as an affront against the very name and nature of God, the One who "will be" (*ehyeh*, Exod 3:14). K's response: "What has been, that is What Will Be."

The injunction to creativity is so misunderstood in Western culture that it is no surprise to find it restricted to poets and artists rather than generally applicable to all humanity. Yet the daily Jewish liturgy is explicit: God, whom we must imitate, "renews through His goodness always and every single day the works of creation." The difficult problem of *how* we imitate God is proposed in a curiously negative way in the very philosophical opening of Kohelet, in its provocative suggestion that what humans see is not the workings of God but of physics, and that the highest perspective we can have, therefore, is a naturalistic one. This may be too bold a way of stating it, however, and the Rabbis' suggestion may be more fruitful: that the sevenfold repetition of vanity hints at the works of the seven days of creation, emphasizing by opposition the distinction between God's creation and creative essence.[19]

(3d) God's Ways: Wayward or Wayless?

"What profit [*yitron*] hath man" (1:3). This is the opening question of the book and, according to at least one opinion (e.g., Zimmerli 1933), the main subject of all of wisdom literature: against the universal context of vanity, what profit can humans derive? "Profit" indicates "what is left over" or escapes destruction. It can thus refer to reward, to remembrance (*zikaron* 1:11), to newness (1:9), to whatever is "better than" something else. Thus, "man has no superiority [*motar*] over the beast" (3:19). The main question, in brief, is whether man is better than, has any advantage over, the rest of nature, or whether he too, as argued by K, is entirely defeated by the rise and fall of time.

This initial formulation is not comprehensive enough, however, because it refers only to man's work, to whatever comes entirely from himself, to *ha-ma'aseh* to the exclusion of *ha-na'aseh*. It locates K's unique concern at the moral level of individual, active responsibility, but in so doing it neglects the role of what comes to humans "from without," as Epictetus put it at the start of his *Enchiridion*. The book's later formulation of wisdom's basic question carries a quite different emphasis:

> . . . what is really good *for* [not from] a man in this life? (Koh 6:12)

The focus now is much broader; it includes not only man's own effort but also what comes to him "from without." This refers to all sources external to the individual, including fate, chance, other people, but in Kohelet the reference is especially to God's actions, to which humans must develop adequate responses and attitudes.

As suggested above in K's anti-Genesis posture, there is in Kohelet as in Job a level of upset against Providence:

> What is done under the heavens is a badly arranged [RSV: "an evil"] affair that God has given. (Koh 1:13)

Some critics have taken this stand as definitive and even chanced the opinion that Kohelet views God as a distant despot (Crenshaw 1987, 30). However, a movement away from this dualism and a softening of the stand against God can be sensed in such notations as the following:

19. Kohelet 1:2, see Rashi and Kohelet Rabbah, ad loc.

> Man has no greater good than eating and drinking and finding
> pleasure in his work itself. I have concluded that *this too is from the*
> *hand of God*. (Koh 2:24 [see below, 3e])

Instead of the italiziced words, one expects to find something like "this
too is vanity" or "this too is a chasing after wind." The substitution is
surprising and leads to the thought that perhaps what comes from God is
not exactly evil or vanity. Slowly, a distinct source of value is advanced
that cannot be reduced to human effort. As we shall see, the most
frequent term for this domain is man's portion, which points to opportu-
nity rather than payment or reward, to whatever comes from God and is
apportioned by Him to the individual.

God's actions are seen as perplexing, unpredictable, thus totally free
(see especially 7:14; 8:17), in radical contrast to the regularity of nature as
portrayed in chapter 1. This is not the same as saying that they are
arbitrary, however, or that chance reigns. There emerges a second sense
of individuality, beyond that of sage and author, for, although man will
utterly perish as a sensual being, from the mere fact of his selection and
the size of his apportionment he achieves differentiation: "Man has no
greater good than eating and drinking. . . . This too is from the hand of
God" (2:24). In other words, enjoyment is a basis for individuation, but
only when sanctioned by the consciousness of the Other.[20]

K's experiment is precisely recounted and seen as motivated not by
mere material greed (2:4–10) but rather by a need to grasp wisdom and
especially the nature and origins of the All-concept. K describes his
expansiveness, his thirst for experience and discovery. He speaks know-
ingly about envy (4:4) and describes his achievements as beyond compare or better than everyone else's (2:9). Gradually, disappointment sets
in, and this sense of individual limitation is a crucial step in a growing
perception: if the individual cannot comprehend "the all" of nature,
either by possession or through understanding, how then can he hope to
grasp Elohim, the Infinite that is their source and the ground of the
totality's limitation? In other words, if man cannot even adequately
comprehend what is under the sun or heavens, how can he possibly
expect to understand what is above the heavens? This reading, which
owes much to Rabbinic exegesis, corresponds to Lévinas's (1969) distinction between a totality and an infinity. Man seems to have a natural
tendency to totalize individual experience by assuming either that the
world is entirely for him, or that the infinite can actually be circum-
scribed by individual experience and concepts. Kohelet is brought to

---

20. That this other need not be God can be seen in 9:9: "Enjoy life with the woman you
love."

reinsert such pseudototalities into the infinite—this is, in fact, what enables us to view them as mere totalities—by the conclusion that God is to be feared.

Maupassant was convinced that we only fear what we don't understand, and the observation can be applied to the start of an inquiry on wisdom such as Prov 1:7: "Fear of the Lord is the first principle [Scott 1965] of knowledge," when the student is overwhelmed at what he or she doesn't know. Such a void can be felt pragmatically, as a glimpse toward the Unknown in which our reality and destiny are entwined. But has no ground been covered, no meaningful knowledge acquired, by the end of such a weighty meditation as Kohelet? However, there is another form of fear, more structured or definable, based not on God's unknowable essence but on the unpredictability of divine action. In each and every circumstance of moment, there is an anxiety as to whether God will judge "justly" (i.e., according to our notions or justice), or whether the inexorable rise and fall of nature will again be operative. Or, will God, in infinite wisdom, do what is right even if we don't at the moment understand?[21]

I do not think that Kohelet sets out to ground such a trust, any more than he intends to portray a personal God. But the book does something perhaps even more basic: it attempts to describe the conditions without which such possibilities are not even conceivable:

> Freedom is not a value in itself, but it remains the condition of any value that man can attain. The sacred that surrounds me and carries me away is violence. (Lévinas 1976, 28–29)[22]

But God's respect for human freedom implies mutual respect, for the God of Hebrew Scripture has all the personal characteristics of the Other, and the necessity of liberating man from God has as its corollary the liberation of God from man. Thus, God's Freedom and Goodness cannot be constrained by His Justice, and this is one of the consequences of the "gift" argument (see the next section).

Further, K's argument that "chance determines everything" is typical, but it must be reduced to the mere possibility that "chance may have a part in" everything. This means that normal deed and consequence is still operative but that God is not bound by His creation or His created justice, that He can overrule things if He wishes. That despair and

---

21. For "fear of the Lord," see also Prov 28:14: "Blessed is the man who fears the Lord always; but he who hardens his heart will fall into calamity." Solomon lost his fear, and this could motivate P's reminder to fear the Lord.

22. Quoted in Finkielkraut (1984, 116), who adds a very pertinent commentary.

questioning of God's justice and providence exist in Kohelet is too obvious to question, but the view that these are rigid conclusions of a totalizing nature has been pushed to absurd limits. The wisdom teachers, following the biblical tradition, had taught control of life and confidence that deeds have their predictable consequences. When this doesn't always happen as expected, the sufferer or perplexed raises questions, and such questions are apt to be exaggerated. To expose such exaggeration is but part of the sage's duty, thus safeguarding the general claim of God's goodness and justice.

But what of the "exceptions"? A comparison may help. The prophets had learned that gentiles do not repent. Jonah's refusal to go to Nineveh is a forceful expression of this conviction. The lesson of the Book, however, is that no nation (and certainly not God) can be bound by rules of thumb. In the same way, without denying divine Justice in general and in the long run, such questions as K's have as their necessary response that God is supremely free; His mercy cannot be limited by humanity's conceptions and expectations. Zimmerli (1962, 139) has described this "very heart of Yahwism," the concern for divine freedom (Crenshaw 1987, 38), by calling Kohelet the "Watchman over God's transcendence."

(3e) God's Presen/ce/ts

God's Holy Presence is not noteworthy in Kohelet, and Roland Murphy's (1990a) recent complaint that in Kohelet God is so far removed from human beings that communion is impossible may be viewed as simply a different way of describing the divine transcendence that, as I have just argued, is one of the Book's arguments. Yet God is most persistently present to humanity, in a positive way, in an area that one would least likely expect, in connection with bodily pleasures. The argument is rooted in creation theology: Kohelet urges us to accept not God's grace but His gifts; or, as a Midrashist might put it, "don't read His presence but rather His presents"!

The subject of eating and drinking punctuates our text, appearing at seven major intervals.[23] Note carefully that each mention of pleasure is followed by the indication that it comes from God:

I. Koh 2:24–26
    Man has no greater good than eating and drinking and finding pleasure in his work itself.
    I have concluded that this too is from the hand of God.

---

23. These seven "epicurean" texts were grouped together and clearly related to their divine sanction by François Rousseau (1981, 210–11); see also Whybray's discussion (1982).

Yet who eats and enjoys if not I?
Yet to the one He favors He gives wisdom and knowledge and happiness,
but to the sinner He gives the task of gathering and amassing, only to hand
it over to whomever God wishes.

II. Koh 3:12–13
I do know that man's only good is to be happy and enjoy his life in
the present.
But I also know that, whenever man eats and drinks and enjoys his work,
this is a gift of God. For I know that all that God does will remain forever.

III. Koh 3:22
That is why I think that man has no good other than being happy
in his work, for this is his portion.
Yet who except God can bring him to ponder what will be afterwards?

IV. Koh 5:17–19 (E18–20)
This is what I have discovered: that it is good and proper to eat and drink
and take enjoyment in the very labor that one does under the sun during the
number of days of one's life that the Lord hath given him, for this is his
portion.

Indeed, every man to whom God has given wealth and possessions
and the power to enjoy them . . .
. . . and to take up his portion and enjoy his toil, this is precisely God's
gift.

Then he should not be overly intent upon the span of his entire life!
Indeed, God answers him through the joy of his heart.

V. Koh 8:15
As for me I recommend contentedness, for there is nothing better for man
under the sun than to eat and drink and be content, and this contentedness
should accompany his labor all the days of his life that God has given him
under the sun.

VI. Koh 9:7–10
Then go, eat your food in contentment and drink your wine with a glad
heart because God has already approved your actions.

VII. Koh 11:8–10
And if a man lives for many years, let him be contented with them all!
But let him also remember that the days of darkness will be many.

All that dies is vanity . . . follow the desires of your heart and the wishes of your eyes.

And know that for all these things God will call you to justice.

The puzzle or contradiction of such passages can be successfully interpreted by recalling the thematic dialectic that underlies Kohelet: the Pessimistic one from $+ > -$, and the opposite one from $- > +$. We thus, again, have two theories of pleasure: one that regards eating and drinking as a *faute de mieux* (2:24), and one that views pleasure as a gift of God. According to the first view, this kind of *simḥah,* viewed as purely temporary, is based on despair over our mortality and has to it a frenzied violence reminiscent of Isa 22:13:

> . . . rejoicing and merriment,
> Killing of cattle and slaughtering of sheep,
> Eating of meat and drinking of wine:
> "Eat and drink, for tomorrow we die!"

In the second sense, happiness or *simḥah* means "contentment," in the Rabbinic sense of "happy with one's lot," *sameaḥ be-ḥelqo;* cf. 8:15; 9:7; 10:19. An important difference between the two views is that the first can only be held during actual pleasure, for carpe diem means the day of pleasure $(+ > -)$. By contrast, the second is a permanent frame of mind, so that even in displeasure one can be contented (thus $- > +$, or perhaps even $+ > +$). Thus, 3:14, the argument that "all that God does *will remain forever,"* occurring right after one of the major joy passages, even suggests that momentary pleasures are seeds of eternity when given by the Eternal and properly received. At the very least, present enjoyment should not be dissociated from the source of pleasure, which is awareness of God's gift.

Two concepts in particular help relate our pleasures to their divine sanction. The first is *ḥeleq.* The concept of one's portion is crucial to the debate, and its ambivalence is well established. On the one hand (see 2:10n), "portion" is associated with "reward, payment," a sense congenial to the pessimist, who from the start wishes to discuss only what comes to humans from their own effort, the *'amal she-ya'amol;* thus "portion" and "reward" are synonymous (see Part Two, xv, 9:6 and 9:5). Gradually, however, a second sense emerges, that of "inheritance," indicating whatever man acquires independent of his own efforts or merit, what he is granted as a gift. This view is the Optimist's because it allows God an active role in one's happiness (see 5:17nn, 18; 9:9; also 2:10n).

The second concept that theologizes pleasure is that of God's communication with man's heart in happiness, since it is asserted that "God
answers him through the joy of his heart" (*ma'aneh-hu' be-simhat libo*,
5:19). To claim that this refers to yet another of God's distractions, to the
divine intent to divert human attention from knowing God, seems to me
to stretch the limits of joy beyond acceptable bounds, for if one claims
that God teases, taunts, tortures us, then one cannot claim that this is
pleasurable, either in fact or in intent.

What then about *simhah*? It covers a range from sensual enjoyment to
refined spiritual pleasure. A proof, say some, that it cannot come from
God (despite Kohelet's sevenfold assertion to the contrary!). But the
opposite could also be argued: that joy is such an important part of life
that no dimension of it could be ignored, and that God can be sensed
with proper understanding even in the body's keenest pleasures. This is
as incredible as Tertullian's believing because it is absurd. Yet it is
broadly democratic in that it is accessible to all humans, as is the gratitude it must stimulate and which is its fulfillment. It suggests that the
universe is indeed FULL of God and that God is good because He FILLS us
at every moment and at every level of our being, even to the "lowest,"
thereby uplifted.

Of the two a fortiori arguments in Kohelet only one has received
proper commentary, the one that justifies the royal fiction: if the king,
highest in wisdom and power, can call everything vanity, then who are
we to contradict (see below, 4d)? There is another argument, however:
God wishes our enjoyment even of His lowliest gifts such as eating and
drinking. If the book praised only wisdom, one could argue withdrawal
from normal existence and asceticism: of course we are to love wisdom,
because of its lofty nature, but surely not coarse bodily pleasures! But it
must be recognized that it is as difficult for God-fearers to eat and drink
in joy as it is, say, for gluttons to meditate on God's wisdom.

4

K versus P: The Dialogue of Characters

Despite its contribution to the essay and to the autobiographical genre, Kohelet is of course not a modern psychological novel. There is a level of personal analysis and confession and characterization that leads in that direction, however, for as the work progresses the points of view or ideologies or voices take on the density of life-interests and personalities.

Among K's many personae in this work, the following stand out: King (Solomon?), wealthy entrepreneur, anti-sage (and, thus, sage), teacher, pessimist, autobiographer, essayist, and perhaps traversing them all: collector. It is therefore essential, in listing and weighing the various themes and topics under discussion, to test the quality of the speaker. Why, for example, the pseudonym? Why the implied relation to King Solomon? Why the extreme bitterness? These qualities of the speaker account for some of the verbal characteristics of the text and must be discussed in any total assessment of Kohelet.

(4a) Wisdom of Experience and Experience of Wisdom

K is a man of knowledge: "I had set my heart to knowing" (1:17), "I and my heart turned repetitively to know and explore" (7:25). Yet, for K as for Socrates, knowledge consists also and perhaps especially in knowing that one does not know.[24] This sense of the limitations of knowledge is especially strong in Kohelet; it is what is usually known as the work's skepticism and is one of its most distinctive features.

Two aspects of this concept in the Hebrew Bible seem especially relevant to our discussion. First, biblical consciousness is profoundly ambivalent about knowledge (da'at). In Eden the tree of knowledge already involved a dialectic: no good without bad. Although this can be taken as referring to man's ability to make judgments of moral value, to distinguish right from wrong, the passage does appear in paradoxical juxtaposition to God's own judgment concerning the "good" of creation. Now, if God saw that the world is good (presumably all good and

---

24. Cf. 6:12: "who can know what is really good for a man"; 8:7: "man does not know what will be"; also 2:19; 3:11; 8:1, 17; 9:1, 12; 10:14; 11:2, 5–6.

with no mixture of bad), one still wants to ask: good for whom? Since man was not yet created, one is required to reply: good for God, perhaps because it is His handiwork and therefore creativity is a good in itself. But this begs the question, or perhaps K would rather say that it forces the question that the work constantly raises and decides cannot be answered: knowledge of good and evil cannot be attained by man concerning the ultimate purposes of God's creation. It would seem, therefore, that this aspect of K's skepticism is consonant with biblical attitudes.

Second, Adam's "knowledge" of his wife (*yada'*, Gen 4:1) further stresses the experiential character of knowing, which includes *connaissance* as well as *savoir*. It is important to notice K's constant effort to attach his knowledge to its experiential origins. In drawing conclusions he often alludes to what he has seen and done, to his personal experiment and experiences. From this perspective, however, Wisdom's programmatic promise to the inexperienced youth or *na'ar* in Prov 1:4 to furnish knowledge (*da'at*) must appear paradoxical, since it is intended precisely to short-circuit the experiential component. Indeed, an important function of wisdom proverbs is to issue warnings about the dangers of existence: physical dangers to survival and spiritual dangers of sin. What wisdom proposes on faith to the inexperienced is rather a substitute experience, with the knowledge-value of real experience but packaged, quicker, easier, and especially safer. Thus again, knowledge discloses a paradox at its heart, since wisdom's knowing is not real (experiential) knowledge and since experiential knowledge can be both dangerous and disappointing.

There is a third ambivalence of knowledge, and in biblical literature we are especially indebted to K for its analysis. It may be summarized by asking what is the knowledge that *knows* that it does *not know*. For K, this more general and firm knowledge is itself experiential, a point made clear by a discourse that constantly enumerates the experiences that have led to his conclusion. His knowledge of ignorance, in other words, is grounded on a description which constantly shifts from the particular to the general, and this is in fact how descriptions proceed: from a reconstruction of things seen or done or experienced ("I did, I built, I collected") to more general formulations, using the well-known techniques of metonymic contiguity (the wind blows to no purpose, so too with man) and synecdoche (the part for the whole, thus allowing partial experience to lead to the quick conclusion that "it has *all* been seen or done or heard or written before"), similar to the paleontologist who reconstructs an entire prehistoric animal from a single molar.[25] But in Kohelet there is no control on the limits of generalization, which, once attained ("all is vanity"),

25. See Hamon (1981, 50–51).

is allowed to proceed in inverse fashion, from the general to the particular, so that imagination is aborted and all of life becomes subject to a sure and predictable knowing. This may account for why K's descriptive (scientific) statements have such an argumentative quality, as if he were trying to persuade (others, and perhaps himself).

V. 1:13, with its two possible views, is a fair summary of the arguments or dialogics concerning wisdom, whether K's experiment is conducted through wisdom or on its behalf. The usual view is that K uses his wisdom to gain an understanding of the world (Fox 1989, 174), but this approach is more descriptive of P, as we shall soon see. K does not set out to explore with his wisdom but rather for it; he wants to acquire wisdom, but from the perspective of his own lived experience. It may of course be true that, even to set out on such a project, one has to be wise to begin with, just as one has to be already a lover of wisdom in order to become wise, or have the fear of God in order to become a God-fearer. But the point still stands: K wishes to test and use experience (as opposed to revelation or tradition or advice) as a means of getting wise. His questions are: What wisdom does experience give? Can experience be the sole and complete basis for wisdom? P's reply is that wisdom cannot be entirely reduced to experiential verification, it presupposes a source from beyond the individual. But K is persistent: he does not use his wisdom to gain an understanding of the world but rather the opposite: he uses the world to understand wisdom.

The interesting thing about Kohelet is that, contrary to modern attitudes, it is the man of faith (P) that is more open-minded than the man of experience. He is doggedly unwilling to foreclose on God's nature or to infer the nature of things in general from particular human experiences, no matter how broad and privileged. For him the all of one's life, the sum total of his acts, as Sartre said, does not allow conclusions concerning the All.[26]

It may be anachronistic, however, to view Hebrew Scripture through the prism of the more modern dialectic of faith versus reasoned experience, and the more appropriate categories may be the debate between empiricism and myth. This possibility is especially evident in the opening debate on the nature of the universe: K's questionable generalizations are always given as the results of observation, while P's refutation resorts to highly complex and evocative metaphors:

1. whereas experience teaches that humans are born and die, the *earth* endures forever (1:4), evoking one of the original "parents" of cre-

---

26. Montaigne was the first modern to argue this reduction when he uttered the paradox: "mon être universel comme Michel de Montaigne" (*Essais*, 3:2).

ation (Gen 1:1) and perhaps too "that Promised Land" at the end of history and which has its scriptural manifestation in the Land of Israel, goal of the wanderings in the desert.

2. the *place* (*maqom*) where the sun and waters originate and to which they go (1:5, 7), thus their point of origin and destination and the coincidence of the two. In view of such passages, it is quite understandable that later Jewish theology referred to God as "the Place."[27]

3. the revolving movement (*shab*) of what K calls the *wind* (1:6) is perceived by P as the spirit that forever "returns," picturing the movement of universal return of repentance (*teshubah*), the chance to try again (cf. ★1:7n *return to their source*).

4. the universal abundance observed by K (1:8) is grasped by P as a *fullness,* perhaps stressing its relation to the Creator, as in such texts as Ps 24:1: "To the Lord belongs the earth and its fullness."

What seems clear is that, as against the empirically based conclusion of K that all is vanity, P counters with a series of concepts that take on the density of myths of beginnings and ultimate ends, challenging the narrowness of experiential empiricism with notions that cannot possibly be verified by the same methods. P creates a tension by reinterpreting K's devalued image of total vanity with a reenergized version of the same: "less than All cannot satisfy man" (Blake).[28]

(4b) The Collector's Greed

The major focus of K's extended autobiographical statement is his vigorous labor in gathering and building and collecting and increasing things for his personal use. It is therefore quite possible that the vanity conclusion is meant to apply less to the All than to these activities themselves:

> I considered the works of my hands and the effort expended, and, behold, all was vanity. (Koh 2:11)

Readers are often willing to overlook the unflattering implications of all this, on the premise that, after all, it was all done for the sake of wisdom and as an experiment, and, following K, pass the blame along and upstairs, to "God the despot," so to speak.

The text speaks quite clearly about this matter, however:

27. "Why is the Holy One called The Place? Because He is the Place of the world, and the world is not His place" (Bereshit Rabbah 68).

28. Quoted in Kolakowski (1989, xii).

I performed great works, built . . . , planted . . . , made . . . , constructed . . . , acquired . . . , collected silver and gold . . . , all human pleasures . . . , grew great and amassed riches beyond all that were before me in Jerusalem . . . , denied my eyes no craving . . . , deprived my heart of no pleasure. (Koh 2:4–10)

This aspect of Kohelet reinforces the inevitable comparison with Solomon; the traditional sources make the point that Solomon collected everything (horses, women, wisdom) and displayed a tendency toward excess and grandeur. But one must reflect further upon the close relation between K's energetic and acquisitive existential project and his various levels of totalization, his constant reference to "all." Scripture makes prominent use of such generalizations, as applied either to God's creative activity in Genesis or to the choices that man must make. Here is one of the best known:

And you shall love the Lord your God with *all* your heart, and with *all* your soul, and with *all* your might. (Deut 6:5)

By contrast, K's use of well-known scriptural categories and language makes his own position and opposition that much more obvious. Indeed, his call to "follow the desires of your heart and the wishes of your eyes" (11:9) seems intended to test such scriptural warnings as the following:

. . . not to follow after your own heart and your own eyes, which you are inclined to go after wantonly. (Num 15:39, RSV; see also 1:13n *explore*)

I submit that it does not require an excessive sensitivity to literary allusiveness to detect the censure implied in such quotations. K has gone too far, and nowhere does his autobiography sound more confessional.

(4c) Pessimism and Gratitude

K's too close or exclusive attachment to experiential reality is related to his humanistic focus on this life, on what happens "under" the sun or heavens. As we have seen, this prevents him from developing perspectives for the future and beyond natural causality. But it also limits his notion of origins to its phenomenal aspect; it forecloses on the possibility of seeing life as a divine gift.

This latter possibility is argued by P in a paradoxical fashion, as seen above (3e), by juxtaposing K's buzzwords "vanity" and "under the sun" with the notion of gift: "Enjoy life with the woman you love . . . which

He has given you all the days of your vanity under the sun" (9:9; also
5:17, 8:15). The argument is presented all the more strongly by quoting
the pet phrases of the opponent, almost in a mocking way. Similarly, P's
concluding call to "in the days of your youth remember your Creator"
(12:1) may also be intended to evoke gratitude.

One of the most resistant differences between P and K is on the
question whether the very ability to enjoy is also God's gift (P) or
whether it depends on humans (K). K's position is stoic: humans should
be able to provide for their own happiness, or at least their merit should
not be imagined as depending on any factor other than their own efforts.
But when men and women extend their activity into the world, they
meet with constant frustration: the concrete results are never satisfying!
In the first phase K gives full rein to his naturally expansive desires; in
the end he questions their usefulness and seems convinced that God has
given them to humans to their harm. The Presenter also acknowledges
the natural desire for fulfillment, but his final position is in essence that
of the Sages: "Who is rich? He who is filled, satisfied, contented, who
rejoices (ha-sameah) in his portion" (Abot 4:1). If this Rabbinic text can
be projected on Kohelet, then the book's frequent mention of simhah
suggests that positive enjoyment of that life given to us is a form of
acknowledgment and gratitude.

(4d) K as King

The quite extensive autobiographical statement from 1:12 to 2:11 begins
by the notation "I, Kohelet, was king over Israel in Jerusalem," and this
has led to referring to section 1:12–2:26 as the "royal fiction." Whether
K's statement is autobiographical in a literal and historical sense is not our
concern here and is at any rate not verifiable at present. Of greater literary
interest is the reason for representing K as a king. The usual explanation
has the merit of psychological consistency, namely, that no one can speak
with greater authority than the king about the worth of wealth and power
(Crenshaw 1987, 70). That is to say, by portraying the King-sage as
highest in both wisdom and power, there is an implicit a fortiori argument
against the further pursuit of experience: If he couldn't, how could you?

There is a question of literary consistency, however, and this question
is usually obstructed by the commonly held view that the royal fiction
applies only to this section of the book.[29] In point of fact, the theme of
kingship pervades the entire dialogue, and later allusions shed a strange
light on the initial section. There is, first of all, the question of the king's
stature: "Woe unto you, Land whose king is a foolish youth. . . . Happy

29. See, for example, Williams (1981, 28).

are you, Land whose king is well-born" (10:16–17). Such a discussion on the quality and qualifications of the king cast a bitter reflection on the earlier boast of uniqueness based on sheer power (2:12), and relative wealth based apparently on conquest (2:8). Related to the pursuit of power is a series of threats emanating from K (= the king):

> Keep the king's commands! (Koh 8.2)

> Don't hasten to leave the king's presence! (Koh 8:3)

> . . . he can do whatever he wishes. (Koh 8:3)

> Do not curse the king even in your thoughts! (Koh 10:20)

Such very explicit warnings may point to weaknesses of kingship, and in fact there is a second series of threats, these not originating from the king but rather directed toward him:

> A mere child, low-born but wise, is better than an aged king who is foolish and no longer able to defend himself. (Koh 4:13)

> Even a king is subject to the soil. (Koh 5:8)

> Wisdom is better than strength. (Koh 9:16, said in reference to the anecdote of the great king and the lowly sage in 9:14–15)

> The quiet words of the sages are heard better than the screaming of the king of fools. (Koh 9:17)

Of course, this last example concerns the opposition between sages and fools, and yet, especially when compared with passages such as 4:13, it reflects badly on kings as well.

We may now be able to grasp the meaning of K's much discussed declaration that "I *was* king" (1:12). What is a king who no longer rules? Barring overthrow, which admittedly may be hinted in such texts as 4:14, kingship is a tenured appointment and one cannot imagine a parent or a pope announcing retirement. Literary tradition, at least, is clearly negative about such decisions, and when the best-known retiree, King Lear, divests himself of power, it is accounted to him as a fool.

In Kohelet the literary figure of the retired king is introduced less for autobiographical purposes than to bring to the center of debate the question and value of withdrawal from public affairs and, by extension, worldly involvement. This is one of the constants of the debate between P and K and the occasion for some of their most biting satire. K's withdrawal is not a philosophical one, nor does he promote contemplative withdrawal à la Charles V. Rather, he has come to the conclusion, through the frustrations of experience, that life is simply not worth the bother. This is not the cool and blasé observation of Voltaire's Pococurante in *Candide* but the cry of anguish of one who passionately desired and tried to succeed, and whose disappointments are real: with women, wealth, wisdom, justice, and the like. He has therefore withdrawn from power while retaining, like Lear, the habit of its use, and this accounts for K's constant ambivalence: his world-weariness and yet keen sense of pique, his recognition of the unfairness of poverty (9:16) and yet appreciation of the advantages of wealth (10:19), his argument on the vanity of power and his threats to keep the king's commands. Thus, on inspection, the royal fiction is both pervasive in extent and remarkably complex. It portrays ambivalence less about the king's political status than about his psychological commitments and reservations,[30] and this portrait is fashioned in dramatic dialogue with the potential usurper of power: the adviser-sage.

(4e) K the Pedagogue

> The students of Rabbi Yochanan Ben Zakkai once asked him: "How is the [rite of the red] heifer performed?" He said to them: "In the gold garments [of the High Priest]." They said to him: "But Rabbi, you have taught us [that it is to be performed] in the white garments [of a common priest]!" He said to them: "You have spoken well. If I have forgotten things that I have done with my own hands and seen with my own eyes, all the more so with things heard with my own ears." But the case was not that he didn't know *but rather that he wanted to stimulate his students.*
>
> And some say that they asked Hillel the Elder. And it was not that he didn't know but rather that he wanted to stimulate his students. For Rabbi Joshuah used to say: "Whoever learns but does not labor [at it] is like a man who sows but does not reap."[31]

Given these positions and portrayals of K or Solomon, the most difficult issue to determine is his own status as a sage. Does K in fact conform to

---

30. A closely related topic is K's age: is K young or old? The commonsensical view is the latter, since he is pessimistic and disgruntled, life-weary from his experiences and not at all hopeful about the future. But the Rabbis disagreed as to whether Solomon wrote the book in his youth or his old age. In favor of the latter view is the statement that "I *was* king over Jerusalem." But the opposite view also has textual support, first in the possibility that all this pessimism is really juvenile and rejected by the later and more mature sage (Presenter). There is also v. 11:9, where the sage turns to K and calls him a youth, thus making K a parody of the *puer-senex* topos: he is old in experience but young in both years and wisdom!

31. Tosefta (on Parah 4:1). The rite of the red heifer is described in Num 19:1–21.

any recognizable image of wisdom? Consider once again his analogies between human hope and natural determinism and his consequent doubt as to spiritual growth; his negativism regarding the creation and the Creator; his rejection of wisdom and faith unless based on his own personal experience. That these positions are deeply felt, that it is possible to speak of K's critique of his real greed for experience and power, means of course the quite positive quality of his being able to learn from experience but hardly constitutes what was then regarded as wisdom. Worldly-wise is not ipso facto wise. Why then does P insist in his summation that "Kohelet was not only himself a sage but also added to wisdom by teaching the people knowledge" (12:9)?

The link between K's wisdom and his role as a teacher may provide a clue. For sages the truth may be all important, but for the teacher it must be presented at the level of the student. Socratic irony is perhaps the most famous literary example of this, but anyone who has ever attended class knows that teacher's tricks are as expected as they are unpredictable. To consider K as the devil's advocate, one must also recall that Satan is also a servant of the Most High; in Job, too, God did not refuse the dialogue or its challenge.

With the image of the pedagogue the representation of K comes full circle: it is here that the argument of the book is reintegrated with the character and professional standing of the hero. It at least suggests a resolution to the pessimist's experiential dilemmas, but the point cannot be fully appreciated from the perspective of modern attitudes. One would need a more traditional view of the spiritual dimensions of debate and contestation, such as the following:

> There is no better companion than a book, nor one even so good; and to pursue an argument with it is worth more than peace.
>
> The more one engages in tenacious dispute with the book, the more good knowledge he will continue to acquire.
>
> (Santob de Carrión, fourteenth century [cited in Perry 1987, 36])

For such a culture dialogue is of paramount importance in its mediation of intellectual doubts that are also lived convictions. I readily admit to have painted an unconventional portrait of the sage Kohelet: a man who without regard to orthodoxies states his experience with full awareness of his limitations, who delights in controversy and in being challenged and corrected because this is the life of the mind and of truth and of dialogue and human encounter. In this view Kohelet becomes an early version of that Montaigne that even the fideist Pascal was forced to admire: the author of the admirable essay on conversation. With this pedagogical image of K we may now return to the original perspective of Hillel and Shammai and ask why *both* sides of the debate have to be represented, why the Presenter felt obliged to preserve as well as challenge K's existential claims.

5

K Versus P: The Dialogue of Topics

(5a) Vanity, Profit, Labor, Enjoyment, etc.

One favorite approach to the interpretation of Kohelet consists in listing its "main topics." The weakness of this approach lies in that the work gives multiple (usually two) points of view for nearly any topic one can identify. It may be helpful to review a typical listing of the topics of Kohelet, but always with an eye to the dialectical structure that gives them meaning. How then do the arguments measure up as the two sides square off?

Many readers take their clue from the opening verses (1:2–3) and therefore list the following as the main topics:

Vanity (*hebel*)
Profit (*yitron*)
Labor or Effort (*'amal*).

However, such a reading is misleading and unwarranted for both textual and generic reasons. First of all, the text is careful to delimit these themes with greater precision. Thus,

VANITY   It is not asserted that "reality" is vanity but rather that "all" is vanity (and, as I argue in my Translation and Commentary, this is first introduced as a question rather than as an assertion). One therefore must go on to inquire what is meant by this "all." For example, it is entirely possible that the content of this question ("Is all vanity?") is specified in the next sentence: everything is vanity because humans derive no profit (see Commentary 1:2, *vanity*). The perspective of human benefit is quite different from the claim that all reality is vanity.

PROFIT   This term is immediately and precisely limited to what comes to a person from his or her own efforts. Second and more important, the decisive limitation of this opening statement of theme is its literary or generic one. Indeed, this initial thematic statement is just that: not a conclusion or even a statement of the work's main theme, but rather an agenda for discussion, a tentative formulation that will become modified considerably as a result of the ensuing debate. To review the lines of discussion, the purely humanistic focus ("man") will be expanded to include God's gifts (if not purposes), and the ideas of LABOR AND EFFORT will lose their exclusive power to define what is worthwhile or beneficial. A good analogy would be a subject proposed at the start of debate in a learned academy, and, as is well known in such debates, initial topics themselves become subject to reformulation.[32]

ENJOYMENT   Though usually taken as a main theme, enjoyment is often viewed in opposition to vanity. K is seen as faced with a choice and must decide either/or. But it may be more correct to see a causal connection between the two, as in the verse "gather ye rosebuds while ye may *for* tomorrow you shall die." There is this strain of thinking in Kohelet, except that K seems to favor stoic over epicurean reasons: pleasure is to be pursued not because it is either enjoyable or tentative but for the reason and to the precise degree that enjoyment may be within my power.

That indeed is K's view, either real or hypothetical, but it is not P's. What needs to be further explored is the religious use to which the two themes may be put. Just as Tertullian said that he believed *because* it is absurd, K asserts enjoyment against the void. We also recall that K's pursuit of enjoyment was not for its own sake but rather for wisdom and knowledge. The dialectic of the text seeks to clarify and deepen this perception, by suggesting that this void is really the Divine Will, for example, by intimating that the future void of death may be but an aspect of the Ground of being that gives man whatever he has. Gradually, enjoyment becomes reattached to its source, and pleasure is seen as sanctioned precisely because it is given (cf. Rad 1972b, 231; also Bergant 1984, 59). As seen in (3e), this is one of P's major argumentative achievements.

WISDOM   K argues that wisdom is experiential and has no value beyond the realm of practicality. His disenchantment with wisdom is rather complex, for beyond the hard work and lack of results that its acquisition involves, there is also for K a distrust of sages, their anger and greed, and especially the claim that they constitute a special class of humanity. For P, by contrast, wisdom is not only or even essentially experiential (personal and based on the past) but rather geared to the future and scriptural promises and hopes.

KNOWLEDGE   K feels he has experienced everything that it is possible for a single person (the king) to experience, and this hardheadedness is also his limitation. P's questions suggest that knowledge is not the final answer—it does not lead to salvation, for example, as Jobling (1986, 37) noted—but K still insists that it is the essential fact of human experience.

JUSTICE   For K justice is shockingly absent, both among men and in

---

32. At the end of the seventeenth century the Spanish poet Miguel de Barrios debated such a question before a literary academy in Amsterdam. The subject: "Which is the greater perfection, beauty or intelligence?" The poet's reply points in the direction of P's views: "Beauty has more perfection than intelligence, inasmuch as beauty is a divine gift, whereas intelligence is a purely human skill."

God. P maintains that there will certainly be a judgment, though He delay.

AUTHORITY   K's insistence on authority shows that he is an absolutist, perhaps because of his conviction that all men are wicked. P seems to prefer the model of the sage-king.

ANGER   Anger is one of the focal points of discussion. The crux is that anger arises from vanity, from the absence of permanent benefit (money, wisdom) from our efforts, and from the spectacle of injustice. Here, there is no use arguing with K that evil almost does not exist, as Maimonides would have it, for his experience proves the contrary, and his reaction is an angry one. At another level there is staged anger (7:3f), not really felt but put on for correctional purposes. K is suspicious, however, for such demonstrations cause the sage to resemble the fool. The correctives are either P's, which is towards faith, or a stoical settling for what *is* within our power, which are the *ways* we think about things. This solution is implicit in both kinds of anger; just as the sage can simulate emotion, one can turn one's thoughts to less painful ways of thinking. However, when P concludes the point on such an inner focus ("remove anger from your heart," 11:10), K adds his typical epicurean flavoring: "And remove sadness from your flesh," so much so that P is compelled to remove to theological ground: "Remember your Creator."

OPTIMISM AND PESSIMISM   K is ready to draw the line, add up his experiences and draw conclusions. He has made as much effort as can be expected and finds life wanting. P believes that all the information is not yet in, and that the past is not a compelling sign for the future.

(5b) Conclusions: Optimism, Pessimism, and the Canon

I have not argued that pessimism is absent from Kohelet but merely that it is not the only voice, that the "all is vanity" assertion is not a conclusion but merely an arguable position, albeit expressed with vehemence. That it is not an absolute position can be seen from other positive aspects of the book: that what humans enjoy from their own labor is good and not vanity (see Rashbam [in Japhet and Salters 1985] on 2:24–27); that human enterprise is to be encouraged (11:1–6); that wisdom is an advantage, though not an absolute one. From our study of the famous "Catalogue of Times" we noted the possibility of an optimistic structure of human time, one that opens toward salvation—not supinely being saved, of course, but rather receiving the God-given chance to save one's self.[33] Indeed, if

33. A splendid recent example of such a concept of time is the Israeli poet Yehuda Amichai's optimism over the eventual peace between Arabs and Israelis: "it will take time. That's why it's so hopeful, because it's just a question of time" (*Jerusalem Post,* international edition, 10 August 1991: 12).

Elohim made all things good in their time, this includes vanity or *hebel,* perhaps even more so in inverse proportion to its appearance of insecurity, as in the daily Jewish blessing that God "suspends the earth upon the waters." In a stunning image the Rabbis have claimed that "this world subsists only because of the breath [*hebel,* vanity] of school children" (Resh Lakish in the name of Rabbi Yehudah haNasi, in BT Shabbat 119b). André Néher (1951, 73) made the attractive suggestion that *hebel* is also the name of the innocent son of Adam and Eve, whose life was useless in that it was violently cut off, and yet it is recorded that his offering was pleasing to God.

There is thus basis for an important distinction between "*hebel* that has sin in it and *hebel* that doesn't" (BT Shabbat 119b). We might conclude this discussion by using one of those reversals so dear to the wisdom writers: if it can be argued that All is vanity, then vanity is at least an essential part of the All. In his beautiful essay on vanity (*Essais* 3:9), Montaigne views his subject alternately as the virtue of the weak and as the absence of evil; in this latter instance he recalls the "vanity" of those Spartan warriors who pared their nails and did their hair before launching into battle.

In conclusion, the Book of Kohelet proposes that our existence is neither futile nor ephemeral; or, rather, that neither of these connotations of vanity (*hebel*) is necessarily pessimistic. Our life is not futile because things can get better as well as worse; even its ephemerality is a source of contented pleasure and thus a way of knowing God, indeed, within the dialogue of a contented heart, a way of feeling God's presen/ce/ts.

In the end the Presenter has also learned an important lesson: he who speaks last does not necessarily speak best, only last and for the moment. Until this point his attitude toward K's pessimism had been oppositional and corrective. He does *not* feel that the world is utter vanity. But now his point of view has changed. He has now come to the conclusions of the Houses of Hillel and Shammai: since it is more than possible that on balance the world *is* vanity, *therefore* one had better watch one's step and fear the Lord. Such fear is no longer a prejudgment of life, not the "beginning" of wisdom viewed as an attempt to avoid the pleasures and especially the pains of existence. Rather, it recognizes the need to live *through* one's existence and to respect the Ground of our transience. K's case has to be presented in Scripture because our last recourse is not faith but our own experience. This is the bottom line, what one turns to when everything else fails, when competing faiths fall short or no longer make sense or shock by their unscrupulousness and vanity. It is not an ideal remedy but, as Montaigne was to argue at the start of his Kohelet-like "De la Vanité," it is the only one available. It occurs at the inner point where a human says "I" and discovers his or her moral nature. It is at this precise moment that one tries to account for one's experience of the world, and here one discovers conflict and contradiction. The Dialogues with Kohelet propose a dialogic model for viewing such conflict as not only livable but also necessary.[34]

Kohelet argues that dialogue is a spiritual mode, a way of living and relating to reality.[35] Dialogue is both the structural essence of Kohelet and the key to the book's spirituality. It includes the effort fairly and respectfully to represent the other's point of view and then challenge it. Dialogue thus bridges the gap between revelation and experience, faith and reason, salvation and indifference; it helps explain religion's interest in secularism and, conversely, how purely human concerns are drawn to ultimate questions. But any alluring reductionism must be avoided; the goal is not the conversion of the other but rather sympathetic coexistence and sharing—better yet, understanding the value of plurality of this created world in the first place. At such a juncture speculation leaps in and various models have been proposed; for instance, the radically theological one of Ben Sirach (33:15):

> See now all the works of the High God: they are paired, the one the opposite of the other.

I personally prefer the more workaday approach of the modern poet Yehuda Amichai (1991, 12), who tries to understand why poets use metaphor (and, I would add, why we use proverbs and *meshalim,* comparisons, which seek to understand things in terms of something else):

> Always comparing. That's why we have two halves, two of everything. Otherwise you'd have one eye, half a nose, no perspective. And you couldn't compare things. This way there's resonance.

Thus, at the root of things there is, in addition to the need for difference, a longing for similarity that constantly, dialogically, bridges gaps. Amichai (1991, 12) continues:

34. I mean morally necessary, very much in the sense of the dialogic observation that claims that "when you are going in the same direction as everyone else, then you may be going in the wrong direction." When, for example, an entire society believes that "richtig oder nicht, mein Vaterland," then the woman or man who challenges this unanimity by questioning this "eternal truth" is precisely the moral person.

35. Brueggemann (1970) has suggestively recaptured and explored this primary function of wisdom literature in "Scripture and an Ecumenical Life-Style," which should be required reading for all students of wisdom and theology. He too views wisdom as "dialogue, not as a technique but as a way of life, as a deep and abiding confidence that the world in which I find myself offers meanings to me if I am open to them" (18).

> Longing is the life-blood of things and ideas. It's another kind of
> metaphoric action. The moment you write 'life is like a poem,'
> you can't stop.

Stylistically, K's and P's canonical experiment involves recording or
"writing" the words of tradition and then correcting or "righting" them.
In Kohelet this also means setting K's report of his experience within a
valuational context, of humanizing facts by values.[36] The words handed
down are thus inextricably composite or dialogic, and they will be further
handed down only on that basis. One is even tempted to argue that, of
these two functions, the adversarial "righting" and the memorative "writing," the latter is the more radical and astonishing, given our hagio-
graphic expectations of Scripture as peopled with one-dimensional heroes
having "all the right answers." Indeed, what motivation did the authors
of the canon have to record such bothersome dissonance as Abraham's
challenge to God's justice (Gen 18), as Moses' refusals (e.g., Exod 4) and
Jonah's outright defection, as David's infamy with Bathsheba and Uriah
(2 Sam 11), as Solomon's royal excess?[37] The question then becomes not
the usual "how did such books as Kohelet and Job and Canticles get into
the canon?" but the more interesting one: "what is the nature of a canon
that includes such books?" The answer to such a question is not to be
found in aesthetics, despite the crucial role of dialogic techniques, but in
what might be called a theology of human experience. Dialogic in its
essence, Hebrew Scripture is perfectly at home with Kohelet because this
dialogue on vanity is but a radical instance of a pervasive attitude. It would
thus seem that Néher's (1951, 12) tag of a "pacte entre la prudence et
l'aventure" could be applied not only to Kohelet but to the Hebrew canon
itself.

36. If I understand Brueggemann (1970) correctly, there is in salvational theology and in
prophetic and cultic authoritarianism a natural polarization and removal from common experience ("as though facts and values could long exist in isolation from each other"), a tendency
that can be set straight by returning to wisdom's dialogic spirit (4).

37. Hebrew Scripture's pervasive avoidance of hagiography and its willingness to portray
heroes in their human dimension, with all their failings, was well observed by Gerhard von
Rad. Taking the heroes of Genesis as an example: "The patriarchal narratives are remarkably
free of that urge to transfigure and idealize the figures of earlier times, which plays such a great
role in popular literature. The patriarchal narratives do not fall short of the rest of the Old
Testament in drawing the picture of man which Israel only found through a long *conversation*
with God" (1972a, 37).

6

The Present Translation, Commentary, and Notes

For reasons of convenience I give the traditionally accepted chapter and verse divisions (those of MT, which differs somewhat from the English), and I further succumb to the practice of dividing the text into thematic subdivisions. Beyond their artificiality, such designations can leave the impression of a work composed of a series of poorly related sections; they also prevent one from seeing the dialogic continuity and interrelatedness of the whole. Their entire usefulness—and this is the reason for their inclusion here—is that they reduce the chances of getting lost in a rather sophisticated text and enable the reader to plot the argument with greater precision. More important for perceiving the unity of the work are the recurrent verbal ambiguities and punning, but except for an occasional coincidence between the English and the Hebrew, the clarification of such instances must be relegated to the Commentary. Kohelet's true unity, as I have suggested, lies in its dialogic methodology, and this alternation of voices is here rendered with the assistance of typography, a technique that proved successful in Falk's (1977) translation of the Song of Songs.

In the Commentary I have stressed those aspects of the text that tend to be overlooked by both the close-up gaze of philologists and the external I-already-have-the-answers approach of theologians, namely, the *literary* dynamics of the text and especially its dialogical nature. We are so accustomed to weak readings and translations of Kohelet, perhaps due to the conservative influence of philology, that we ask in desperation: Where is precisely the literariness, where the puns, the sharpness, the goads?[38] My main dogma is that I take the Massoretic Text (MT) as it is (what is currently known as "texts in their present form"), less because "that's the way the author wrote it" than because its authenticity is

---

38. Koh 12:11. One may of course waive the importance of such criteria and admit that in the usual flat translation "much in the way of subtlety, connotation, and deliberate ambiguity is lost," all to benefit "only one aspect of Qohelet's meaning—its literal, propositional content" (Fox 1989, 166).

buttressed by its antiquity and its literary unity. It is of course always possible to imagine a different text and to revise accordingly. Many critics have done so, thus revealing their allegiance less to higher criticism than to midrash.

I have tried, perhaps unsuccessfully, to avoid the trend of anthologizing that now passes for commentary in academic criticism, mainly because the pleasure of acknowledging my debts to others had to be balanced by the necessity of reducing the bulk of commentary. I have kept constantly before my eyes the commentaries of Gordis (1968), still of great value, and of Crenshaw (1987) and Zer-Kabod (1973), each anthological of different traditions of scholarship, and each judicious in interpretation. Crenshaw (1987) presents a reliable overview of academic research; Zer-Kabod (1973) offers a generous sampling and discussion of Rabbinic and modern Jewish scholarship. Both consider literary as well as philological and theological questions. For pointed relevance Whybray's (1989) commentary is difficult to surpass, and a number of other recent efforts (Ogden [1987], Fox [1989], Lohfink [1980]) are well worth the reading. I have also drawn constant inspiration from medieval research, notably from classical Rabbinic commentary such as Rashbam (Rabbi Samuel ben Meir, twelfth century), too often neglected by current fashions of scholarship. Rashbam is credited with a quite modern interest in literary aspects of the biblical text, although in this he is regarded as rather the exception than the rule among his contemporaries (see Japhet and Salters [1985, 37]).

In order to reduce the bulk of commentary, some material had to be relegated to the section entitled Additional Notes on Kohelet, here referenced by an *. In view of some insuperable textual difficulties of Kohelet, these Notes provide different perspectives, for one inevitably reaches a point of throwing up one's hands and becomes willing to consider midrashic alternatives—as the Rabbis might exclaim: "this verse calls aloud: 'give me a midrashic interpretation!' " The Additional Notes section makes a modest attempt to address this need.

Part Two

Dialogues with K
Translation and Commentary

I (1:1–3) The Presenter P[1] Announces K's Motto and Thesis

1:1 *The sayings of Kohelet, son of David, King in Jerusalem:*
2 **VANITY OF VANITIES.**
Kohelet has spoken a vanity of vanities! Is everything vanity?
3 **What profit hath man from all his labor at which he labors under the sun?**

Commentary

Note: ⋆ refers to Part Three 1, Additional Notes on Kohelet

1:1   Since "Kohelet" speaks of himself in the first person in 1:12 and uses the first person throughout, there is general agreement that these opening words, which speak of him in the third person, are those of an editor or Presenter, and in fact the voice of a Presenter reappears in 7:27 and at the conclusion of the work (12:8–10). But our passage presents two difficulties to this view. On the one hand, the Presenter's editorial addition "Kohelet has spoken" (v. 2) appears superfluous, since it is sufficient to have stated "[these are] the sayings of." On the other hand and more difficult still, how does one explain the repetition of "vanity of vanity," which is not repeated in the parallel summation in 12:8? Rashbam's parallels are not entirely convincing (e.g., Ps 115:1, 93:3) in that they are all poetic ones, for although repetition characterizes elevated styles such as poetry, it is unclear why the prosaic Presenter would use such discourse. The best solution seems to be that v. 1 is entirely said by the Presenter in order to introduce the theme that has made Kohelet famous: "vanity of vanities." At this point the Presenter marks the return of his own voice by "Kohelet has spoken," followed by a *mock* repetition intended to undercut Kohelet's general view, with which he disagrees. The procedure wherein the original sage's words or sayings are preserved along with a critical reply, as epitomized in v. 2, is a paradigmatic example of the creation of the "sayings of the sages"; cf. 12:9–10nn.

sayings⋆
Kohelet⋆ Usually taken as a proper name (but why not simply refer to him as Solomon, as at the start of Canticles and Prov-

---

1. As previously noted, I adopt the following conventions for designating the two voices of the Dialogues: K, for Kohelet, the wise and disenchanted sage and king; and P, for the (more orthodox and perhaps tolerant!) Presenter. In order to distinguish the biblical work from the character K the designation "Kohelet" is used here only for the work and K only for the character.

erbs!), the epithet is also related to the root *qhl,* referring to the king's
activities at "gathering or collecting" wisdom from many different
sources. Rashbam cites as a parallel the example of Agur (Prov 30:1)
because he too collected (*'agar*) wisdom. Since Kohelet gathered much
more than wisdom, however (see 2:26n. *gathering . . .*), it is likely that
the name is used by the Presenter in an ironic sense: The Cohellector. See
Introduction 4b, "The Collector's Greed."

    King★   The identification with Solomon is inescapable
when one adds the crucial notation in 1:12: "king over [all of] Israel in
Jerusalem." In view of the split of the unified kingdom that occurred
among Solomon's successors and the fact that Jerusalem then became
capital of Judah but not of the Northern Kingdom, Solomon is the only
candidate who fits these qualifications. This being the case, one must
again ask what is the purpose of the nickname (see the preceding n.),
especially if, as is often argued, Solomon's authority was needed to gain
the book's acceptance into the canon!

    in Jerusalem★

1:2   *VANITY*   *hebel*   The meaning of this crucial term is specified by the sequel, as in 2:11: "all is vanity . . . and (= because) *there is
no profit.*" A similar view is expressed in Jer 16:19: "worthless things
(*hebel*) in which there is no profit."

    OF VANITIES★   Kohelet's superlative is patently a ploy of
argument, but it is probably deeply felt, since totalization is a "natural"
tendency both of the distressed and of those who use their experience as
the sole basis of their knowledge (see Introduction 1).

    has spoken   *'amar*   This word is usually used either to intro-
duce a direct quotation or to say to whom a statement is being made.
Here it is synonymous with *le-hagid,* "to speak, to speak of," as in Ps
40:11 10E: "I have spoken of (*'amarti*) thy faithfulness and thy salvation"
(RSV). The sense is close to 5:5 (see n.): "to declare solemnly." The
perfect tense here expresses what Kohelet usually says, thus further
emphasizing that this is his motto. But the perfect also attaches the usual
saying to the dialogue, thus "just now spoken" in addition to "has
always spoken." Congenial to the dialogic rendering is Crenshaw's
(1987) preference for "says," like the Greek aorist.

    a vanity of vanities   This is not K's repetition, which would
be tautological (albeit quite consonant with his love of rhetorical emphasis), but P's ironic mimicking indicating disbelief; after all, on one level
K's superlative is absurd—can there be degrees of emptiness? P's argument, typical of his forensic style of "going one better" than his opponent, is that words (*debarim*) can be as vain (cf. 1:8, 5:6, 10:14, 12:12) as
things and events, also *debarim;* thus, empty words that describe vanity

could only be a "*vanity* of vanities," and K has, unwittingly, demonstrated his own thesis.

Is everything vanity? Viewed dialogically, the *h-* is not the definite article but the interrogative *h-*. The question anticipates a negative answer: Surely everything is *not* vanity (cf. Num 11:12; Job 1:8). P's question begins the exegesis of K's motto: when K says "vanity of vanities," does he refer to everything, and is this a true superlative? Crenshaw (1987) takes the universal claim "all is vanity" as a categorical assertion, but then he asks the necessary question: "Would not its readers have promptly set to thinking about life's good things that might escape Qohelet's harsh censure" (58)? His solution is political rather than pedagogical, arguing that readers might be willing to accept such categorical nonsense on Solomon's (i.e., K's) authority. Whybray (1989, 35) correctly senses that this verse is "an *interpretation* of his [Kohelet's] thought, but may well be a *mis*understanding or at least an over-simplification of it" (italics Whybray's).

For the interrogative *h-,* see Isa 28:24 and Jonah 4:4, 9. That the vocalization may be a simple patach even before a nonguttural, see Gen 27:38, Lev 10:19, Job 23:6, and especially Deut 32:6, which recaptures the same sense of astonishment: "Do you *thus* requite the Lord!?"

everything   kol, "all"   The term often refers to all the works of creation (see below, 5:8n. *of all*), in which case it anticipates K's complaint against the Creator, "Elohim, who makes everything, *ha-kol*" (11:5). In any event, this is an outstanding example of how a totality seeks the disguise of Infinity; cf. 1:3n. *under the sun.*

1:3   This verse states not the theme of the work but rather the opening topic of debate, the "programmatic question" (Ogden 1987, 28). The difference between the two is that the first would subsume all subsequent thematic development, which is patently not the case, whereas the opening topic of a debate is but a focus of discussion which itself undergoes reformulation. It is unclear whether the verse is spoken by P or by K, although, surely, it is one of K's burning issues, especially in its stoical focus on human control over one's destiny and its implied exclusion of sources of value beyond human beings.

What profit hath   K likes to wax poetic, whether through repetition of key words and phrases (e.g., "vanity of vanities"), through rhetorical questions such as here, or through a diction that has resonances in other poetic passages of Scripture such as Ps 30:10 9E: "What profit is there in my blood?" The question is ironically quoted by P in 6:11.

As to why K begins his discourse with a question when assertion is his usual mode, it might be said that he has a penchant for rhetorical questions, which are assertions in essence. His question would thus imply an answer: "None at all!" Or, in a debate situation, K's question seems an appropriate response to the preceding question. Indeed, the provocations of debate account for many a stylistic feature of these *Dialogues*.

    profit   yitron   Occurs only here in the Hebrew Bible. It may be an ironic calque on *yeter,* as in Jacob's blessing to Reuben: "Preeminent (*yeter*) in status and pre-eminent in power" (Gen 49:3). K wishes to contest the possibility of any human preeminence whatever, but he cannot take the biblical text head-on. The neologism is close enough to recall the original sense but different enough to allow a way out. The meaning may be: "what benefit accrues to one who labors over one who does not?" A large majority of words related to this root in Kohelet have comparative force. This is especially so because Kohelet's inquiry concerns the basis of human values, and these are established comparatively, as, for example, when one seeks to establish what is "better than" or "worse than" something else.

Alternatively, a passage in Sirach (18:6, 8) provides an interesting perspective: "There is no diminishing or increasing or penetrating the wonders of the Lord. . . . What is a human, what is his value (*yitron*)?" It is possible that this was a traditional context for discussing man's *yitron,* his inability to penetrate the final purposes of God's creation (see 12:14nn.).

    man   I.e., human beings and not God. The opening assumption is that human beings are the proper focus of the inquiry. As the dialogue develops, the hidden agenda will gradually emerge, which is not what comes from man's own effort but rather what comes to him from God (cf. 12:14nn.). There may be a further argument in the word in that it is intended to include man in his generality and without exception, thus purely natural and experiential man and with no allowance for special categories such as the sages.

    all his labor at which he labors   *'amal* in Scripture has strong associations with "man is born to trouble" (Job 5:7; 3:10; also Deut 26:7; Judg 10:16), to whatever the world brings him by way of anxiety and pain, to what comes from without and which it is man's duty to assume. However, since for K the stoic it refers to human effort, to what he himself puts into something, he is careful to specify this active sense of the term ("which he labors"), which otherwise is superfluous (he could simply have said: "all his labor under the sun"). The possessive "*his* labor," beyond indicating the source, also designates the beneficiary of the effort, what is *for himself* as opposed to, say, slave labor, which is always *for* another. In this regard the possessive reinforces the irony of "*all* his labor," since it is suggested that he benefits from nothing. In 2:18 a further distinction will be made between the act of labor and its result.

under the sun*   I.e., in this mortal world, since, just as the sun rises only to set (v. 5), everything is fated to die. Zer-Kabod (1973, 1) limits the expression to human society, arguing the partition of the universe into three sectors: "God is in heaven and you are upon the earth" (below, 5:1), while the dead are in the place of darkness (11:8). However, although the expression is unique to Kohelet, it is parallel to, and therefore synonymous with, "under the heavens" (1:13, 2:3, 3:1). This latter expression is commonly not exclusive but inclusive, an extension of Kohelet's All: "Under all the heavens" (Gen 7:19; Deut 2:25, 4:19). Exod 17:14 is an especially interesting parallel, in view of 1:11 below, with its command to *utterly* blot out *the memory* of Amalek "from under the heavens." The area under the sun or heavens is thus the total area of human activity. Whether this includes the natural world as well is one of the subjects of the first debate.

II   (1:4–11)   Prologue on the Nature of Things:
                     Analogies from Nature

1:4 **A generation goes forth, only to die!**
     But the earth endures forever.

5   **The sun rises, only to set!**
     Yet it pants to return to its starting point, where it rises
6   *again. Moreover, it goes southward but returns northward.*

     The wind goes forth around and around!
     Yet it can reverse its direction.

7   **All rivers flow to the sea!**
     But the sea is not filled. And the rivers must return to their
     source, since they continue to flow to their destination.

8   **All things are weary . . .**
     . . . things that a person cannot say!

     The eye is never sated with things to see.
     Or the ear filled with things to hear!

9   **What will be has already been, and every action is**
     doomed to be repeated.
     But is there nothing new under the sun?
10   *Surely there is something about which one can say: "Look,*
     this is new . . ."

     It has already been in the ages that went before us.
11   *Is there then no remembrance of former great men? And of the*
     next generation of sages will there be no remembrance by
     those who come after?

Commentary

1:4–11   This section contains two equal parts of four verses each and
articulates a carefully crafted debate on the lessons of nature.

1:4–7   In these verses K will seek support for his vanity argument
from analogies with nature (cf. Prov 25:13–14). The Presenter's reply
will be that, if anything can be learned from such analogies, it is that
nature's repetitiveness is more a subject of wonder and even encourage-
ment than of despair; whereas K looks at the end of each cycle, P focuses
on its (new) beginning.

Alternatively, whereas modern commentaries see man as one with nature in their cycles of futility, Rashbam sees a strong opposition in that only man does not have a stable place or natural habit. He thus reads "the wind," "the rivers," etc. as exclusions: the *winds* return but not humans, the *rivers* continue but not humans. My alternative to both of these views is that opposing arguments cancel one another, meaning that no proof can be adduced from such natural analogies. However, this does not cancel their value as analogies or possibilities.

Though he does try to adjust to the ongoing argument (e.g., in v. 6), K's point is quite elementary and is hammered home in four verses of four stresses each:

A generation goes forth, only to die.
The sun rises, only to set.
The wind goes forth around and around (until it dies).
All rivers flow to the sea (where they die).

K's point is that everything is vanity and there is no profit because everything dies (cf. Introduction 3a), thus parallel with his closing poem on death (12:1–7) and vanity conclusion (12:8). Thus, viewed literarily, K's opening and closing arguments on vanity and his negative lessons from his analogies with nature form a pessimistic *inclusio* of the entire book. Note carefully that the notion of cyclicality is not part of the pessimist's argument here but rather its refutation, thus appropriately ascribed to another voice (here P). Indeed, it is only when K's negative argument of linearity or continual flow toward death is countered by P's optimistic notion of ever-renewed cyclicality* that this latter notion will become the topic of discussion in the second part of this section (vv. 8–11).

1:4   *generation   dor* All living things that dwell (see n. *the earth*) upon the earth. The focus of the argument at this point is not individual human existence but human life in its continuity. The cycles of nature are introduced only as argumentative parallels.

   goes forth/to die   holek/ba' The usual rendering "goes" is misleading, for in English it implies "goes away," thus forcing the parallel "comes" as "comes into the world." However, *halak* often (not always) has the positive sense of "going forth," of intentional motion towards a goal, of progress (whether real or imagined). This progressive sense is well expressed in Prov 4:18, which narrates (as does our next verse) the increasing force of the sun in its first phase: "But the way of the righteous is like the light of dawn, which shines ever brighter (*holek wa-'or*) until the fullness of noon." For the precise sense of our verse, see Ibn Ezra: "This verse speaks of the earth, for all that are created *from* it will return *to* it, as it is said: 'You are dust and to dust you shall return.' " Thus, the antithesis represents rise and fall or going forth and returning to the point of departure respectively, analogous to the movement of the other three elements (see Introduction 3a). Even those who see *ba'* as meaning "coming into the world" (e.g., Crenshaw 1987, 62) agree that in the next verse it means "to set or die," and they therefore have the burden of explaining why the word is used in opposite senses in adjacent verses. More convincing is Whybray's (1989, 42) principle that such a recurrence of key words "suggests a certain parallelism between them and the probability of an identity of meaning in each case for these words."

only to die   I propose that the *waw-* be taken here in the sense of "so that," as in Jonah 1:11: " 'What shall we do to you, that (*waw*) the sea may quiet down for us?' " Or perhaps "*Just as* it is born, *so too* it dies," similar to the connective between the A and B sections of the parallelistic line (Kugel 1981, 13–14), as in 7:1 below: "Just as good standing is better than good oil, so too the day of a man's death is better than the day of his birth." K's point is that there is no profit because we are born but also die, birth leads only to death.

But   It is curious that most major commentaries correctly take the *waw-* connective as a "but" contrastive but fail to note both the contradictory purpose of the argument and also its persistence through all four natural analogies. The sense of the reply is that, although generations die, the (people of the) earth continue to produce further generations.

the earth★   ha-'arets   This means "the people of the earth," as in Gen 9:19: "These three were the sons of Noah; and from these the whole *earth* was peopled"; also Gen 11:1: "Now all the [people of the] earth had one language." The argument is that although individual people and generations pass, the earth will always be peopled with humans. More specifically, the reference is to "those that currently *inhabit* the earth," and P's response seems motivated in part by the relation between generation (*dor*) and *dar,* "to dwell."

endures★   'omadet, "stands"   This means "does not disappear or cease but remains in existence," and there is little support for the meaning "remains the same" (Scott 1965; Fox 1989) or "is unchanged" (Gordis 1968).

1:5   *The sun rises, only to set!*   The analogy is made all the more persuasive by recalling that we all dwell and labor *under the sun* (v. 3).

pants to return   sho'ep   Fox conflates the two senses as: "goes panting." This "going" is a "returning," however, not because of a misreading *shab 'ap* but because the sun's "place" is its point of departure, and this not only for the past but also for the future; cf. next n.

starting point   Literally, "place," which is the east (Rashbam).

1:6   *it goes southward but returns northward*   Rashi and Targum Jonathan take this as referring not to the wind but the sun, presumably because, although the sun travels in an east–west direction, over the course of a year it migrates on a north–south circuit. Others take it as referring to the delayed subject, the wind, which travels in this direction (see 11:3). In either case, in the context of the ongoing argument, this introduces a further complication to K's attempt to establish that all motion is simple, unilinear, and end-stopped, as it were.

     around and around   With sarcastic insistence K points out that cyclicality, which P observes in nature, does not defeat his argument of fateful movement forward ("goes forth") to death but is rather modeled on the local motion of the wind, perhaps like atoms which circle around a nucleus and are yet bound to the overall motion of the atom, thus not a true cyclicality. Thus, *sobeb sobeb,* meaning "here and there," does not continue, and certainly not introduce, the argument of cyclicality, as some would wish, but merely acknowledges the previous point that some direct motions do indeed include deviation or zigzagging but that this does not refute its fateful forward movement, which here is the wind's going forth (again *holek*). For this meaning of *sbb* cf. Cant 3:2: "I will arise now and go about (*'asobebah*) the city," which means, since she is looking for her beloved, that she will certainly look around, here and there, but continue in a straight direction. Or, in a related sense, in the following verse (Cant 3:3) *sbb* refers to "making the rounds," i.e., going along a specific route and, while looking around, certainly not reversing direction.

     it can reverse its direction   Literally, "But it returns upon its tracks," which I interpret as "in the opposite direction." Or, it could mean "it returns to (*'al* = *'el*) its circuits," to its point of departure, where, like the sun and the rivers and the generations, it starts again. Again, a further complication is introduced into K's model of simple, forward, and end-stopped motion.

1:7   *All rivers*   Here again is K's characteristic "All" argument; by the plural "rivers" he may be alluding analogically to individual existences.

     flow★   Again *holkim*   They "go forth" but can only advance toward the sea, where they die.

     But the sea is not filled   The meaning seems to be that the rivers are not exhausted by their forward motion and that their wish to fill the sea does not result in either frustration or self-destruction (there are always rivers!). Another possibility is that, just as the earth is never full of generations but continues to put them forth, the sea does not detain the waters but rather allows them to flow continually. P perhaps stresses, despite K's wish to establish natural laws, that this example is *against* the laws of nature, for water flowing into a container will eventually fill it.

1:8–11   K now admits the possibility of cycles but asks again (cf. v. 6) whether they are anything more than mere, monotonous repetition. In these verses K also becomes more explicit about his use of nature analogies, already implicit in "generation" and "earth" in v. 4 (see nn.), to explain human affairs.

1:8   *All things   kol ha-debarim   All* things that we see in the physical world and, by extension, in the human world or history, corresponding to Latin usage of *res* ("things") for *res facta* ("human deeds"). This summarizes K's analogy between nature and human nature, as well as his argument of totality, sustained by "all," as in v. 7 and often.

          weary   i.e., with this endless and fruitless activity. The frequent translation "wearisome" seems to be based on a haplography, reading *meyag'im* from the preceding *debarim*. However, elsewhere in the Hebrew Bible (Deut 25:18; 2 Sam 17:2) the sense is "weary."

          things   The second use of the word does not occur in the Hebrew and is usually supplied as a direct object (it, them). But it is likely that it is P's repetition, in order to acknowledge K's dual use of *debarim*: "things" and "things spoken, words" (*1:1 *dibrei*).

          a person   'ish   Perhaps as opposed to *'adam* (1:3) or human beings in general. If Crenshaw (1987) is correct in seeing this as applied to a specific individual, then that individual could only be the interlocutor K, and the ironic sense would be compounded by the Rabbinic insistence that *'ish* always refers to an important person (see Rashi on Num 12:3). Thus, again referring to the royal fiction: "there are things that even a person of your rank cannot say!" This usage seems to recur in 7:5; see also the next n.

          cannot say   lo' yukal le-daber   The suggestion is that human speech doesn't conform to the universal weariness of "things" and thus forms an important exception (cf. 12:12). Within the context of dialogue, this remark is an ironic aside: "This universal weariness of things doesn't seem to prevent *you* from saying things." Or, more directly: "If *all* things (= words) are weary, then we had better shut up!" There may be further irony if P is seen as reacting to K's more theological complaint. Recall the similar language of Mal 2:17: "You have wearied [*hoga'tem*] the Lord with your words [*be-dibereikem*]. Yet you say, 'How have we wearied Him?' By saying, 'Everyone who does evil is good in the sight of the Lord, and he delights in them'; or by asking, 'Where is the God of justice?' " Through the language of indirection typical of both the courtier before his master (the king!) and the student before his teacher, P warns K against going too far when speaking about God. But it is also an instance of elegant self-reproach: "your teaching method is dialogic; are there then to be limits on what can be said?!"

the eye/the ear   K continues to talk about things in the world out there, the realm of visible experience, whereas P stresses things human such as speech. The eye is not literally intended but rather as the privileged organ of the soul's desires (see 1:13, 2:10, 11:9). There is perhaps also an evocation of the full extent of human misery, as suggested by the proximity of *'amal* (1:3): ". . . nor hid trouble (*'amal*) from my eyes" (Job 3:10); or, as the spiritual puts it: "Nobody knows the trouble I've seen," i.e., experienced.

filled with things to hear   By taking the previous remark as referring literally to the physical organ, P gives an ironic rejoinder to K's complaint (1:7) that things lack filling or fulfillment. In the context of dialogue this alludes to K's endless complaining: "my ears are full of this nonsense!"

sated, filled   tisba', timmalei'   Both mean the same thing, see below 6:7 and especially their synonymy in Deut 33:23.

1:9   *what will be/every action*   Zer-Kabod (1973) sees in these carefully crafted expressions an important distinction, the first as referring to God's creative activity, and the second to *human* action; somewhat similarly, Scott sees the distinction as between the natural and the human world. If the first is the case, then K is pursuing his hidden agenda, through his language of indirection, against God's creation. From Scott's perspective, K would be pursuing his analogy between natural and human events. Parenthetically, Zer-Kabod's notion seems based on God's self-definition in Exod 3:14 as "the One Who will be."

doomed to be repeated   Literally, "what has been done is what will be done" (RSV).

nothing new   K's argument to this point has been that patterns or directions or possibilities do not change: things proceed on a straight line, with no chance of returning and starting again. The negative particle in combination with *waw* often means "yet" (e.g., Prov 13:7), which would make no sense coming from K. It thus seems better to avoid this statement as an assertion and to take the remark as a question placed by P as a possible inference from K's position. Note that P is trying to maneuver to easier ground, for if it is asserted that *nothing* is new, then he has only to prove a single exception.

1:10   *look   re'eh*   Crenshaw (1987, 68) makes the attractive suggestion that this particle, like *hinneh,* often signals a shift in point of view. It may also serve as a code word here, an indirect reference to such passages as Deut 11:26 in which *re'eh* serves as a particle introducing a weighty announcement: "Behold (*re'eh*), I set before you this day a blessing and a curse." Its most obvious reference, however, is to K's empirical or experiential method.

   this is new . . . It is not certain what P's example will be, since he is interrupted. He may be thinking of wisdom, as the sequel to the discussion seems to indicate.

1:11   *Is there then* Taken as a question, this verse both draws the correct inference from what precedes and elicits K's concluding answer in the following monologue: there is no remembrance of the sage over the fool (2:16) and thus, a fortiori, there is no possible profit or *yitron* from *any* human endeavor.

   former great men *r'ishonim* and *'aharonim* Probably refer here to people (although in 7:10 they refer to days); cf. Jer 11:10: *'abotam ha-r'ishonim,* "their forefathers." This reading is consistent with the movement of the argument: in v. 9, K intimated an analogy between the repetitiveness of nature and the futility of human action, and here P meets the claim head-on. That this subject was on K's mind can be seen in his rejoinder in v. 14 ("all the deeds that men have done").

   An attractive alternative is to understand the passage as part of K's long diatribe against wisdom. Thus, "all words [of wisdom] are weary" (1:8). When a sage thinks that his saying is new (v. 10), it has all been said before, except that it seems new to us because there is no remembrance of earlier wisdom sayings and there will be none of later ones either. In Chronicles *r'ishonim* and *'aharonim* refer to words, *debarim,* no less than nine times (1 Chr 18:17; 2 Chr 20:34, etc.).

   next generation *'aharonim* Does not mean "later ones" but "the next ones" in succession; cf. Deut 24:3; 29:21 22E; Ps 48:14 13E.

   of sages This is added in the translation, since it is the probable reference to P's notion of greatness.

III   (1:12–2:26)   The Experiment with Experience

12 **I, Kohelet, was King over Israel in Jerusalem.**
13 **And on behalf of wisdom I allowed my heart to investigate and explore all the things that happen under the heavens: it is a badly arranged affair . . .**
      . . . a fair arrangement that God has given to men to wrangle over.

14 **I saw all the deeds that are done under the sun. Look, they are all vanity and an affair with the wind:**
15   **"What is crooked cannot be made straight."**
       And what is absent cannot be counted, I suppose!

16 **I spoke with my heart: "Look, I have greatly added to the wisdom that preceded me in Jerusalem" (my heart had seen much wisdom and**
17 **experience, for I had set my heart to knowing both wisdom and experience, madness and knowledge). I now know that this too is a chasing after wind. For:**
18   **"In (too) much wisdom is much angry frustration!"**
       Greed for experience is greed for pain!

2:1 **I said in my heart: "Come now, I'll test you with enjoyment: Have a good time!"**
       But surely this too is vanity!

2   **About pleasure I said: "Madness! And as for enjoyment: What does it do?"**
3   **I explored in my heart how to sustain my body with wine (all the while conducting my experiment on behalf of wisdom) and take hold of foolishness until I could discern what good people themselves can acquire under the heavens during the numbered days of their lives.**
4   **I performed great works: built me houses and**
5   **planted vineyards, made gardens and orchards in**
6   **which I planted fruit-trees of all the varieties. I constructed pools of water in order to irrigate tree**
7   **forests. I acquired servants, both men and women, and even reared up my own; also, my herds and**

flocks were more numerous than any before me in
8　Jerusalem. I also collected silver and gold for myself, and the treasure of kings and distant prov-
inces. I got me singers and musicians and all hu-
9　man pleasures: women one and many. And so I
grew great and amassed riches beyond all that
were before me in Jerusalem, and my wisdom
10　even assisted me. I denied my eyes no craving,
and I deprived my heart of no pleasure. Indeed,
my heart rejoiced in all the labor, and that was
my only portion from all my labor.
11　　Yet I considered the works of my hands and the
effort expended, and, behold, all was vanity and a
striving after the wind, for no profit remains under the sun.
12　　I then turned to consider wisdom in relation to
madness and foolishness, for who is the man that
can outdo the king?
According to you, others have already done it!

13　And I saw that, like light over darkness, wisdom
has an edge over foolishness.
14　*Of course! As the saying goes:*
　　"The sage has his eyes in his head,
　　but the fool walks in darkness."

Yet I also know that one and the same fate will
befall both. I said in my heart: it will happen to
15　me too as it has happened to the fool. Of what
value then is my greater wisdom? So I reproached
my heart that this too is vanity.
16　*Just as there can never be remembrance of the sage along with*
　　the fool . . .
　　. . . since even in the near future all will be forgotten!
　　. . . how can the sage die like the fool?

17　So I hated life because it saddened me that what
happens under the sun is all vanity and a chasing
18　after the wind. I even hated all the fruits of my
toil under the sun, which I would leave to one
19　coming after me; and who knows whether he will
be wise or foolish? Yet he will control all the
fruits of my toil and wisdom under the sun. This

20 **too is vanity. So once again I caused my heart to despair over all the results of my labors under the sun.**

21 *Yet, a man can sometimes toil with wisdom and knowledge and success . . .*

And He will give his rightful portion over to one who has not labored for it! This too is vanity and
22 **a great evil. Yet, even in the present what does man have from all the toil and anxiety that he**
23 **expends under the sun? For all day long his endeavor is full of pain and grief, and even at night his heart does not rest: this too is vanity.**

24   **Therefore, man has no greater good than eating and drinking and finding pleasure in his work itself.**

I myself have concluded that this too is from the hand of God.

25 **Who eats and enjoys if not I?**

26 *Yet to the one He favors He gives wisdom and knowledge and happiness, but to the sinner He gives the task of gathering and amassing, only to hand it over to whomever God wishes.*

Commentary

1:12   *I Kohelet*   There is a touching irony to K's naming himself precisely at the point in the debate at which memory is introduced, given the close connection between the two themes: "This is My name (*shemi*) forever, and this is My memorial (*zeh zikri*, "this is my remembrance") throughout all generations" (Exod 3:15).

was King   This begins what has been called the royal fiction, the portrayal of K as royalty, most probably Solomon, a fiction by no means limited to this section but rather characteristic of the entire work (cf. Introduction 4d). The past tense is surprising here but probably should not be construed literally: "and no longer rule." Rather, a contextual reading seems appropriate. In view of the theme of memory just introduced, he continues to view his entire life as a whole and thus as a record of the past: during all my years as King I have been able to achieve no more than this. Alternatively, the statement can be read as "I am Kohelet I was . . . ," thus distancing present identity from past experience. Like nature itself, he no longer is what he was; he has fallen or departed from his high status.

King over Israel   I.e., king over *all of* Israel, cf. 1:1n. *King.*

1:13   *on behalf of wisdom*   It is common to construe "wisdom" as
an instrument, as in Ps 104:24: "how manifold are Your works! in wisdom You have made them all." The strong reading "for the sake or
purpose of wisdom" seems preferable, however, since Kohelet's intent is
that of evaluation, of testing the advantage or permanent human value
(called in this text the *yitron*) of wisdom itself (cf. Introduction 4a). This
meaning of the prepositional *b-* is close to one Rabbinic reading of Gen
1:1 *be-re'shit,* "in the beginning = for the sake of *re'shit.*"

    I allowed   Cf. "I did not let you (*lo' natati-ka*) touch her"
(Gen 20:6, 31:7; also Job 31:30). Given the heart's independence and
waywardness, this permissive sense is preferable to the usual "I set,
devoted," which, however, is consistent with his project on behalf of
wisdom.

    under the heavens   See 1:3n. and 3:1n.

    I allowed my heart   Rather than the usual "mind." Kohelet
indulges in a bit of metaphysical conceit-making here by introducing a
"dialogue with his heart"; see the next n.

    to explore   la-tur   The spies' exploration of the Land is
relevant (Num 13:2, 16, 17), whether in the sense of military reconnais-
sance or simple "tourism," but even more important is the Toranic
warning (Num 15:39) "not to follow (*lo' taturu*) after [the desires of]
your own heart and your own eyes, which you are inclined to go after
wantonly" (RSV). Crucial here is the link between the "heart" and illicit
seeking, on the one hand, and the independence of heart and eyes on the
other (see below, 2:10 and especially 11:9, where a warning is issued
against such desires). Since the heart needs no prodding toward such
activity, "allow" is to be preferred over the usual "devoted." Indeed, K
almost allegorizes his heart (what we would call his self) and, to a lesser
degree, his eyes, as he makes a pact with them to explore his experience.
The possible randomness of such a search was well expressed by the
French metaphysical poet Scève (sixteenth century), when he compared
his adolescent eye to a weathervane.

    things that happen   ha-na'seh   Everything that is done by an
agency outside of himself and of man, and thus to be distinguished from
human deeds in the next verse. This is the area of chance happenings but
also of God's actions, thus "the human *condition* in general." For K the
ultimate instance of this is death (cf. 2:17); for P it is the gift of life.

    it   The antecedent of the pronoun *hu'* is usually taken as *ha-
na'aseh,* the human condition. However, Whybray (1989) and Zer-
Kabod (1973), following others, refer the pronoun back to the wisdom
enterprise in general and to man's insatiable curiosity, thus equivalent to
the pronoun *zeh* in 12:13 and anticipating the work's conclusion (12:14).

a badly arranged affair . . .   *'inyan ra'*   "An unhappy business" (RSV), with my English version revised to allow the wordplays on *ra'*, "evil," and *'anah be-*, "to wrangle over."

a fair arrangement   *'inyan ra'*   These words are added in the translation. P willfully misinterprets *ra'*, "evil," as *re'a*, "fair" (literally, "friend"), and pursues his corrective pun in "to argue with one another" (*la'anot*), see the next n.

that God has given to men   The stress on God's gifts is prime P throughout Kohelet, so that even a "bad" affair must somehow be "fair" and even "wrangling" must lead to some good result such as truth. In this regard P is very much attuned to gratitude toward God, even when the bad side seems to dominate, since "one is obliged to bless for the evil as well as for the good" (Mishnah Berakot 9:5).

to wrangle over   This is my attempt to render the wordplay on *'inyan/'anah*, "arrangement/wrangle." *'Anah* has the meaning of "to answer," often in an argumentative context, and, perhaps related to this, of singing responsively. Even in the latter case it can retain the debating sense of going one better, as in 1 Sam 21:12 11E: "Did they not sing to one another (*ya'anu*) of him in dances:

'Saul has slain his thousands.'
'But (RSV: "and") David his ten thousands.' "

To indicate the contestatory nature of the two responses, each should be set in its own quotation markers.

Alternatively, this wordplay based on *'anah* plus the preposition *be-* anticipates 5:19, thus "through which to answer (him)."

1:14   *I saw*   Given the close relation between heart and eyes in the previous verse, this action is quite expected, all the more so in that it stresses K's experiential method. Thus, "I myself saw, I didn't merely speculate or hear about them" (cf. page 13, note 10).

all the deeds   This refers most probably to all those kinds of deeds that can be done by someone such as himself. These include both his activity of acquisition (in pursuit of pleasure and glory) and his morality or acts of goodness. K will now discuss the first and return to the question of morality in 3:16f. Less likely here is the allusion to God's own deeds (contrast 7:13, cf. n. *the things that happen* in the previous verse), although the vagueness here is perhaps deliberate, thus both allowing or forecasting the theological critique and veiling it.

an affair   re'ut   "Friendship," with perhaps sexual overtones (Cant 1:9, 15). The word in the present construct case already exists in the Hebrew Bible (Exod 11:2; Esth 1:19) with the sense of "another, one another," thus close to the Mishnaic noun *re'ut*, "friendship." Not to be outdone, K returns to the pun over *ra'*, which here may be either the abstract noun of *re'a*, as in later Hebrew but already perhaps in the name of Ruth (*rut, reʿut*). Close to the *reʿut ruaḥ* of our text is Hos 12:2 1E: "Ephraim chases (RSV: "herds") the wind (*roʿah ruaḥ*), and pursues the east wind all day long," thus "desires." Others have understood it as based on *raʿah*, a "shepherding."

1:15   *"What is crooked . . ."*   The opening Prologue on the Nature of Things has prepared the way for the formal characteristics of this verse, which is the first of many examples of a "debate in proverbs" in Kohelet in which the second half of a verse contradicts the first half or goes one better (see Introduction 2b and Excursus 2d). As to content, K seems to have in mind the crookedness of human deeds (v. 13), since he directs the same observation to God's actions in 7:13. Or, more likely and in accordance with K's findings, it is wisdom itself that cannot be made straight. Translators have wavered on whether these sayings are applied to a general truth (RSV: "What is crooked cannot be made straight") or to the particular case: "a crookedness not to be straightened" (Gordis 1968). Both are possible, depending on the speaker. I quote the RSV, just as K quotes a well-known popular source to reinforce his general claim, quite preposterous in its generality, since, as will be noted in 12:13, K himself was able to correct or make straight many proverbs.

      And what is absent   In responding with his own parallel truism, P expresses his exasperation over both the triviality of what was perhaps a popular saying and perhaps also the recourse to such "authorities" as a method of argumentation. He in fact goes one better in suggesting that K argues not only no *yitron* or positive balance on the ledger but an actual lack.

      cannot be counted   This apparent truism (one commentator asks how one can count the missing elements of a thing) is to be viewed as part of the warning to "in the days of your youth remember your Creator" (12:1), which also takes on the pathos of being addressed to an aged person. To sense the bitterly ironic overtones of this remark, one has to view K's anguish over his waning days and lack of remembrance in the context of wisdom's program as outlined in Ps 90:12: "So teach us to number (*li-mnot*) our days, that we may get a heart of wisdom." P's lesson to his interlocutor: "You should have been wise by numbering your days while there was still time: count your days rather than your money!" For a different twist, recall that one of the blessings of the sons of Abraham (Gen 13:16) and Jacob (Num 23:10) is to be beyond counting. By suggesting that there is no remembrance of former ones (v. 11) and that, in consequence, these will be recorded only as absences, is K treading on the dangerous ground of denying or denigrating divine promises?

I suppose   This is added in the translation to emphasize P's
sarcasm.

1:16–2:24 Solomon's dual program of wisdom and riches is paralleled
by 1 Kgs 10:23.

1:16   *I spoke   dibarti 'ani* For the pleonastic use of the subject
pronoun to mark a change of speaker as well as an objection to what was
previously said, see Excursus 2c. See also the next n.
        with my heart   'im libi I.e., my self, a continued "personifi-
cation of the heart" (Barton 1908, 86) but with a tinge of preciosity that
allows K to continue his inner dialogue; see 1:13n. *my heart*. Note the
preposition *'im*, "with," which stresses that what follows is a dialogue
(within a dialogue) rather than an interior monologue ("I said *to* myself"
or "*in* my heart," 2:1); that is to say, at the start of his experiment he has
somewhat of a distance from his self or desires. Another variant in this
formulaic statement of "words in or with the heart" may be the alternation between the conversational *'amarti* (2:1, 15) and the more stern
dibarti here and in 2:15 ("words of reproach," cf. ★1:1 *sayings*).
        Look   hinneh This particle may again signal a change of
speaker and perspective (cf. 1:10n. *look*). In this case K reports an inner
dialogue in which he took the position of P against the heart's desires
and in favor of the heart's wisdom. Dialogically, this is a powerful tactic,
which in effect says: "Look, I used to think like all you proponents of
wisdom."
        I have greatly added to the wisdom★ Linguistic evidence does
not support the tradition of reading a comparative here (RSV: "surpass-
ing all who were over Jerusalem before me"), but one must still acknowledge a strain of greed in K and a well-developed notion of envious
competition (cf. 4:4; 2:7, 9; 9:6). His point here, rather, is that he does
not see the acquisition of *wisdom* as an expression of it. Surely, when the
Queen of Sheba notes that Solomon has amassed wisdom (*hosapta
ḥokmah*, 1 Kgs 10:7), there is a clear tone of admiration. From our verse
it seems that K is simply carrying out what was to be regarded by the
Rabbis as the duty to add to the sum of previous knowledge, either
incrementally or perhaps by seeing something new, a *ḥidush*. This reading does not emphasize the great superiority of K's wisdom but rather its
organic continuity with previous local tradition, which he admires ("all
the wisdom that preceded me"), and his place within (rather than above)
that tradition. Such an image of K is consistent with P's concluding
appraisal below (12:9–11).
        in Jerusalem   'al has the sense of "in" Jerusalem, as in Ps
68:30 29E.

my heart had seen   The expression *r'h ḥokmah* occurs only
three other times in Scripture. In 2 Chr 9:3 it has the sense of "observe,
experience by direct observation"; in 2:12 below it means "consider,"
and perhaps "experience"; in 9:13, "to see an example of, to reflect
upon." Thus, "experienced," since *ra'h* approaches this sense in our text
(cf. 1:8; 2:1 and nn.).

1:17   *wisdom and experience*   K's new experiment is to examine the
relation between worldly experience and wisdom, how one leads to the
other. His conclusion is that all wisdom is experiential, but that even this
is won at too high a price (cf. 2:11n. *for no profit remains*). For a brief discussion of the two wisdoms, the experiential and the mysterious, see Bergant
(1984, 3–6). The nontheoretical nature of *da't,* experience, is in evidence
already in Adam's "knowledge" of Eve (Gen 4:1; see Introduction 4a).
        madness and knowledge   holelot we-siklut   MT makes good
sense and should be retained. Grammatically speaking, this doubling of
nouns is close to Gordis's (1968) double accusative after verbs of perception, although it seems simpler to view the second as an appositional
pairing, functioning as a valuational mirror of the first.

K, as previously stated, is pursuing both wisdom and experiential
knowledge, *ḥokmah we-da't,* a pair stated three times in three successive
verses (1:16–18). His judgment is that *ḥokmah we-da't* are, successively,
madness and knowledge; that is to say, from this point on he judges the
former negatively but clings to the latter, experiential knowledge, as the
sole basis of wisdom, as can be confirmed by his frequent use of the
verbal form (especially here in v. 17: *la-da't, yada'ti*). It is thus unneces-
sary to emend K's *siklut* "knowledge" to *siklut* "folly." This might be P's
(playful) misreading, but it does not represent K's point of view.
        I now know   "I have learned from experience," with "now"
added in the translation to stress the conclusion. This brings to a close
his present words of reproach to his heart.

1:18   This verse continues the "debate in proverbs" begun in v. 15
in which an authoritarian summation in proverb form is countered in
kind.
        (too) much wisdom   *rb* can connote something excessive, as
in: "You have gone too far *(rab)*" (Num 16:3; cf. also Ezek 45:9). K never
completely denies the value of wisdom. For example, it increases the
chances of survival (cf. 7:12), but he cannot admit that it has value for its
own sake or that its possession places one in a special category.
        Greed for experience   The *waw* contrastive ("but") indicates a
change in voice or perspective, as often in wisdom sayings. The verb *le-
hosip* + direct object can take on negative connotations; in Ps 120:3 and
Prov 19:4, for example, the context is one of greed. P too makes a sharp

distinction between experience and wisdom, by ascribing greed and pain only to the former.

2:1   *I said   'amarti 'ani*   Note again the pleonastic pronoun to indicate change of speaker (cf. 1:16n. *I spoke*).

          in my heart   be-libi   K continues the inner dialogue with the self or, to pursue the literary fiction, with the heart. However, the preposition suggests less an exchange than a contact or consultation with his deeper self or desires; for the negative connotations of this, see n. *vanity* below.

          test   For the root *nsh*, see 7:23; also 1 Kgs 10:1, where the Queen of Sheba comes to test Solomon (*lenasoto*) with riddles. The French *expérience* expresses both dimensions of this concept, the experimental and the experiential.

          enjoyment   The Hebrew *simḥah* covers a range of pleasures from sensual (see 2:24n.) to spiritual: "The hope of the righteous is gladness" (Prov 10:28); "everlasting joy" (*simḥat 'olam* Isa 35:10). It is appropriately proposed in the heart, since that is its usual location ("on the day of the gladness of his heart," Cant 3:11; cf. below 2:10).

          Have a good time   Literally, "see, experience the good." Kugel (1981, 5) argues that the idiom here is not *r'h b-* but *r'h (b)tob*, "enjoy," meaning that the preposition is incidental, as confirmed below in 3:13; 5:17; 6:6; 9:9. Here the expression specifies the level of *simḥah* proposed; see the preceding n.

          But surely   Note again (cf. v. 10) the use of *hinneh* to indicate change of speaker.

          this too is vanity   This text seems to share in the scriptural suspicion concerning whatever is said "*in* the heart," as in Ps 14:1: "The fool has said in his heart: 'There is no God' "; also Ps 10:6, 13. This negative judgment cannot refer to the enjoyment of life, which both speakers advocate. Perhaps P is objecting to pleasure as a pursuit, since in his view it should be accepted (as a gift of God) but not "tested."

2:2   *pleasure   seḥoq*   Here the word does not have its usual meaning of "laughter, sport," unless the reference is to amusement or entertainment, akin to Pascal's *divertissement*. For the present context, see below, 10:19; also Targum Onkelos on Gen 21:6, which translates Sarah's *tseḥoq* as *ḥedwa'*, "pleasure" (cf. Gen 26:8). Prov 14:13 may shed some light on K's distinction: "Even in pleasure (*seḥoq*, RSV: "laughter") the heart is sad, and the end of joy (*simḥah*) is grief." That is to say, since the negative quality of pleasure/laughter is immediately felt, K says that anyone who fails to see it is mad. Since joy or enjoyment (*simḥah*) can be tested only by its results in the future, however, it is the subject only of the implied negative of a question beginning by *mah* (see next n.).

What does it do?   The negative answer is implied: "Nothing at all" and therefore of no value. Like many "doers," K confuses external activity with doing. His natural impulse is to "act" and build and expand and acquire and increase, whereas P will argue that the true locus of action is in the will and the mind, that contentment, for example, is a higher form of doing because its actions are victories over the heart. Note that the criticism of *simḥah*, enjoyment, is less extreme than the condemnation of *seḥoq* or pleasure. Indeed, it may have positive qualities; cf. Introduction 4c.

2:3   *I explored in my heart*   For the heart's independence regarding what critics like to refer to as K's "experiment," see also 2:1. The verb *tarti* suggests that his experiment also has a confessional tinge; see 1:13n. *explore* and also 11:9.

        sustain   mashak b-   Cf. Job 24:22: "He sustains [RSV: "prolongs the life of"] the mighty by His power."

        wine   Probably taken here as the prototype of pleasure (cf. 10:19), wine is elsewhere applied to the heart and plays an important and legitimate role: "wine that gladdens the heart of man" (Ps 104:15).

        take hold of foolishness   I.e., to remain in control and not let foolishness, arising from either frivolity or drunkenness, take hold of me (e.g., as was the case in Exod 15:14: "Trembling has taken hold of [*'aḥaz*] the inhabitants of Philistia"). For the use of this verb with the preposition *b-*, see also below 7:18; Gen 25:26.

        can acquire   This particular phase of the experiment involves man's own actions, the *tob 'asher ya'asu* that is enumerated by no less than nine verbs of action in the next six verses, placed usually at the start of each clause. Note, however, that this activity is directed not to doing good deeds but rather to the acquisition of objects of pleasure and power, as summarized in 2:9. For this meaning of the verb *'asah,* cf. Gen 12:5: ". . . and the souls that they had acquired [*'asher 'asu*] in Haran"; also Gen 31:1.

        under the heavens   I.e., in this world. See also 3:1n.

        the numbered days of their lives   Literally, "the number of days of their life." Most commentators take the expression as a limitation, thus consistent with K's pessimism: "during the few days" (RSV); "during the brief span" (Gordis 1968). The phrase recurs twice in our text: "during the number of the days of his vain life" (6:12), with negative and limiting implications; however, 5:17 avoids these negative connotations: "during the number of days of one's life that God has given him." Note that K's version here avoids P's later stress on the divine gift.

2:4–11   The parallel with Deut 8:12–13 is close, both in the details and their order of presentation: "Lest, when you have eaten and are filled, and have *built fine houses* and lived in them, and when your *herds and flocks* have multiplied, and your *silver and gold* have multiplied . . ." The entire passage thus becomes condemnatory and confessional in nature.

2:4   *I performed great works   higdalti ma'asai*   Literally, "I made great my works," as in 1:16. This caption will now be explained by nine verbs specifying the kinds of great works he has in mind, three of which (*'asiti*) echo the root *ma'asai*. Ibn Ezra makes the attractive suggestion that K is here describing his new project *ad extra,* in the external world, as opposed to his previous exclusive concern with wisdom; thus, "I increased my external activity," i.e., what is summarized in v. 11 as the "works of my hands."

Another possibility is that *ma'asai* means "acquisitions," thus anticipating *qaniti* in v. 7; cf. the parallel in Ps 104:24: "How manifold are Your works (*ma'aseka*) . . . , the earth is full of Your acquisitions (*qinyaneka,* RSV: "creatures")"; for *'sh* meaning "to acquire" cf. 2:3n. *can acquire.* Ibn Ezra, alternatively: "I increased my wealth"; cf. 2:8n. *got me.* This makes it more possible to understand his disappointment expressed in 2:11, since the things he has acquired either have no permanence or he has no control over them after his death.

built me   Hebrew *li*   Construed as an indirect object by RSV and Crenshaw (1987, "for myself") and as an untranslatable ethical dative by Gordis (1968)—which can however be rendered as "I built me houses." It is possible, however, that the preposition here is synonymous with *l-shmi,* "for the glory of my name," as in the synonymous alternation in 1 Chr 17:4 (*li*) and 22:10 (*l-shmi*), which is also a context of housebuilding. At any rate, the stress is not on K's need but rather on his projected fame among men, on his wish to "make a name for himself."

2:5   *fruit-trees of all the varieties   'ets kol peri*   Recalls Gen 1:11, 29, as often noted, but making the point not so much that K has at hand all the delights of paradise but rather that his creativity parallels, and is perhaps in competition with, God's own works in the creation of the world. K's creativity thus becomes another test of his vanity theory, another form of his question to God, Who delights in creating a world in which nothing of permanent value remains.

2:6   *all the varieties*   Again, K's use of his key word "all" has its typical ambivalence. On the one hand it designates an almost scientific inclusiveness, thus parallel to the "all is vanity" stated as an argumentative posture; on the other hand it suggests excess and thus forms part of K's ostentatious activity, whether on behalf of fame or pleasure or experiential knowledge.

tree forests   "Forest causing trees to sprout," thus apparently
trees that do not produce fruit but only cause other trees to sprout. This
may be another suggestion of pointless behavior, since nonfruit-bearing
trees had a status lower than those of direct benefit to man (Deut 20:20).
This is a good example of the tail wagging the dog as, once the decision
has been made to have forests, then large quantities of a vital resource,
"pools of water," have to be provided for their maintenance.

2:7   *I acquired   qaniti*   This notation begins a complex conceptual pun based on one meaning of Kohelet's name ("one who acquires or
gathers or collects," see 2:26) and is related to Cain (*qayin*), the one
whom "I acquired" (*qaniti,* Gen 4:1). In 2:26 below the collector's behavior is attributed to the sinner and the benefits are given over to *hebel,*
"vanity" (which, ironically enough, is also the name of Cain's brother
Abel or *hebel,* Gen 4:2).

          and even   Again, the suggestion is one of superfluous acqui-
sition. Thus, "in addition to" (Scott 1965) or, better, "although" (Gordis
1968).

          more numerous than   harbeh   Best construed with the follow-
ing preposition *m-* and as a comparative, as in Jonah 4:11: "that great city
in which there are more than (*harbeh m-*) a hundred and twenty thousand
persons." This comparative, spoken in a confessional context, may be
less an indication of external grandeur than of inner motivation, making
the additional point that the king's motive was not only pleasure but also
envy and power.

          before me in Jerusalem   See 2:9n.

2:8   *collected   kanasti*   Another conceptual pun on Kohelet's
name: "I kohellected." In Esth 4:16 it refers to one of the extensions of
the name, that of gathering people together; in 2:26 below it is synonymously paired with *'asapti.*

          silver and gold   This order, rather than the reverse, is fre-
quent in the Pentateuch when a major condemnation is implied or explicitly stated: Exod 20:23 and Deut 29:16 17E (idolatry); Num 22:18 and
24:13 (Balaam's wealth); Deut 7:25 (covetousness); see also Ps 115:4;
135:15. This notation therefore continues K's self-accusation and recalls
the warning to kings: "nor shall he greatly multiply for himself silver
and gold" (Deut 17:17).

          got me   'asiti li   "I acquired"; this meaning is well attested
to; cf. 2:3; 2:4n. *I performed.*

          women   shiddah we-shiddot   There is no consensus on the
meaning here, but a plausible approach is to stress the synonymy with
ta'anugot, "pleasures" (see Gordis 1968 for all the possible etymologies).

This would be consistent with the image of Solomon in 1 Kgs 11:1–8. Rashi thinks that the allusion is to chariots (cf. 1 Kgs 4:26; 10:26).

one and many   shiddah we-shiddot   The interpretation of this combined singular and plural form is difficult. One interesting possibility is Fox's (1989) citation of Ps 72:5, *dor-dorim,* which is seen as a hendiadys expressing multiplicity, thus "in abundance" or "many" (RSV). This example approximates our text but lacks the *waw* connective. A more likely possibility is Ibn Ezra's citation of Judg 5:30, which is a singular followed by a dual form: *raham rahamatayim,* "a maiden or two (for every man)." This example can also be questioned on the absence of the *waw* connective but not on the dual, since the dual is not literally intended but means simply "more than one," as frequently (see below, 4:9: "two are better than one," which may mean "the more the better"). It may also be that this expression is to be taken as a variant of formulas of numerical heightening such as "seven or eight" (11:2), frequent in the Hebrew Bible and usually indicating multiplicity: three and four (Amos 1:3–11); six and seven (Job 5:19); etc. Or the emphasis may be on paucity or a limited multiplicity, as in Job 33:14: "For God speaks in one way, and in two," that is to say, "in a few ways." At any rate, this expression may mark the start of an ongoing debate on the relative value of the "one and the many" that may be summarized by two contradictory proverbs: "Better one . . . than two" (4:6); "Two are better than one" (4:8). In the present context of pleasure, the discussion would concern the relative value of quality versus quantity. Is it true, as the bumper sticker asserts, that "life is too short to drink bad wine" and that one good glass is therefore better than many bad ones? Then the expression would mean: "I got me one or two good women," somewhat in keeping with the call to spend one's life with the woman you love (9:9). Or, if the stress is on quantity, as exemplified by K's acquisitiveness, then, indeed, *many* are better than one.

2:9   *I grew great and amassed riches   gadalti we-hosapti* (the interpretation "riches" is added). I grew great by adding to my worldly riches. To be distinguished from the *hif'il* use in 1:16.

beyond all that were   For a possible sense of this comparative, see 2:7n. *more.*

before me in Jerusalem   If taken in a temporal sense, as it usually is, this notation cannot refer only to Jewish rulers, which would only be David, but also to all previous rulers, Jebusite and others, such as Melchizedek (Gen 14:18). The more usual sense of the term, however, is "within view of, in the presence of," referring especially to divine or royal presence. The reference would therefore be to all his contemporaries in the known world, and especially to those who stand before him (1 Kgs 10:8). It was not axiomatic that kings need be the wealthiest persons in the nation, or indeed that they are above envy, as can be seen in the tale of Naboth's vineyard narrated in 1 Kgs 29.

    assisted me   *'amdah li*   The meaning is not only the passive "remained with me, did not abandon me," indicating merely that he escaped a drunken stupor, but also, as the Targum translates, a more active collaboration as well, as in Esth 4:14 (perhaps also Ps 109:31): "Salvation will assist the Jews (*ya'amod la-yehudim*) from another place." Surely, the statement that Solomon "excelled all the kings of the earth in riches and wisdom" (1 Kgs 10:23–25) does not in the slightest suggest a contradiction between these two pursuits. But K's notation of this apparent advantage of wisdom—that it helps increase pleasure and possessions—is soon undercut by the feeling of the vanity of these pursuits.

2:10   *eyes/heart*   On the relation between the heart and the eyes, see 1:13–14. The enterprise is criticized in 11:9.

    my only portion   I.e., "my reward." The stress is on the pronominal suffix: *my* portion, because it is what I myself have produced through my own efforts. In view of what follows, the "only" is added to indicate a further emphasis here: "and that was my *only* portion," since nothing remained and my only enjoyment was in the present.

    The concept of one's portion is crucial to the debate, and its ambivalence is well established. On the one hand, "portion" is associated with "inheritance": *helek we-nahelah* (Gen 31:14; Deut 10:9; 1 Sam 20:1), thus with whatever man acquires independent of his own efforts or merit, what he is granted as a gift: "But to the Levites they *gave* no portion in the land" (Jos 14:4). On the other hand, however, the term means "reward, payment" as in Gen 14:24: "And the portion of the men who accompanied me." K holds to the second sense of the term (see below 9:6 and 9:5, where "portion" and "reward" are synonymous), while P holds the first view because it allows God an active role in one's happiness (see 5:17nn, 18; 9:9; Introduction 3e).

2:11   *Yet I considered*   *U-paniti 'ani*   The sense required here is not "then" but the contrastive "yet." This is expressed by the repetition of the personal pronoun subject, which is an aspect of K's style (cf. 1:16), as in Ezek 16:59–60: "I will deal with you according to your deeds, when you despised the oath in breaking the covenant; yet I will remember [*wezakarti gam 'ani*] my covenant with you in the days of your youth" (cf. also Dan 5:16). The emphatic use of *'ani*, which suggests to Crenshaw (1987) that man is the measure of all things, seems nevertheless more stylistic than ideological. Indeed, when K does use the emphatic "I" for ideological reasons, it is to diminish the self, as in 2:15. For the use of this verb see 2:20n.

the works of my hands   I.e., those performed in response to the desires of his eyes and heart.

vanity   The satisfaction of his desires brings pleasure in the present but no lasting benefit; cf. also the next n.

for no profit remains   we-'ein yitron   The *waw* connective has the sense of "seeing that, since," as in Ps 72:12: "He delivers . . . the poor, since he has none to help him." But is this statement credible? Doesn't his wealth remain, capable of prolonging pleasure in the present? Perhaps K means that although the heart is glad, it is not thereby improved. This would give support to Fox's (1989, 178) understanding of *yitron,* which may be K's: "there is no *adequate* gain" (cf. 1:17n. *wisdom* . . .).

2:12   *I then turned*   This repeats the initial verb of the previous verse and perhaps also the contrastive: "Despite the vanity that I discovered I *yet* turned to consider . . ."

in relation to   This unusual rendering of the *waw* connective (*ḥokmah we-holelot*) was proposed by Galling (1969 [1940]) and is required by the context.

madness and foolishness   The two go together, since madness is the final result, whereas foolishness is the initial quality, as per 10:13. But K suggests that perhaps these should also be inspected as values, especially given their high connections with wisdom (1:17; 10:1). Perhaps there should be such a thing as a praise of folly. At any rate, in terms of a search for definitions (of wisdom), the procedure of considering a term's opposite is well taken.

outdo   ba' aḥarei   The sense of "physically entering a place after someone." Rashbam (in Japhet and Salters 1985) gives the unusual suggestion that the expression means "to come after someone before the king to beg mercy," apparently based on the contextual meaning of 1 Kgs 1:14. The preposition usually occurs with other verbs and has the sense of "following after, in support or imitation" (cf. 2 Sam 20:14).

the king   The reference is to the speaker himself.

According to you, others have already done it   Literally, "what they have already done." The second half of this verse is difficult and has been subjected to hopeless emendation. I take it as an ironic rejoinder to the king's claim to uniqueness, which, it is now suggested, is in contradiction with his previous complaint on the sameness of things (1:10b). The connection between the two verses, as well as the signal of a change of speakers, lies in P's ironic repetition of the unusual word *kbar* from v. 1:10. The present verse begins a continuing debate on the nature and privileges of kingship, a debate which K, alias Solomon, takes very personally.

2:13   *wisdom has an edge*   This is an important admission, for if there are levels of *yitron,* then ALL is not vanity, at least not in the same degree.

    like light over darkness   For K this means: "like life over death." Like the two trees in Eden, light and darkness are ambivalent in this book. For K they symbolize life and death; for P they mean good and evil. This comparison is therefore important for defining the book's two meanings of wisdom and foolishness.

2:14   *The sage*   The sage/fool topic is here presented within the broader evaluation of wisdom in its relation with other values. In 7:4–12 it is developed with regard to how it is practiced by its holders or practitioners. Further, here the emphasis is on what happens to sages: from the point of view of fate they are only human. The later inquiry will focus on their moral qualities, on what they can do for themselves and others.

    has his eyes in his head   The sage exercises prudence, "knows what's the score," a view with which K would not disagree. In view of the moral meaning of the second part of the verse and given K's decision to "follow his eyes," P could not utter these words without sarcasm: The sage's eyes are in his head but not in collusion with the desires of his "heart." The phrase "in his head" is thus read as an exclusion: "*in his head* and not, for example, in his belly."

    the fool walks   halak   "To walk" has a frequent moral sense and is thus more appropriate to P. For the moral sense of *halak,* cf. Ps 1:1: "Blessed is the man who does not *walk* in the counsel of the *wicked.*" It was paired with "darkness" to signify immorality: "who forsake the paths of uprightness to walk (*laleket*) in the ways of darkness (*ḥoshek*); who rejoice in doing evil" (Prov 2:13–14); cf. also Prov 4:18; Isa 9:1 2E.

    Yet   For the adversative use of *gam,* see Excursus 2c.

    one and the same   Literally, "one."

    fate   miqreh   "Chance," which for K always means "death"; see below, 3:19; 9:2. In Scripture the concept is often a veil for divine intervention to which God gives the appearance of chance: Ruth 2:3; Gen 24:12; 27:20; Num 23:4, 16. This being the case, the use of the term by K is but another covert criticism of Providence.

    both   Literally, *kullam*   "All of them"; for the meaning of "both," see also below, 7:18. These opposites obviously include all intermediate levels. Thus, the "all" become "one" as even the greatest of distinctions among men is nullified before death and mankind's unity has a purely negative foundation.

2:15   *me too*   I.e., K the sage.

Of what value then . . .   It is best to take *yoter* as a comparative with a suppressed *m-,* since the whole purpose of this passage is comparative, stressing K's (vain) superiority in both wisdom and possessions.

    greater   yoter   K expresses the highest irony with this wordplay that recalls his opening complaint on the lack of profit: Even of wisdom, a *yoter* brings no *yitron.*

    I reproached   dibarti   Cf. 1:16n. *with my heart.*

2:16   This verse is a good instance of how a dialectical solution can rescue an otherwise difficult text. Whereas K argues the limited nature of wisdom—limited to its source in experience and to its purely practical importance—P's thought is based on the total, essential disproportion between the sage and the fool.* In v. 13, P won a grudging concession and now wishes to press his advantage. K claims that all differences are obliterated by death, common to both sages and fools, but P here objects that sages are remembered beyond their death (and thus, in this sense, do not die). Like most of Kohelet's critics, K does not understand (or pretends not to) and hears: ". . . the sage *like* the fool," which is a highly unusual usage of the preposition *'im,* "with."

    Just as . . . [in the same way] how   For a similar use of *ki . . . waw-,* see 5:2. Or perhaps *ki* has here its frequent dialogic function of marking a change of voice.

    never   the negative particle + *le-'olam*   Cf. Ps 15:5: "He who does these things shall *never* be moved." However, K understands the expression in the more restrictive sense of "after death" (BDB 2.j.), whence his reaction: "even in the near future."

    remembrance   This refers to one's "name"; cf. 3:1.

    even in the near future   Gordis (1968) explains this rendering.

2:17–23   The transition from death's universality to the lack of control over one's inheritance and the fruits of one's labor is succinctly expressed in Ps 49:11: "For he shall see that even the wise die, the fool and the brutish alike must perish and leave their wealth to others." Such an attitude is not one of complete self-centeredness (Crenshaw 1987, 88) but rather a natural concern of biblical man. K's fear that his wealth may pass to an unworthy person (2:19) is based on the legitimate desire to enjoy what one has earned (2:18). Deut 20–28 takes the repeated view that such a state of affairs will necessarily arise for those who neglect the commandments (also Isa 62:8–9), and in a remarkably apposite passage Job regards this as punishment for lust: "if . . . my heart has gone after my eyes . . . , then let me sow and another eat" (31:7–8). Such parallel passages increase the likelihood that K is still in a confessional mood.

2:17   *So*   This is a *waw* resultative (Crenshaw 1987).

I hated   I came to dislike. The verb covers a wide range of emotion, from deep disgust to simple negation, rather than contradiction, of "love" (thus, "unloved, disliked" rather than "hated"); cf. Deut 21:15; Judg 14:16. At any rate, K does not come to hate life to the extent that he wishes to leave it, as does Job (6:8–9).

it saddened me   ra' 'alay   Apparently the equivalent of *ra' lepanaw* in Neh 2:1: "For I had not seemed sad in his presence." The opposite is *tob 'al* (Esth 3:9): "to seem good to someone."

everything that happens   ha-ma'aseh ha-na'asah   The ultimate instance of what "happens," according to K, is death; cf. 1:13n. *the things that happen.*

2:18   *I even hated*   Note the emphatic "I" pronoun, to stress that this is a more radical hatred, since it extends even to the area of his personal responsibility, as opposed to the "what happens" described in the previous verse.

all the fruits of my toil   'et kol 'amali   I.e., the wealth that he strived to accumulate, the results of his labor and not the labor itself, since he has already stated (2:10) that the act of labor was his only source of pleasure.

2:19   *fruits of my toil and wisdom   'amali she-'amalti we-she-ḥakamti*   This is usually taken as referring to wealth acquired through the application of wisdom, thus "the earnings . . . that I was ingenious for" (Crenshaw 1987). However, this may also refer to his wisdom itself, such as the proverbs he will leave behind and that will not only be used by others but corrected as well (cf. 12:9n. *righting*).

2:20   *once again   saboti*   This action is to be distinguished from *panah* (2:11, 12), which means "turn to a different subject." Scott (1965) got it right here and in 9:11 (but not in 4:1, 7): "once more." Ibn Ezra sees that *sab* indicates a change in the direction of the discourse, but he fails to notice that the turning is not toward another subject but upon itself. Thus, like the wind that repeats its action (1:6 *sobeb*), K, who had argued the analogy between natural and human actions, uses the same verbal root to describe his own repetitious behavior.

to despair   K's first despair (hatred) was over the vanity of external events (2:17); now he extends this feeling to his own actions. This rather *précieux* figure of "causing his heart to despair" brings to an end the fictitious experiment that began in 1:13, where he allowed his heart the independence he now takes back and that led him to experimental activities of equal boldness (e.g., 2:3).

2:21   *Yet   ki*   Indicates a change of speaker and has the meaning
of German *doch,* "nevertheless"; see Isa 8:23 9:1E.
        success   kishron   As in 4:4.
        wisdom and knowledge and success   These seem to be not con-
junctives but explicatives: "success that comes from wisdom and knowledge," or perhaps "wisdom and knowledge that lead to success." The
final conjunctive is thus a kind of qualifier of purpose, such as: "to eat
and drink and be [for the purpose of being] content"; "Go from your
country and your kindred and your father's house" (Gen 12:1): go from
the first two so that you can free yourself from the third.
        He will give   Especially in wisdom texts (but see also, for
example, 1 Sam 3:17), the subject "God" is often understood but omitted: "but the desire of the righteous He will grant" (RSV: "will be
granted," Prov 10:24; cf. Prov 12:14; 13:21; also below, 9:9). This introduces the central subject of God's gifts, and the tone of complaint gives
another reason for not mentioning God's name. There is perhaps a
further complaint in the word "give," since K would prefer the merit
system (see 2:17–23n) over God's gifts, which strike him as arbitrary.
        his rightful portion   The word *rightful* is added in order to
clarify that, for K, "portion" is what one earns through one's labor and
therefore deserves.

2:22   *even in the present   meh howeh la-'adam*   "What is to man,"
i.e., what does he have. This use of *howeh* anticipates a later meaning of
the term. The argument has progressed from the denial of profit *in the
future* to the assertion that *even in the present* man has no reward for his
pains. Verse 5:11 repeats this argument and reinforces an important
distinction between two senses of "present": the one that is still committed to future reward and hence hopeful or fearful of results, and the one
in 2:24 that thinks only of the present in the present.
        anxiety   ra'ayon libo   "His heart's pursuit," perhaps related
to *ro'eh ruaḥ,* the chasing after wind (cf. 1:14n. *an affair*).

2:23   *all day long   kol yamaw*   Literally, "all his days." This accusative of time is balanced by *ba-laylah,* with which it forms a conceptual
pair meaning "always, all day and all night," as in 8:16. The "all" is
again a dominant characteristic of K's argumentative vocabulary.

2:24   *Therefore*   This is added in order to clarify the conclusive
function of the pleasure argument in K's way of seeing things.
        no greater good   'ein tob sh-   "There is no good except,"
construed correctly by Zer-Kabod (1973, 55 n. 10) as a superlative.
        eating and drinking   The debate focuses on whether eating
and drinking is to be regarded only as a *faute de mieux,* or whether it is a

gift of God. According to the first view, this kind of *simḥah* is viewed as purely temporary (cf. Introduction 3e).

finding pleasure Literally, "causing himself to enjoy," based on the expression "seeing the good" (cf. 2:1n. *enjoy yourself*).

I myself Again (cf. 1:16n.), the inversion of verb and personal pronoun subject indicates a change of speaker. P takes strong issue with the view of pleasure as a goal in itself and always (see Introduction 3e) insists on its divine sanction.

2:25   *Yet* Again *ki* signals a change of voice.

who eats and enjoys if not I? K perhaps intends the stoic sense that only I am responsible for my happiness since my perceptions are entirely within my power. Early in his career Montaigne wrote a brief stoic piece entitled "That the Taste of Good and Evil Depends in Large Part on the Opinion We Have of Them" (*Essais* 1:14).

2:26   *happiness simḥa* "Contentment," in the Rabbinic sense of "happy with one's lot," *sameaḥ be-ḥelqo;* cf. 8:15; 9:7; 10:19.

gathering and amassing In this hardly veiled accusation P takes on the role of Job's three challengers. K had described himself as one who gathers (*kanasti,* 2:8), and Solomon is similarly pictured in 1 Kgs 10:26: *vaye'sop.* Indeed, cannot Kohelet's name ironically refer to such behavior? It is now suggested that such actions are those of a sinner; see 2:7n. *I acquired.*

IV (2:26b–3:8) The Two Times or Directions:
Human Nature Versus Nature

This too is vanity and a chasing after wind, for
3:1 **this means that fate rules over everything!**
Yet every thing has its appropriate time under the heavens.

2 **There is an appointed time to be born inevitably
followed by death!
Whatever is planted is eventually uprooted!**

3 *There is an appropriate time to kill but also a time to heal,
A time to destroy but also a time to build up,*
4 *A time to weep but also a time to be happy,
A time to mourn but also a time to dance.*
5 **A time to disseminate your stones
but a longer time to hold them in!
A time to embrace but always followed by
separation!**
6 **What is pursued is inevitably lost!
What is retained is inevitably scattered!**

7 *But what we tear we can also sew up.
He who is silent will have his time to talk.*

8 **What we love we end up hating!**
There is indeed a time for war, but also a time for peace.

Commentary

3:1   *fate   zeman*   "Fixed time," thus "preordained" and close to
the meaning of "fate" that it acquired in medieval Arabic and Hebrew
poetry. That K intends this sense can be seen in his insistence that it is
over All, the entire universe. The eighteenth-century exegete Yehiel
Hillel Altschuler in his commentary Mezudat Ziyon comments on this
verse that "nothing happens by chance . . . but rather in its own time
[*zeman*] because of a previous cause." K's argumentation alternates between the view that everything is due to chance or, as here, that it is all
determined, i.e., that God acts with no consistency or power or with too
much. In his view it is all the same, since man no longer has control over
his own happiness.

   rules over   la-kol   The preposition *l*- has a possessive sense
here and also somewhat the sense of "upon," as in Ps 145:9: "God's

goodness is toward/upon everyone (*la-kol*) and His mercies upon ('*al*) all
His creatures."

    everything . . . every thing   To K's attempt to totalize (*la-kol*)
P opposes the distinction of limitation: *kol ḥepets*, each and every (desirable) thing (cf. also 3:11n. *everything*). In later wisdom texts the meaning
of this term evolved from "pleasure" and "longing" to "business, affair,
thing," but the concept can be made yet more specific. In a wisdom
context a *ḥepets* is what one makes *time* for, what one desires or to which
one attaches value. In Prov 3:35 ("Wisdom is more precious than pearls,
and none of your things [*ḥepetseka*] can be compared to it," also 8:11),
the decisive factor is not the comparison but the possessive *-ka*, "things
of *yours*," i.e., whatever you desire or to which you attach importance.

    an appropriate time★   '*et*   And it is one's duty to find that
appropriate time. The debate here focuses on whether all is preordained
(cf. 9:1) or, as P will later maintain, whether the wise can discern the
proper time of things, if only to adopt the appropriate attitude (cf. 3:11n.
beautiful . . .). Or, if P is asserting that there is an appropriate time for
each desire or *ḥepets*, then K cannot be surprised if fools toil in vain.

    under the heavens★

3:2–8   For the importance of the rigidly ordered chiasmus of these
verses, see Introduction 3a. The crucial difference between the two dis-
putants is the *order* of events, from positive to negative (K), or vice versa
(P). The technique of argumentation is basically the same as in the
"Prologue on the Nature of Things" in chapter 1. For all negative examples listed by K, P offers an equal number of contrary instances. It
should be noted that K continues his confessional stance here, for, although his concepts are general enough to include any human existence,
they also recall his previous complaints and activities: dying (1:4; also
3:19); planting (2:4, 5); pursuit of pleasure (2:8); disgust and hatred (2:17,
18).

3:2   *appointed*   Compare the ominous tones of Ezek 7:7: "The
[appointed] time ('*et*) has come, the day is near." K continues to stress
the predetermined and fateful aspect of time.

    to be born   The Hebrew usually means "to give birth," but
the traditional translation has perhaps been influenced by two factors: (a)
the influence of such texts as Job 39:1: '*et ledet;* and (b) the parallel with
"to die," which is passive in meaning. A further problem is that this
would be the only pair in the series that does not speak of human *actions,*
and therefore the series as a whole could not be construed as good advice
on what to do (Ibn Ezra in fact alludes to this problem). However,
wisdom sayings in general and Kohelet in particular deal not only with
actions but with attitudes. For example, such a remark as "there is an

appropriate time to live," understood as "it is good to be alive, in spite of difficulties," might be most fitting to someone like Job, sick of life and wanting to die. In addition, no pair of concepts better illustrates the Pessimist's main point of man's passivity in face of an all-powerful Fate. And if P's previous remark asserts that there is an appropriate time for each desire (*ḥepets*), who ever expresses a desire to be born? Are humans ever consulted?

death This is K's most serious complaint, to be compared with Job 14:1f. His point is that everything is in pairs and that therefore everything that is born must perish.

planted This may refer to vineyards (2:4) but most probably to trees (2:5). The juxtaposition of human beings and trees probably rests on their comparison: in Job 15:7–10: "For there is hope for a tree . . . but man dies"; also Deut 20:19: "For is man a tree of the field?"

3:3–4 P agrees with K in that "all the works of the Most High . . . are in pairs, one the opposite of the other" (Sirach 33:15), and he is also willing to consider the *temporal* succession of opposites. However, he disagrees on their *order* of succession and thus on the meaning of their structures.

3:5–6 K's speech seems to be structured in pairs. The first refers to the creation of human beings and then the love for them; the second pair refers to the acquisition of material things and then the care of them.

3:5 *disseminate le-hashlik* Literally, "cast, scatter" as in Ezek 28:17. My translation attempts to capture the wordplay on "stones," suggesting sexual congress. K's disappointment over life's contradictions expresses itself in two verbal ironies. In the first instance his speech opens with a positive use of *le-hashlik* and ends with a negative use of the same verb (3:6b); second, his favorite and most typical activity of "collecting" (*kanasti* 2:8) is totally subverted in this new context (*knos 'abanim*) and now connotes its opposite, the *loss* or "holding in" of pleasure.

stones 'abanim Probably *'obnayim*, the vagina: see Jastrow (1950).

embrace ḥbq The erotic sense is possible (Cant 2:6; 8:3; or, in an illicit sense, Prov 5:20) but not required, since it can also refer to affection, either maternal (2 Kgs 4:16) or familial (Gen 29:13). Later, P will chide K for his love of embracing by implying that what he really loves to "embrace" or fold is his own arms, in laziness (4:5).

3:7 Dialogically, this can be interpreted as a quiet and dignified attempt to cast a positive light on K's strenuous advocacy of withdrawal and his violent complaining: K could have withdrawn completely by being silent but instead he has chosen to begin the repair (the figure of sewing) by speaking up.

3:8   *hating*   This is a fitting summation of K's quest since it describes his progression from engagement to withdrawal (see Introduction 4d). It is moving in its view that the opposite—really the contradiction—of hatred is not indifference but love, with which it is still tied. This is why K's withdrawal is not total and why he can still engage passionately in the debate; just as life and death are inextricably related, his love is still a part of his hatred.

          war and peace   Since K has just admitted that love is a part of his hatred, P proposes that the two can be reversed and that even the hatred of war can be neutralized.

V   (3:9–15)   God's Hidden Purposes

9 **But what is the agent's profit from all his effort?**
10 *I have reflected on this "badly arranged affair" that God has*
11 *given humans to argue over: God has made every thing beautiful in its proper time.*

He has also given in their hearts a love for this world!
Except that it is not given to man to know, from beginning to end, what God has made.

12 **I do know that man's only good is to be happy and enjoy his life in the present.**
13 *But I also know that, whenever man eats and drinks and enjoys his work, this is a gift of God. For I know that all*
14 *that God does will remain forever.*

But,   "to it there is no adding . . ."
and   "from it there is no subtracting."
And God has seen-to it that men should fear Him.

15 **What's past is past, and what's to be is already fore-seen!**
Yet God will exact punishment for our pursuits.

Commentary

3:9   *the agent's profit*   K wishes to return to the original topic of discussion (1:2). He is unconvinced that events can progress (3:2–8), uninterested in what is done (*ha-na'aseh* 1:13) because it does not relate to individual merit, and reconciled to accepting the intrinsic pleasures of labor itself as the sole kind of reward (2:10). He still would like to discuss, however, whether the agent's labor has any further fruits (2:18).

from all his effort   ba'asher hu' 'amel   "Inasmuch as he labors." K's question is now one of degree. If one's only pleasure is from one's actions themselves, will greater effort increase pleasure? If not, why drive yourself crazy? And perhaps there is also pleasure in *no* effort. From the sages' warnings against laziness (e.g., Prov 6:6–11), one infers not only a strong human tendency but perhaps also a powerful argument. Of course, K has a hidden agenda, since his real complaint is that God has devised an unworkable situation.

3:10   In a more explicit way than K, P is unwilling to consider the question so narrowly as to exclude the extrahuman and superhuman context of our deeds. His deeper point seems to be that recognition or acknowledgment of this context, especially in the form of gratitude for gifts bestowed, is in itself a human action and perhaps one that carries its own intrinsic reward. He returns to this subject by quoting their previous disagreement concerning the *'inyan . . . la'anot bo,* the *badly arranged affair . . . to wrangle over* (1:13).

3:11   *every thing*   Debate rages around this central issue of totality, and the challenge is issued by quotation of K's battle cry: "All, everything," which P defuses by its resolution into "every thing" (cf. 3:1n. *everything*). As against K's absurd claims to total knowledge based on his private experience, P counters with an argument of deep trust in divine Providence, a position equally absurd from K's empirical perspective.

          beautiful in its proper time   yapeh be'ito   There is a classic biblical notion that God gives things, often sustenance, at the appropriate time: "I (RSV: "he") will give the rain for your land in its season" (Deut 11:14, also 28:12); "They all look to You to give them their food in due season" (Ps 104:27, also 145:15, 1:3). In these and similar examples, the concept of *be'ito* ("in its season," or possibly "in his season") was taken by Rabbinic commentators to refer to the beneficiaries individually: what is appropriate to each one (Rashi, Radak), and this may in fact be the view advanced by P.

          given   natan   The more usual English translation would be "placed," but the debate continues over what God "gives" and the questionable status of those gifts.

          a love for this world   I follow Ibn Ezra in taking *'olam* as referring to "the desires for the things of this world." K possibly agrees that things are appropriate to their own times but notes that man's desires for them, placed in him by God, do not correspond to these times but function according to their own rhythms. Thus, K translates *be'ito* not as "at the time appropriate to each person" (see n. above) but rather "in its own good time." This interpretation is strengthened by K's notation that this desire is placed *in their hearts,* which, as already seen, has its own independent cycle of desires. K's focus on the desires of the heart, especially his own, continues unabated.

          except that . . .   P continues his interrupted statement but also responds to K's interjection by deliberately misreading the latter's *'olam,* "world," as *he'elem,* "what is hidden or enigmatic."

          from beginning to end★   P does not argue that we know nothing of God's works (as Fox [1989, 194] argues), but rather that we do not understand *every* stage in the process. Note that his skepticism is not used against religion but for it: it is precisely in the blocks of unknowing that God's fuller purpose is concealed, and it is precisely because we do not have knowledge of ends that we are able to live each "time" or event appropriately, in joy or grief. The remark is ambivalent, however; cf. the next n.

3:12   *I do know*   K misinterprets the previous remark as one of complete skepticism, that "we cannot really comprehend anything" (Crenshaw 1987). His reply therefore begins with an emphatic verb to stress that at least something can be known.

    man's only good   Literally, "there is no good in them except."

    enjoy his life in the present   *la'asot tob be-ḥayyaw*   From the context, this expression constitutes a synonymous pair with *li-smoaḥ*, "to be happy," and thus establishes a parallel with the synonymous pair in P's reply: "eats and drinks and enjoys."

3:13   *But I also know*   *we-gam*   The repetition of the verb is implied (it is repeated at the start of the next verse) as the debate continues over what one can really know.

    man   *ha-'adam*   The article implies the collective sense.

    enjoys   *ra'ah tob*   See 2:1n. enjoy . . .

    gift of God   P returns to his previous argument (2:24) and, through his use of the collective, seems to make two points: that God gives enjoyment to all and that the mere existence of enjoyment is to be considered a divine gift.

3:14   *I know*   The repetition of the verb in the starting position is emphatic.

    will remain forever   Cf. Introduction 3e.

    to it there is no adding   K reluctantly concedes that one must be contented with what one has, but only because one has to and not out of gratitude. His use of *lehosip* adapts this general advice to his disappointment with his own activities (cf. 1:18, 2:9). This is yet another instance of a debate in proverbs. Here K accepts Agur's advice (Prov 30:6: "Do not add to his words") concerning God's words, except that he reads *debaraw* as "things, affairs."

    and from it there is no subtracting   Since the talk is of God's things/words, P refers to another use of the adage to bolster his own point: "Don't add to His word [*ha-dabar*, also "His thing"] and don't subtract from it" (Deut 4:2, also 13:1 12:32E). Noteworthy also is the context of these passages, with the reference to God's gift in Deut 4:1 and the fear of God in Deut 13:5 4E. P is suggesting that K's attitude is a detraction.

    seen to it   *'asah she-*   "Caused," as in Ezek 36:27: "I will cause you to walk in my statutes."

    men should fear Him   In this context the idea seems to be that fear of God is yet another of His gifts. That acceptance of this gift is obligatory may be seen from the conclusion (12:13): "Fear God and keep His commandments."

3:15　　　　K now explicitly applies his physical determinism of 1:9 to humans. He asks to what purpose man fears God if everything (including the fear!) is preordained.

　　　　exact punishment for　　*biqesh*　　With the accusative, as in 2 Sam 4:11; Ezek 3:18, 20.

　　　　our pursuits　　Literally, "what is pursued (by us)." The word was used in a bad as well as a good sense: pursue peace (Ps 34:15); righteousness (Deut 16:20; also 1 Sam 26:18); but also: pursue bribes (Isa 1:23); wickedness, evil advice (Ps 119:150); "Ephraim herds the wind and pursues the east wind all day long" (Hos 12:2 1E).

VI   (3:16–22)   The Place of Justice

16 **I have also observed under the sun that the place of justice is also the place of wickedness, that where righteousness should be that is where wickedness abides.**

17 *I have thought to myself: "God will judge the righteous and the wicked." Surely, there is an appropriate time for every matter, and He will bring judgment upon every deed there.*

18 **I have thought to myself concerning human beings and God's judgment of them, and I have observed that they act as beasts toward one another.**

19 **Thus, there is a kind of justice, since man and beast have a common lot: as the one dies, so dies the other! They all share the same spirit and man has no superiority over the beast, for all is vanity.**

20 **Everything goes to the same place. As it is written,**

> **"everything is from the dust
> and everything returns to the dust."**

21 *Who knows, perhaps man's spirit will rise upwards and the beast's spirit will descend below the earth?*

22 **That is why I think that man has no good other than being happy in his work, for this is his portion.**
Yet who except God can bring him to ponder what will be afterwards?

Commentary

3:16   The doctrine of reward and punishment is a backbone of the Hebrew Bible, but frequent is the observation or complaint that experience proves the opposite: *tsaddiq we-ra' lo, rasha' we-tob lo!* If God will indeed, as P claims, require an accounting, K wants to know when, since the evidence of his experience proves just the opposite.

that where righteousness should be   umeqom ha-tsedeq   The two statements form a single topic, and the *waw* is not conjunctive but comparative (*waw-adequationis*).

3:17   "Many have taken 3:17 to be a note by a later reader because of its orthodox tone" (Scott 1965), but one should go on to notice that this is true of half the book, notably that half spoken by P.

God will judge   See Deut 1:17: "For judgment is the Lord's" (RSV: "For the judgment is God's").

Surely, there is an appropriate time   One could easily ascribe this remark as spoken sarcastically by K, since in his experience the appropriate "time" never occurs. Since both interlocuters view judgment as a good, however, then this seems yet another expression of P's optimism that, in the long run, justice will triumph.

He will bring judgment   This is added in the translation because it seems implied in the previous statement.

there   sham   This cryptic allusion probably means "in the grave." In Job 1:21, 3:17, 3:19 the term refers to Sheol, as it does below (9:10). Gordis is right in seeing here an early allusion to judgment after death. Crenshaw objects that 9:10 "denies any work to that land of darkness," but that verse excludes only human work and not divine judgment.

3:18–20   K denies the possibility of divine judgment on ethical grounds: since humans behave like beasts and since beasts cease completely to exist at death, therefore God cannot judge men after their death.

3:18   *concerning human beings   'al dibrat*   An Aramaism for *'al dabar* (Gen 20:11).

and (concerning) God's judgment of them   l- with a verb of saying: "Say concerning me (*li*): 'he is my brother' " (Gen 20:13). Like Gordis (1968), I take *'elohim* as the subject of the shortened infinitive *bar* (= *barer*). This statement is in line with the ongoing discussion of God's justice and in direct response to the previous remark.

I have observed that   we-li-r'ot   This is an infinitive absolute used as a continuation of a preceding finite verb; cf. GKC 113.4. As in 9:1 below: "I have set my mind to this entire matter and I have decided (*we-la-bur*)."

3:19   *there is a kind of justice*   This is added in the translation in order to clarify the relation of the passage to the ongoing debate.

They all   As elsewhere in Kohelet (cf. 2:14; 7:15), "all" can refer to the *two* cases under discussion.

3:20   *As it is written*   What follows seems to be a free quotation of Gen 3:19, and one can imagine K's joy at bringing a proof from Scripture itself.

3:21   *who knows?*   This verb in the present is heavily weighted in Hebrew Scripture. It often refers to divine knowledge (Gen 3:5; Ps 1:6, etc.); in the interrogative it thus creates a space of doubt into which the possibility of God's free intervention or unfathomable power is implied, as in Esth 4:14: "Relief and deliverance will arise for the Jews from another quarter. . . . *And who knows* whether you have not come to the kingdom for such a time as this?" The point is whether God can be constrained by man's desires and concepts, and P's answer to the rhetorical question is at least "perhaps."

3:22   *that is why*   "Therefore," a *waw* resultative. K's answer to the rhetorical question is obviously "no one" (except God). He thus argues "carpe diem" on the basis of total human ignorance of the future.

except God   These words, added in the translation, help clarify P's position, which is that man's not-knowing protects God's freedom of action. P will argue that it is precisely God's unpredictability that keeps man "on his toes"; K feels that, since this has the appearance of injustice, it has the opposite effect.

to ponder   This carries overtones of "with fear" *lir'ot be-;* literally, "to look upon," thus using a verb of perception to contradict K's claim to know the common fate. We have already seen that this verb, when constructed with the preposition *b-,* means "to look upon with (a certain) emotion," as in 2:1: *li-r'ot be-tob* (to enjoy). The nature of the things seen determines the emotion, and often it is of an ominous quality. In Hab 5:1 what is looked upon is God's astonishing acts. In 1 Sam 6:19 it may suggest a sense of awe and impending disaster. Below (11:4) Rashi understands the action of "looking upon the clouds" as expressing the fear of not reaping, a connection that seems conditioned not by the similarity of the two verbs (cf. 3:14) but rather by the preposition, as in Ps 64:9–10: "all who see them (*ro'eh bam*) will wag their heads and fear." P previously argued that focus on present enjoyment should not be dissociated from the source of pleasure, which is awareness of God's gift; he now adds that such a focus should not become an obsession that denies the future accountability of one's actions.

afterwards   I.e., in the grave.

VII   (4:1–16)   A Debate in Proverbs: On the One
                          Versus the Many

4:1 **Again I considered all the oppressed under the
    sun. Behold the tears of the oppressed, and they
    have no comforter.**
    *Yet He will remove strength from the hand of their oppres-
    sors. And they have no comforter?*

2   **Then I should praise the dead who have already
    died over those who yet live!**

3   *And even more than these two: he who has never yet existed
    and never seen "the evil deeds that are done under the sun"!*

4   **I consider that all effort and achievement arise
    from envy of one's neighbor, and this too is there-
    fore vanity and a chasing after the wind.**

5   *"The fool folds his arms
        and eats away at his own flesh."*

6   **"Better one handful with repose
        than two fistfuls with effort
        and chasing after wind."**

7   *But I would reconsider this "vanity under the sun."*

8   *If a man is always alone and acts as if he had no son or
    brother, then I would say that there is no end to his toil and
    his wealth brings no satisfaction.*
    **But for whom do I toil and deprive myself of plea-
    sure if not myself?**

    This too is a vanity and evil arrangement.

9   *Two are better than one if that produces rewards for their*

10 *joint efforts. For instance, if they both stumble the one can lift
    up the other, whereas a single person will have nobody to lift*

11 *him up. Also, if two lie together they will be warm, but how*

12 *can a single person warm himself? Again, if an enemy at-
    tacks, the two will stand against him.*
    **And "a triple cord cannot quickly be severed,"
    as the saying goes!**

13 *I would agree, however, that a mere child, low-born but
    wise, is better than an aged king who is foolish and no longer*

14 *able to defend himself. For such lads have emerged from
    prison to rule, even if born poor in that very kingdom.*

15 **I have seen all the living who move about under
the sun throng to the side of such a lad as will**
16 **reign in his stead. There is no end to all the people
who preceded them in a similar endeavor, nor
will those who come later take pleasure in this second lad. Surely, this too is vanity and a chasing
after wind.**

Commentary

4:1   *Again I considered*   I.e., from a different perspective. In this
transitional verse K seeks to return to the subject of 3:16 but now considers the topic of injustice from the point of view of the victim.

He will remove strength   I supply subject and verb in order to
reconstruct this elliptical verse on the basis of *miyyad,* "from the hand
of," assuming such an expression as 1 Kgs 11:35: "But I will take the
kingdom out of his son's hand"; also v. 34; Num 21:26. Here the ellipsis
of the subject, frequent in wisdom texts when the subject is God, is
extended to the verb, which is implied, however, in the preposition *min*
of *mi-yyad.*

strength   koaḥ   The point is constantly made in the Hebrew
Bible that the wicked and the strong will not be saved by their strength;
cf. 1 Sam 2:9; Amos 2:14; Deut 8:17; Ps 33:16.

And they have no comforter?   As often in Kohelet, the repetition signals a change of speaker and implies an ironic rebuttal. To avoid
the repetition, Scott (1965) reads *menaqqem,* "avenger," for *menaḥem.*
Perhaps the word already has both senses and P is again playing on
words (see Lam 1:16).

4:2–14   In this ongoing contest, which progresses in part through
"debates in proverbs," this section is unique in that it forms a veritable
string of "better-than" sayings, thus structurally "going one better" in a
genre that has one-upmanship as its very mode of operation. I study this
string sequence in Perry (1993a).

4:2   These words are argumentative and spoken in derision,
since in Kohelet there is little support for the view that death or nonexis-
tence is better than life. On the contrary, "a live dog is better than a dead
lion" (9:4), and the claim that the day of death is better than the day of
birth (7:1) is advanced only in the context of the value of a good name.
The view therefore cannot be ascribed to K, who feels on the contrary
that, despite life's vanity, there is still pleasure in one's present labor and
in eating and drinking. In context, his point is that the Comforter/

Avenger waits so long that one might as well be dead, since the dead seem to have as much hope of relief as the living!

the dead who have already died   This apparent tautology is intended to establish a distinction between two kinds of nonliving: those mentioned here who have lived and died, and those to be mentioned immediately, who have never lived, the unborn.

4:3   *more than these two*   Literally, "better than both," an interesting variant of the "better-than" formula; cf. Sirach 40:18.

        yet '*aden*   Perhaps from *'ad hen*. This unusual word is once more a dialogic reaction to the hapax *'adenah* in the previous verse.

        "the evil deeds . . ."   Rather than *"all* the evil deeds . . . ," as K would have stated it, P questions whether evil perpetrated by humans is an argument against creation.

4:4   Note the emphatic inversion of verb and pronoun subject indicating change of speaker (see Excursus 2c), as well as K's characteristic "All" argument. Here again the "All" argument forces theological considerations; if indeed all deeds are evil in their very principle, then this must point to a defect in their manufacture, so to speak. However, the subject has subtly shifted from the victims to the perpetrators, to what men *do* (*ha-ma'aseh,* v. 3) as opposed to what is *done,* and for the first time K impugns the motives of our deeds.

4:5–6   The debate in proverbs rages on. These two proverbs may appear complementary from a wisdom perspective, since each expresses a vicious extreme of the virtuous mean of industriousness. Dialogically, however, they are contradictory.

4:5   P uses this popular-sounding proverb to react to the severe implications of the view that all our motives are sinful, since in that case even the wise and righteous would refrain from action and become lazy and starve. The proverb also offers strong argument against K's epicureanism, since the negative results of withdrawal from activity, eating away at one's own flesh, is just the opposite of pleasurable eating and drinking and, ironically, enjoying one's activity. By implication P also points out the positive features of envious competition, namely that it discourages laziness and motivates a person to support himself or herself.

        folds   ḥobeq   Compare Prov 6:10–11: "A little folding of the hands to rest, and poverty will come upon you like a marauder"; also 24:33–34. P's example is also ironic. In 3:5 K had projected "embracing" as a positive value. P now notes the negative effects of "embracing" or folding one's arms. For the portrait of the fool see 4:17 and n.

        eats away at his own flesh   "devours his own body"; for the expression see Num 12:12; Isa 49:26.

4:6   *handful, fistfuls*   I.e., of sustenance, continuing the discussion and in response to the eventual skinniness of the lazy person. K's response also has the sound of a proverb, perhaps to mimic the previous point and to continue the game of debating in proverbs.

          with repose/with effort   naḥat/'amal   RSV has "of rest/of labor." But since it would be self-evident that a little rest is better than a lot of labor, and since the metaphor seems excessive (see Gordis), it is preferable to interpret these as adverbial accusatives.[2] So too Rashbam: "it is good for a man to have a handful of money with contentment . . . , for a little money is better for him than a lot of it with toil."

One should carefully note the progression of K's argument, or perhaps the self-realization that it implies. K the builder and energetic collector began the discussion by an intense interest in the rewards of one's *'amal* or labor (1:3). The motto for his acquisitive behavior was clearly "more is better than less." He now sees the limitations of such exaggerated pursuits and is willing to admit that repose may be superior.

There is another assumption, however, that K is unwilling to abandon so quickly. It also could be stated as a motto: "one is better than two," which structures his preference for *one* handful over *two*. This is a totally consistent structural statement of K's stoical position (e.g., 2:25) and makes more explicit his solipsistic tendencies. These will now become the focus of P's attack.

4:7   *reconsider*   Cf. 4:1n.

4:8   *If . . . then*   The particle of existence *yesh* introduces a condition (Crenshaw 1987, 88, on 2:21).

          acts as if   The attack, surely, is directed against one who voluntarily separates himself from his fellow and acts only on his own behalf. Rashbam interprets in this sense: "*He does not want* to have a second man with him to help him."

Alternatively, the allusion is to the lack of real inheritors. Zer-Kabod (1973) points out that a son and brother are first in the line of inheritance according to the Torah (Num 27:8–9). The complaint would thus not be unlike Abraham's in Gen 15:3, especially as interpreted by Rashi: "THOU HAST GIVEN ME NO OFFSPRING: And of what avail then is all that Thou hast given me?" This would then provide K with yet another question against the divinity.

---

2. Another reason for this is in the structure of "better-than" proverbs, which seem to require strong predicates. Thus, although two portions of sustenance would be considered "better than" a single portion, yet a single portion with *repose* would be better than a large amount if accompanied by its opposite. For the thought as well as the structure, see Prov 17:1: "Better a dry morsel with quiet than a house full of feasting with strife." For further elaboration, see my *Wisdom Literature and the Structure of Proverbs* (1993a).

no end to his toil   Without help he has to work harder.

no satisfaction   P's sense of enjoyment is that it must be shared. Thus he advises one to "enjoy life with a woman you love" (9:9).

but for whom   *waw* followed later by *gam* has an adversative use (see Excursus 3), although in this verse Gordis (1968) and Crenshaw (1987) see its use in the previous clause ("neither son nor brother. Yet . . .") rather than here.

if not myself   These added words help stress K's ideological egoism, based on the stoical notion (see 2:25n. and Introduction 5a) of self-reliance, as well as on the epicurean truism that enjoyment is always personal. See also 6:7.

4:9–12   P refuses to dissociate results from effort and now lists examples of how "two" may be more effective than "one." However, his examples are all negative, proving only that there's at least defensive strength in numbers.

4:12   *as the saying goes*   These words are added to bring out the aphoristic character of what may have been a popular saying. It is true that the context does not support the point of the aphorism, for of the three things just mentioned one is the adversary! However, the strategy of quoting a proverb that is absurd in context is to explode the opponent's myth according to which "the more the merrier" and that quantity can be a valid substitute for quality.

4:13   *I would agree*   P is offering a concession to his point that "two are better than one." Or he may be merely making the point that not all "one's" are alike, that (as he loves to argue) the sage, even disadvantaged by poverty and youthful inexperience or powerlessness, is always superior to the fool. However, the topic of a king's folly is not likely to appeal to K, who has a personal interest in excepting this category of humans.

4:14   *for such lads have emerged*   Literally, "he emerged," referring to a particular event no longer known. Since the intent is to demonstrate the possible, I generalize the event.

4:15   K quips that power is less a proof of wisdom than of popularity and that such a sage is soon overthrown by a more popular favorite. In so doing K returns to his argument that all plurality is only apparent and can be reduced to monotonous sameness: all "two's" are really "one's" and there is no real difference between sages and fools.

4:16   K returns to his claim that, like nature, history repeats itself and there is nothing new in human society either.

VIII   (4:17–5:8)   On Sages and Fools: Let Your
                          Words Be Few and Fear God

17 **When you go into the house of God and He is near
    at hand, keep your foot from the sacrifices of
    fools, for these do not know even how to do evil.**
5:1 **Do not be rash with your speech and let not your
    heart be quick to speak a word in God's presence.**
    *God is in heaven and you are only upon the earth, and this is
    why your words should be few:*

2   *"Just as a dream has too many topics,
           the voice of a fool has too many words."*

3   **I would agree that when you make a vow to God,
    don't delay in paying it, for God has no delight in**
4   **fools: Pay what you vow! It is better to say noth-
    ing than to vow and not pay it.**
5   **But beyond this, don't let your mouth lead you
    into sin and then declare before God's messenger
    that it was only a slip. Why give God the opportu-
    nity to be angry with your speech and destroy the
    work of your hands?**
6   *Just as with too many dreams and vanities, so it is also with
    too many words and complaints. Fear God!*

7   **If you see oppression of the poor and distortion of
    judgment and right in the judicial district, don't
    express astonishment over the matter . . .**
    As high as one is there is always a higher Avenger.

8   **And, as you said, the "earth" is the highest of all!**
    Yes, even a king is subject to the soil.

Commentary

4:17–5:8   This is a continuation of the debate introduced in 4:5, 13
over the relative value of sages and fools. It argues prudence, self-
restraint in speech, avoidance of fools, and respect for God's punishment. It does *not* express reluctance to offer sacrifices and preference for
obedience, as, for example, in 1 Sam 15:22 ("to obey is better than
sacrifice"). Rather, it urges propriety while in God's presence, however
differently the two interlocutors define this presence. At any rate, it is
difficult to understand how one could interpret this earnest argument as

representing an upper-class viewpoint and a concern for "good form" only.

4:17   *keep your foot from*   The root of the problem in interpreting this verse seems to be the desire to construe the *m-* of *mi-tet* as a comparative (GKC 133e), when in fact it is easily construed as the prepositional component of *shmor ragleka . . . m-,* which is a frequent expression in wisdom literature: "He will keep your foot from being ensnared" (Prov 3:26); cf. similar verbs in Prov 1:15 (*mena'*); Prov 4:27 (*ḥasar*); Prov 25:17 (*ḥokar*), all constructed with the preposition *mem.*

        and He is near at hand   "and [He is] near to hearing." One might have expected the repetition of the subject, e.g., *we-hu' qarob.* However, omission of God's name as the subject of the verb is not uncommon (see 2:21n.). Alternatively, the subject is carried over from the previous word *'elohim.* At any rate, God's nearness is an important concept, especially in such texts as Ps 145:18: "The Lord is near to all who call upon Him." Grammatically, the expression is similar to Isa 13:22, where the adjective is also construed with *l-* and the infinitive: "its time is close at hand," *qarob la-bo'.* K's meaning is that God will hear because He is close at hand, i.e., the divine presence rests in the house of God. By contrast, P expands the meaning by reading a temporal emphasis here: God is close to hearing, He is about to hear.

        the sacrifices of fools   tet ha-kesilim zebaḥ   Literally, "fools' giving or distribution of sacrifices." The specific expression *natan zebaḥ* occurs in Ps 51:18 and there seems to refer to a burnt or sin offering. However, the context here is the peace offering, only part of which was burned on the altar and the rest "given" as food to the priests (Lev 7:32) and the worshipers. This sacrifice was especially appropriate in fulfillment of vows made in times of distress (e.g., Jonah 1:16). This sacrificial context, as described in Ps 116, has important parallels to our passage: the salvation from distress and the vows made and then acquitted in the presence of all the people (including fools). This would somewhat limit Zer-Kabod's (1973) plausible suggestion that the warning is against joining fools at their sacrificial meal.

        fools   This is a definitive description of fools, presented as an a fortiori observation: don't expect fools ever to do good, since they don't even know how to do evil ("they walk in darkness," 2:14). Their defect, therefore, is not their wickedness but their ignorance: "they *know* not." However, fools are not virtuous skeptics but rather ill-behaved boors: they don't know *how to act.*

5:1–6   The two verbal activities appropriate to God's house are now considered: prayer and vows, i.e., the sacrifices in payment thereof. Given the context of the peace offerings (see previous nn.), it is possible that this includes a warning against boisterousness at such sacrificial gatherings.

5:1   *in God's presence*   Not "to God" but rather "before God." Fox's (1989) desire to limit this verse to "circumspection in uttering vows rather than caution in speech generally" accurately describes K's own intent, whereas P will pursue his more general advice of watching what you say about God in general (see the next n.). To limit the ambivalence of this verse is to misread P's language of indirection.

God is in heaven   And He therefore can hear all that is said everywhere, not only in the house of God; cf. 8:12n. *who constantly . . .*

you are only upon the earth   While this can be heard as a general reference to all humans, thus getting P off the hook so to speak, it is also, dialogically, a direct reminder that ALL words are heard, not only those uttered in the Temple.

5:2   For the comparative use of *ki . . . waw,* see also 2:16 and Zer-Kabod (1973, 27 n. 8).

dream   It is difficult to explain the introduction of dreams into this context, unless it is assumed that it is dragged in through quotation of a popular proverb on the loquaciousness of fools. By relating the topic to the vanity argument, however (v. 6), P will make the point more explicit.

too many   rob   Cf. 1:18, 5:6.

5:3–4   The other defect of fools (the first being their ignorance and perhaps also their lack of decorum) is their contempt for speech (and for God). Again, the proper behavior is that of Ps 116:14: "I shall pay my vows." K seems also to be reacting to the veiled criticism of his remarks, since P is arguing that he talks too much and that all loquaciousness is foolish.

5:3   *I would agree that*   These added words help understand how K admits the previous point only in its precise application to vows; it is to his purpose to conceal his underlying critique of the divinity.

when you make a vow   Some have used these verses to prove that K discourages vows, but the case seems to be the opposite. V. 3 is an almost literal citation of Deut 23:22–23: "If you make a vow to the Lord your God, do not be remiss in paying it, for the Lord your God will surely require it from you and there will be sin in you. But if you refrain from vowing, there will be no sin in you." It is clear that here Deut does not "encourage the making of vows" (Crenshaw 1987, 117) but rather uses the optional "if" (*ki,* cf. Lev 30:3) and goes on to stress that vows are *not* required. But K is more definite and therefore replaces the ambiguous *ki* by *ka'asher,* "when." Note that K reproduces both commands

of these two biblical sources: Vows must be paid (v. 4, Lev 30:3) and on
time (v. 3, Deut 23:22).

    God has no delight in fools   Literally, "there is no delight
(*ḥepets*, cf. also 12:1) in fools." Note again the omission of God's name
(see 2:21n.). God's delight is mentioned explicitly in 1 Sam 15:22; Mal
1:10: " 'I have no delight in you,' said the Lord."

5:4   From the context of Jonah 1:16 and Ps 116, as well as from
the paradoxical nature of all such "better-than" statements, the implications of this wisdom-saying are hair-raising: It is better not to vow, *even
if your life is endangered,* than to vow and not pay. The consequences are
that the latter is even more life-threatening, as the next verse goes on to
explain.

5:5   *But beyond this*   These words are added in the translation to
clarify the movement of the dialogue.

    sin   I.e., by neglecting the advice of Deut 23:23 to "perform
what has passed your lips."

    declare   t'omar   As in Deut 26:3: "And you shall declare
(*we-'amarta*) to him."

    God's messenger   Probably the officiating priest, consistent
with K's wish to limit the context of God's action. But the Septuagint
reads "God," which clearly records P's attempt to expand the context of
divine action in this passage.

    why give God the opportunity to be angry   Literally, "why will
God be angry . . . ?" The thought is that of "tempting Providence"
(Barton 1908).

5:6   *just as . . . so   ki . . . waw*   Cf. 5:2n.

    too many (dreams and vanities)   rob   As in 2:18, 5:2. The
dreams mentioned in 5:2 are now related to K's favorite topic of vanity,
and both are now used as a springboard for P's underlying point: since K
has admitted to necessary limitations on speech, he may now wish to
consider the excesses of his own speech behavior.

    too many   harbeh   As in 5:19, 7:16.

    words and complaints   debarim   Words of reproach. See *1:1,
dibrei.

    Fear God   And stop complaining!

5:7–8   This continues the theme of God's justice from the previous
section and 3:16f and 4:1, as suggested by the repetition of the key words
mishpat, tsedek, ḥepets.

    judicial district   Literally, "province," as in 2:8, but here the
author seems to be thinking also about the etymological connection
between *medinah*, "province, city," and *din*, "judgment."

express astonishment The verb *tmh* refers here not merely to one's emotional reaction but also to its expression. I find attractive Zer-Kabod's (1973) suggestion that this expression takes the form of a question, a sense frequent in Rabbinic Hebrew. Such questioning is portrayed in Mal 2:17: "when you say . . . : 'Where is the God of justice?' "

the matter ḥepets However, in 3:17 above, the reference is to God's justice: "God will judge . . . every matter (*ḥepets*)." This word allows P to make explicit the theological context of such a discussion (whether it is implied by K's critique is entirely possible). Here P emphasizes that, although God is in heaven (5:1), or rather precisely because He is in heaven, He is still in touch; indeed, He oversees everything.

as high as one is . . . Literally, "each watchman is higher than the next and there are higher ones above these." I take the plural (contrast GKC 124h) as one of majesty, as referring to God the Judge. Crenshaw (1987) agrees in part, except that he sees the reference to the highest official, i.e., the king.

Avenger Literally, "watchman," which is a complex notion including providential care (the "Am I my brother's keeper?" of Gen 4:9), waiting for the right moment (Gen 37:11), noticing or remembering for purposes of retribution (Ps 130:3; Job 14:16: "You wouldst not even watch for my sin"), and perhaps even the more sinister lying in wait of Ps 56:7 where the enemies "watch my steps." The general thought of being "higher than" and therefore "looking down" and observing all human actions is expressed in Ps 33:13–14: "The Lord looks down from heaven, He beholds all the sons of men . . . and understands all their deeds."

5:8 *the "earth"* In this difficult verse K seems to render ironic the point implied in 1:4, according to which only "the earth" has eternity; cf. ★1:4 *the earth,* also Rashi ad loc.

the highest yitron b- In this comparative use of *yitron* one would have expected the preposition *min,* as in 2:13. For the use of *b-* see the next n.

of all ba-kol★

Yes, even a king . . . Literally, "a king is subject to the soil." This continues the discussion of kingship; see 2:12n. *others . . .*

soil sadeh Literally, "field." P does not insist on his homiletic midrash on "earth" (= humility), and this choice of a synonym allows him to direct the discussion toward another of his favorite subjects, the universal dignity and importance of labor and the happiness of earning one's own bread.

is subject to neʿebad Literally, "is enslaved to." In Kohelet irony is occasionally expressed over the paradoxical reversal of lords and servants (10:7), and in v. 10:17 it is implied that not even all kings are free men. By contrast, the king's enslavement to the earth is regarded here as not only proper but in the nature of things. Grammatically, the participle *ne'ebad* is perfectly ambivalent here. I read it as modifying *melek,* the king, since this makes explicit his paradoxically meritorious servitude, and also because "soil" (*sadeh*) already implies that the ground is tilled or *ne'ebad*. However, many commentators follow this latter interpretation because *'bd* occurs in the *nif'al* only with this meaning in Hebrew Scripture.

　　　　is subject to the soil★

IX   (5:9–6:9a)   What Is True Wealth?

9   *And*
   "He who loves money will never be satisfied."
   And
   he who loves abundance: no increase!
10 **This too is vanity: When wealth multiplies, so do its spenders.**

   But what benefit can owners derive except from what is
11 *within their range of vision? Sweet is the sleep of the poor laborer, whether he has eaten little or much . . .*
   But the full belly of the man of wealth is not enough to let him sleep!

12   **I have observed a sickly evil under the sun: wealth stored up for its owners to one's own**
13 **detriment. For his wealth is lost in an unhappy venture and all the while he begets a son but has nothing to leave him.**
14   *"Just as he issued from his mother's womb naked, he will return" to go again as he came.*

   But neither will he carry off anything for his
15 **labor! And this too is a sickly evil . . .**
   That he should go forth again exactly as he came?

   What is his net profit? He labors in vain!
16 **In addition, during all his days he eats in darkness and much travail, sickness and anger.**
17 *This is what I have discovered: that it is good and proper to eat and drink and take enjoyment in the very labor that one does under the sun during the number of days of one's life that the Lord hath given him, for this is his portion.*

18 **Indeed, every man to whom God has given wealth and possessions and the power to enjoy them . . .**
   . . . and to take up his portion and enjoy his toil, this is precisely God's gift.

19 **Then he should not be overly intent upon the span of his entire life!**
   Indeed, God answers him through the joy of his heart.

6:1   **There is an evil I have observed under the sun,
and it is widespread among men: a man to whom**

2   **"God has given" wealth and possessions and honor
and anything he could possibly desire, but God
does not give him control over them, rather a
stranger will devour them. This indeed is vanity
and an evil sickness.**

3   *If a man begets a hundred children and lives a long life: despite the length of his days, if he does not take satisfaction in
these good things . . .*

. . . **and have a proper burial, I would say that the
stillborn child is better off than he.**

4   *Yet, as you would argue, in vanity he comes and in darkness
he goes forth . . .*

5   . . . **and in darkness his name is covered over.
Though he has neither enjoyed the sun nor experienced its warmth, his rest is still to be preferred to
the other.**

6   *Even had he lived a thousand years twice over but did not
enjoy himself, do not all humans "go to the same place," as
you put it?*

7   **All man's toil is for his own sustenance.**
And this is why his appetite is never filled?

8   **How then is the sage better than the fool, or your
poor man who knows how to take and enjoy life
on its own terms?**

9   *Surely, a joy at hand is better than excessive desires.*

Commentary

5:9   The transition to a new section takes the form here of a
dialogic continuation of the discussion of God's justice. P points out that
not all punishment is judicial and exemplary, that, as the Rabbis said,
"the reward for sin is sin," that greed, for example, is self-defeating
because, by its very nature, it thwarts the enjoyment that it seeks. Two
distinct but related attitudes are criticized here: (a) greed for money for
its own sake or as the goal of labor, as opposed to the love of work itself;
(b) the love of abundance in any of its forms, perhaps since this goes
beyond human need. There is thus an initial issue of quality or direction
of one's desire, but even when this is correct there still remains the

problem of quantity, since one certainly can have too much of a good thing (e.g., 1:18). In terms of the dialogue, whereas P's analysis centers on psychological factors such as dissatisfaction, K prefers to discuss physical and external realities, especially wealth. Note again the sharp debate in proverbs in this verse.

He who loves money . . . Two stylistic features give this saying the ring of a popular proverb: the repetition of *kesep* in the rhyming position (cf. 10:11), and the aphoristic tightening of syntax as exemplified by the omission of the subject *mi,* "one who," in explicit contrast to the reply.

and he who loves This is the only use of this verb with the preposition *be-* in Hebrew Scripture and is therefore often dismissed as a dittography (a careless scribal repetition of the final letter of the previous word). However, others have pointed out the analogy with synonymous expressions such as *ḥapets be-* and *ratsah be-,* which of course could have been used here except for two reasons. First, the close semantic connection between the two halves of the verse is accentuated by the repetition of the same verb (in a verse that already uses the repetition of *kesep*). Second, the synonymous use of this preposition allows the author to enlarge the meaning of *hamon* so that it refers not only to material wealth but also to exaggerated acquisition ("abundance") of whatever objects, even including people (cf. 2:7 above). What we have here, then, is another criticism of Solomon's acquisitive habits, accentuated by the (rather clumsy) mimicking of the form of the previous proverb.

no increase lo' tebu'ah The repetition of the verb *yis-ba'* from the first hemistich is understood, as often in proverbs. The reference is not only to agricultural produce, however, but rather to whatever issues forth from something else (from the verb *ba'*) and is thus able to yield enjoyment or satisfaction. Thus: "He is satisfied by the yield of his lips" (Prov 18:20); "whatever is gained from productive labor" (Deut 16:15). It is thus a loose synonym of *yitron.*

5:10   K may be arguing that man is *naturally* a predator, created as such, and thus that the punishment of greed derives from its own structure and therefore from God, the ultimate creator of that structure. Or this may be viewed as an answer to the last point, namely that abundance of material goods itself is evil, perhaps because of the additional maintenance involved (see above, 2:4–7).

its spenders Literally, "its eaters or consumers," who act predictably and according to the normal course of things, as opposed to the sudden and unexpected loss referred to in 5:13.

what benefit "How can one enjoy except what is near at hand?"

within their range of vision   Literally, "the seeing of his eyes," perhaps referring to what can be watched over. However, in the context of K's constant dissatisfaction (5:9), P is arguing that, as against K's view of the endless dissatisfaction of the "eye" (= desires; cf. 1:8nn. *eye, sated*), the soul's desires are not infinite but rather have a natural range. Cf. Seneca, *Epistles to Lucilius,* end of Letter 16.

5:11   For the two thoughts of this verse, see 2:22n.; or, as LaBruyère put it: The poor are "contents du nécessaire," whereas the rich are "inquiets et pauvres avec le superflu" (*Les Caractères,* "Des Grands,*" no. 25). P observes that the premise has consequences not only for the "haves" but also for the "have-nots." He points out that the poor, who have little to watch over, are happy with their lot, but he implies that their lack of anguish is to be ascribed either to their productiveness or, more likely, to their general contentedness.

      poor   This word is not in the text but is implied by the comparison that follows.

      *the full belly   ha-saba*ʿ*   The sense is more specific or concrete than either "satiety" or even "abundance" (see Gordis 1968 and also Prov 25:16). K continues to contemplate the paradoxes of existence: how can a hungry man sleep well and how can his case be compared to that of one who is well-fed! Specifically, he renders ironic Deut 8:10 (also 6:11; 11:15), which he translates as "you shall eat and be filled (but not satisfied)!"

5:12   K continues the discussion of wealth but addresses his real concern, which is not the present but the future and the profit that it can bring. There is an implicit criticism here of the view that one can enjoy only what is at hand and that there is no protection against loss, robbery, and the like. Surely, experience teaches that some do have success in storing their material belongings. But he now argues that, even when storage and protection are successful, other evils lie in wait.

      sickly evil   raʿah ḥolah   Crenshaw (1987) translates the phrase (in v. 15 but not here) as "serious injustice," in which case K is pursuing his indictment of God's justice. The Rabbis (in Kohelet Rabbah) were properly puzzled by the adjective (is there such a thing as an evil that is not sickly?). The adjective may therefore be for mere emphasis (Zer-Kabod 1973), although the particular emphasis may actually be a doubling: the wealthy person will have no benefit either in this life, by way of enjoyment, or after this life as an inheritance to others. That is to say, there will be a double evil in that the reasonable expectations of both father and son are defeated. This dual perspective helps explain the curious alternation of singular and plural in this verse.

      stored up   I.e., successfully safeguarded against its spenders or "eaters" (5:10).

for its owners   This refers to both father and, eventually, the heir. Gordis (1968) rejects the translation "*by* its owners" on the basis of the requirements of context, but he then goes on to change the context by translating "owners" as a singular!

one's own detriment   I.e., his detriment, that of the original owner, which seems to be the "man of wealth" in the previous verse. It is he who bears the onus of the evil injustice since he is the one who earned the money in the first place. Or, the singular may refer to the son in the next verse.

5:13   *For*   This verse is an elaboration of the case (Crenshaw 1987) and not an illustration (Zer-Kabod 1973).

unhappy venture   As examples Kohelet Rabbah lists the loss of wealth of Korach, Haman, Job, and Naboth the Israelite.

he begets a son   The point seems to be either that he had a son for the purpose of preserving his heritage, or he first had a son and then worked in order to leave him something. In both instances the focus is on the inheritance.

he has nothing to leave him   Literally, "there is nothing in his hand." For "hand" with the meaning of "possession" see Num 21:26, where to "take the land out of his hand" obviously means "out of his possession."

5:14   *from his mother's womb naked, he will return*   The speaker seems to be quoting Job 1:21 from memory, since the parallel is too close to suppose a mere coincidence. And the literary reminiscence both invites the reader to recall the example of Job and also suggests a similarity of meaning. Indeed, P is teaching a lesson in patient understanding and acceptance of God's ways. His argument is that, although nothing was gained, nothing has been lost since there was nothing at the outset.

The parallel deserves even more scrutiny, since the slight differences reveal that P is quoting a well-known text for his own purposes. Job 1:21: "*Naked* I came from my mother's womb and naked I shall return *there*." K: "Just as he issued from his mother's womb, naked, he will return . . ." The first point is that "naked" is only used once and it may therefore serve as the first "naked" in Job (so Barton 1908; Fox 1989) and not be attached to the end of the sentence, as often translated. The second point is that, as Crenshaw (1987) has noted, the Kohelet text omits Job's euphemism "there" (*shammah*), but the reason for this is not to express preference for another euphemism (*halak*, "to go"; i.e., to die) but rather to free the latter part of the verse for reinterpretation.

to go again as he came   Literally, "to return to go as he came." This repeats the language and curious dialectic of 1:7 and would seem to suffer the interpretation of what the Rabbis called "intimations of the resurrection of the dead from Toranic authority" (BT Sanhedrin, chapter

10). At the very least, it again takes up P's observation of cyclicality in nature (vv. 1:4–7).

But neither will   Literally, "nothing that he can take in his hand will he carry off for his toil" (Gordis 1968). This verse gives an additional ("this too" in the next verse) reason, beyond lack of legacy, why his work and storing were in vain: granted that he started from zero, he still added something of his own, and that is precisely what he should be entitled to keep. There seems to be also a debate with the point expressed in Ps 49:18f 17E. On the one hand, he agrees that "For when he dies he will carry nothing away," but he also argues that even during his life he is constantly unhappy, as opposed to Ps 49:19 18E, which goes on to assert that "Though, while he lives, he counts himself happy."

carry off   I read *yolik* for *yolek*, following Rashbam (Japhet and Salters 1985).

from his labor   be-'amalo   For *me-'amalo*, as noticed earlier by Ibn Ezra, who cites Lev 8:32: "and what remains of the flesh (*ba-basar*)."

5:15   *this too*   This is the second evil; see n. *But neither will* to the previous verse.

that he should go forth again exactly as he came   I.e., that he should begin again from nothing. There is no formal indication of a change of voice here, and the words could be ascribed to K. However, the change of voice indicates the possible unreasonableness of the assertion. Here, continuing his semantics of going and coming (cf. 1:4n. *goes forth . . .*), P cannot fathom why this circumstance can be charged to God, since nothing has been lost (he had nothing to start with!) and, due to the cyclicality of the process, there is always another chance.

net profit   K still deplores that no thing in this life can be carried over into the next round of existence. Death therefore signifies the absolute end of his worldly goods, both in this world (when left to his son) and in the next.

in vain   la-ruaḥ   Apparently equivalent to *hebel*.

5:16   *In addition*   He adds yet a third evil, namely that even his present life, the period of acquisition of wealth, is painful. Note again K's fondness for accumulation at the end of the verse, here the piling on of synonyms.

all his days   I.e., during his entire life. Perhaps moved by the argument of paucity, by K's tendency to diminish and minimize his blessings, Ibn Ezra attaches this expression to "in darkness" and interprets that, because of overwork, the wealthy man is unable to eat until nighttime.

darkness   The sense here is probably that of "lack of understanding" (cf. "the people that walk in darkness" Isa 9:1) and thus appropriate to the fool of 2:14 above.

5:17   The transition to a discussion of one's portion or *ḥelek* is quite natural, given both the preceding complaint over the son's loss of inheritance and also the synonymy of *ḥelek* and *naḥalah,* inheritance (cf. 2:10n. *my portion*).

    I   The emphatic repetition of the personal subject (see 1:16n.) is further accentuated by *hinneh,* "behold."

    in the very labor   See 2:10. P would agree with K that one's main pleasure (perhaps not his only one) comes from one's own activity, intrinsically and not as a result, but he will insist that this portion always comes from God.

    the number of days of his life   Despite the general preference for interpretations denoting paucity (see above 2:3n. *the numbered . . .*), the sense here is definitely not pessimistic. Gordis (1968) cites Job 14:5: *mispar ḥodoshaw,* "the number of his months." However, even this example does not argue limitation in the sense of "few" but rather the more relevant sense of a providential determination, a numbering that God performs at birth or from the beginning. It is also possible, however, that the one who numbers or counts in this passage is not God but man and especially the sage, as in Ps 90:12, where this activity is the very criterion of wisdom: "Teach us to count our days, so that we may get a heart of wisdom." This reading directly addresses K's program of experimentation on behalf of wisdom. In the same sense and more generally, Zer-Kabod (1973) pictures K as exercising his mission to teach knowledge to the people (12:9).

    the Lord hath given   P continues the quotation of Job 1:21 begun in 5:14.

    portion   See 2:10n.

5:18   *Indeed   gam*   Seems to be used adversatively; see 4:8n.

    and the power to enjoy them   K is now arguing like P, except that he observes that, since there is no limit to God's power, if enjoyment comes from God this must include the very power to enjoy.

    and to take up his portion   la-se't 'et ḥelqo   In turn, P now argues like K by granting that man does have a measure of control over his enjoyment. The crucial phrase, the condition of "taking pleasure in one's labor" (*lismoaḥ ba-'amalo*) is, in an active sense, *la-se't 'et helqo.*

5:19   *he should not be overly intent*   This is given as ironic advice, that one should not spend too much time brooding on the number of one's days. K pursues this point in the second half of 11:8, with the same meaning of *yizkor* (and a different one of *harbeh*).

overly   harbeh   "too much," as in 5:6; 7:16.

God answers him   I.e., in the present; he does not have to wait for some distant future. The unusual verb *ma'aneh,* occurring in the expression *ki ha-'elohim ma'aneh,* would seem to be a reply to some such statement as Micah 3:7: *ki 'ein ma'aneh 'elohim:* "for there is no answer from God." Commentators take it as a *hif'il;* Rashbam, for example, translates it as "to cause to sing or rejoice," citing Exod 15:21 and Deut 31:21. The sense seems to be that God responds to man's effort to assume his portion by granting him a grateful heart.

through the joy of his heart   besimhat libo   The preposition *be-* indicates not only "at the time of" but also the means, as in Gen 15:8: "How *(be-mah)* am I to know that I shall possess it?" The meaning would then be that the joy itself, probably the feeling of gratitude over God's gifts, would be sufficient proof of God's response.

6:1   The previous case involved a man with an heir but no inheritance to leave him: he has lost his benefit and enjoyment even in the present. The present case is that of a man with inheritance but no heir: he retains present enjoyment but has no future, while retaining the desire for (and hence the frustration over) the future.

6:2   The continuing allusion to Solomon's career is made explicit here by the reference to "wealth and possessions and honor" (cf. 2 Chr 1:11, 12; also Prov 8:18), but the termination of these goods may be hinted in the parallel passage in 1 Kgs 3:13: "I have given you wealth and honor . . . all the days of your life." All the days *of your life,* as the Rabbis would say, but no longer. This would then be an allusion to Solomon's loss of most of his kingdom since it did not pass as an inheritance to his son. In this verse K attempts to point out a contradiction in P's argument of God's gifts.

honor   To the material benefits listed in 5:18, K adds the element of honor *(kabod),* as befits a kingly personage. Or, it might be stated that in the case of a king, wealth is a distinct form of glory, as in Esth 1:4: "He showed the riches of his royal glory"; a king's generosity is therefore distinctive, "according to a king's bounty" (Esth 1:7 and especially Solomon's gifts to the Queen of Sheba mentioned in 1 Kgs 10:13).

anything he could possibly desire   I.e., in the present.

control   Literally, "the power to enjoy (eat) them," that is to say, to exercise control over them.

a stranger   And not his heir, presumably his son.

will devour them   Literally, "will eat them," perhaps in the sense of waste.

6:3   P offers a more extreme example to prove his point that enjoyment, which in agreement with K occurs only in the present, results not from external goods but rather from spiritual satisfaction, as manifested in a sense of gratitude for God's gifts.

   take satisfaction in   tisba' min   Used only here with this preposition.

   and have a proper burial   The conditional that starts the verse is continued by *we-gam*. For the importance of honor see 6:2n. Granting such importance to a decent burial may seem hyperbolic (better than long life and children, the two signs of divine blessing in Hebrew Scripture!), yet it is well documented. The point seems in contradiction to K's philosophical insistence on enjoyment in the present and on his skepticism concerning the value of fame after death (cf. 7:1), yet it is consistent with his main personage, the king (cf. *).

6:4   *in vanity he comes*   He dies without personal profit or *yitron*. For this meaning of *ba'* see 1:4n and 5:14–15. The expression *ba-hebel ba'* may be an ironic calque of *ba' ba-yamim,* "to get along in years," precisely what this infant does not do.

   he goes forth   yelek   To the netherworld.

   darkness   This is an interesting case of diaphora (use of the same word in a slightly different sense). The first refers to the darkness of the netherworld; the second, to the absence of enduring fame in this world.

6:5   K has been confronted by a comparison of two of his most secure values, pleasure and fame, and now chooses the latter (here presented in its negative form as the absence of dishonor) as "better-than" the former.

   enjoyed/experienced   shemesh lo' ra'ah we-lo' yada'   Literally, "the sun he did not see or know." Seeing is often synonymous with enjoyment (cf. 2:1; 9:9), and here the verb "to know" is close to the notion of "experience" in Gen 4:1 and Judg 3:1–2.

   his rest is still to be preferred   nahat la-zeh mi-zeh   At the least, this strange expression repeats the "better-than" formula of v. 3, but it may also add the idea of rest, indicating that K's rhetoric of nothingness after death was only that, and that he does hold to some idea of afterlife. The stillborn is preferable, in his view, because, although he never acquires honor, he does not lose it (through an improper burial). Worse than a *yitron,* therefore, is nothing, but worse still is a deficit.

6:6   *a thousand years twice over**   I.e., two thousand, not used perhaps (Zer-Kabod 1973) because "thousand" is sufficient, being frequently used in the Hebrew Bible to express a high number (below 7:28).

   the same place   P sarcastically quotes K's argument in 3:20, since K has just admitted to degrees of benefit—or lack thereof—after death. The question is, again, whether anything survives the death of the individual. The subject will be pursued momentarily, in the discussion of fame.

6:7   *All man's toil . . .*   The thought seems to echo Prov 16:26: "A worker's hunger works for him alone (RSV: "for him"), for his mouth urges him on." K's negative evaluation of this situation is also expressed in another proverb: "for a piece of bread a man will transgress" (Prov 28:21). Again through his characteristic "all" argument, K pursues his attack against the Creator, for if *all* human behavior can be explained by selfish motivation, then there must be a defect in the creation itself.

    his own sustenance   Literally, "his own mouth" (see the preceding n.). For a further instance of K's selfishness, see 4:8n. *if not myself.*

    and this is why . . . ?   The initial *we-gam* not only indicates a change of speaker but also the cause (cf. 9:3). Since the retort expresses surprise and disbelief, it is best rendered by a question. Note P's ironic use of quotation: of "appetite" (*nepesh,* see the preceding n.) and, more directly, of K's argument on universal dissatisfaction in 1:8.

6:8   K resumes the debate (cf. 1:11; 2:14–16 and nn.) on whether any category of humans can be considered as superior.

    take and enjoy life on its own terms   This is a guess for the unusual expression *la-halok neged ha-ḥayyim;* literally, "to walk against life" (RSV: "the living"). As used in this book, the verb means "to go forth according to one's natural desires or motion" (cf. 1:4n.), and I understand the sense dialogically, since P had previously argued for the special status not only of sages but of the poor (cf. 4:14; 5:7; 9:15–16; and especially 5:11).

6:9   *a joy at hand*   This is Gordis's (1968) excellent rendering of *mar'eh 'einayim,* the "sight of the eyes, what the eyes can see." Beyond the connotation of experience and enjoyment associated with sight in our text, P seems purposefully to limit such desires, as opposed to K's more expansive notion of "whatever the eyes can see."

    excessive desires   halak-nepesh   The appetite's going forth, thus "the wandering of desire" (RSV). Zer-Kabod (1973) quotes Ps 131:1–2: "I do not occupy myself (*lo' halakti*) with things too great and too marvelous for me. But I have calmed and quieted my soul (*napshi*)" (RSV). Indeed, this text recapitulates the two desires of K that come in for much criticism in Kohelet: grandeur and knowledge.

X   (6:9b–11)   Transition: What Is Man?

This also is vanity and a chasing after wind.
10 **Everything that exists has already been called by
name. Thus it is known that man is called** ADAM
because he is from the ADAMAH, **the ground . . .**
   *. . . and he therefore cannot argue with One stronger than
   he.*

11 **There are so many things that increase vanity!**
   Yes, for example the question "what profit hath man?"

Commentary

6:9b   *this also*   This may refer to what K would regard as a fiction, the distinction just made between proximate and distant desires
and the possibility that humans are indeed capable of containing desire.
However, I take it as introducing the next vanity argument.

6:10   K restates his argument: since all men are from the earth,
there are no substantial distinctions (such as sage and fool, v. 8) between
them. And since their natures are already given, as implied by their
generic name, there is no possibility of change and all criticism must be
referred to their original creation.
        'adam/'adamah   "God formed man (*'adam*) of dust from the
ground (*'adamah*)" (Gen 2:7; cf. 3:19 above).
        because he is from the ADAMAH, *the ground*   These words do
not appear in the MT and are added here to bring out the etymological
argument.
        One stronger than he   The emphasis on the etymology of
'adam leads P in the opposite direction and allows him once again to
introduce his religious warning: "Humans (*'adam*) and not God (*'El*)"
(Isa 31:3).

6:11   *Yes, for example the question*   This dialogic remark is not in
the original. P again plays on the ambivalence of *debarim*, "things,
words," and humorously agrees that his opponent's words are to be
included in the proliferation of universal vanity.
        what profit hath man?   This is K's fundamental question,
here quoted ironically; cf. 1:3 and n.

XI   (6:12–7:12)   Beginnings and Ends (Again the
                          Two Directions)

12 **Yet, who can know what is really good for a man
    in this life during the number of the days of his
    vain life that he spends like a shadow? And who
    can tell man what will be after him under the sun?**
7:1 *But there's reputation:*
        "Better a good name than good oil!"

    Then for such a person:
    Better the day of death than the day of his birth!
2   *Yes, it is better to go to the house of mourning than to the
    banquet hall, since this is man's end, so every living person
    had better remember this:*
3   *"Anger is better than laughter."*

4   **Can an angry face rejoice the heart? The sages can
    think only of houses of mourning!**
    And fools can think only of houses of mirth.
5   *Surely it is better to hear the reproof of a sage than for a
    person to hear the song of fools, for*
6   *"like the crackling of thorns under the pot," such is the
    laughter of fools.*

7   **Yet this too is vanity, that derision can make a
    sage foolish.**
8   *And gifts can destroy him. . . . Let's at least agree that*
        "the end of a thing is better than its beginning":
    a patient spirit is better than a haughty spirit.

9   **Then do not be quick to put on an angry face, for
    "anger in the bosom of fools abides."**
10 *But don't say: "how can it be that the old days were better
    than these?" For such questions do not arise from wisdom.*

11 **Such "wisdom" is always better with wealth, a
    definite advantage to those who would enjoy life.**
12 **For the protection of wisdom is the protection of
    money.**
    And the advantage of experience?

    **Let's conclude this by agreeing that wisdom pre-
    serves the lives of its holders.**

Commentary

6:12   This magnificent, rhapsodic verse is an apt conclusion to K's pessimism, summarizing the brevity of human life, the foolishness of effort, and especially the inability of even the sage ("who can know, who can tell?") to discern either the good of this life or the nature of the next. The rest of the book will rebound from this position, attempting both to define the limits of this skepticism (is there really *no* good? what about fame?) and its positive and religious uses.

   like a shadow   The comparison recurs in 8:13.

   who can know, who can tell   The questions imply a negative response, as K continues his assault against wisdom and its practitioners.

   spends   ya'aseh   See BDB *'asah,* end.

7:1–12   It is destructive to delete or rearrange this series, as some have done, and hardly adequate to explain its retention on the basis of its being a "collection" of proverbs, which is often another way of asserting that it has no unifying theme. Rather, it is of a piece with the continuing debate, except that its formal device, that of a "debate in proverbs," is more patent here (see Excursus 2d). Kohelet is a living and lively dialogue, and to overlook this point is to miss the connectedness of the text.

   The specific form of debate here is that of "better-than" proverbs, a current and typical stylistic formula that K finds uncongenial to his attack against wisdom. This is because such comparative formulas beg the question: to admit that a given value is "better than" another is to grant the argument of value and by implication to reject the leveling denial that "ALL is vanity" and valueless.

   As to content, the central issue is again (cf. 2:26b–3:8) the two directions that life can take: the direction of natural causality ($+ > -$) or of human nature ($- > +$). However, the vocabulary has now shifted from that of direction, either of decline or progression, to that of the terminal points, of beginnings and ends.

7:1   *But there's reputation/then for such a person*   These words are added to clarify the development of the arguments.

   Assent to the first of these apparently traditional sayings is not difficult: would not most of us agree that certain pleasures, here symbolized by oil, must often be suspended or deferred for higher purposes such as a good name? However, the interpretation can lead in two different directions.

   better a good name   For P this means a good reputation in the present, and it directly responds to K's previous worry about "what will be after" (6:12). P's reply: you should worry more about present repute and stop brooding about death!

Alternatively, instead of the usual interpretation of "name" as "good name" or fame, one can take the first statement literally: in view of the finality of death just argued, *any* form of survival is preferable to even the best pleasures of this life. At any rate, the remark directly addresses K's doubt in the previous verse concerning what will be after a person's death.

good oil   P recalls the wisdom perspective of the warnings against the stranger woman in Prov 5:3–4: "Her palate is smoother than oil, but her end is bitter as wormwood." Here oil symbolizes the tempting sweetness of present pleasures, and an a fortiori argument is implied: a good name is better even than good or permissible pleasures.

better the day of death   K reads the popular proverb differently, or (willfully) misreads it in accord with the exegetical tradition that stressed the aromatic qualities of oil: "your anointing *oils are fragrant, your name* is oil poured out" (Cant 1:3). From this perspective, oil does not symbolize present pleasures but rather fame after death.

better/better   Despite its similarity with P's quotation, K's retort would itself not qualify as a traditional or popular saying because it would not achieve a consensus. What K is quoting, by way of parody, is the *form* of the saying. Through his mimicry he is also challenging proverbs' presumption of authority, the right of literary structure to impose assent through its very form rather than its content.

day/day   The repetition of the word emphasizes the (false) identity and thus accentuates the paradox: all "days" are not alike; indeed, they are opposites, since one's final day is radically unlike any of the others.

his birth   This personal suffix has proved embarrassing to critics, who have deleted it or, like Gordis (1968), postulated an impersonal ("day of one's birth"). However, it refers more naturally to the (possessor of the) good name of the first hemistich. It thus has a dialogic function, making the rejoinder all the more caustic and pointed.

7:2   As typical of his way of wisdom reading, P explains that the importance of the day of death is not only literal but has a daily application for the living. This metaphorical extension will be called into question in v. 4.

man's end   This quibble anticipates Montaigne's famous distinction between death as the goal (*le but*) of life and as the simple termination or end (*le bout*) of life. K had advanced the first, implying that all of life derives its importance, or rather the absence thereof, only from the moment of physical death. P counters that it is life itself that is important, since the end will also terminate man's existence as a *human* being: since death "is the end of man as such."

every living person   The apparently superfluous adjective seems intended to exclude the dead, since "the dead do not praise the Lord" (Ps 115:17), thus continuing the debate over the status of the dead begun in 4:2. The emphasis here is that the idea of death is for the living.

had better remember   This begins the advice that will culminate in the more specific and touching "in the days of your youth remember your Creator" of 12:1. Similarly here, the emphasis is on reflection deepened by memory, and the apposite expression is not *sim leb 'el* (Gordis 1968), to "pay attention," but rather the deeper and more permanent mental and emotional attachment of placement *upon* (understanding *'al* for *'el,* as frequently) the heart (Deut 6:6), of knowing "*where* one's heart is," as v. 4 will put it.

Alternatively, the statement can be taken as a declarative, definitional of the sage: "every truly living person will remember this" (see below, the midrashic reading of 9:5).

7:3   *anger*   I.e., the sage's anger; cf. the next verse and 1:18.

Can an angry face . . .   Here *ki* signifies an interrogative "perhaps" and expresses surprise, introducing a dialogical rejoinder. It is thus the equivalent of our question mark. Rashi explains this usage in Exod 23:5, also on Deut 7:17.

7:4   *the sages*   Here begins a debate on the value of the sages. K dislikes their chastising and gloomy spirit; P retorts that fools are worse and thus the distinction is still valid.

can think only of   Literally, "the heart of the sages is in the house of mourning," that is to say, even when they cannot go there (7:2), "the house of mourning is always with them" (Ibn Ezra), perhaps because "in this way they set their minds upon the day of death and do not sin" (Rashbam, in Japhet and Salters 1985).

7:5   *a person*   This seems to refer to the individual being addressed, K, an important person (cf. 1:8n. *a person*).

song of fools   P seems to be alluding to K's acknowledgement in 2:8: "I got me singers . . ."

7:6   *this too is vanity*   The reference is unclear. To refer it, as does Ibn Ezra, to the laughter of fools is to have too easy a time of it. However, it may have a more general reference to the superiority of the sage and thus be of a piece with the continuing critique of the sage's special status, already introduced in 2:14 and continued in the next verse. Or, in the same spirit, it can refer to the sage's reproof in the previous verse. I take it as referring to what follows.

7:7   *derision   'osheq*   In the two previous verses the point was made against the social pressures of the fool: not only is it corrupting but

perhaps intentionally so. Thus, the fools' *seḥoq* is now read in its mali-
cious sense, not merely as laughter but as mockery, and it is now
glossed, in a distant but recognizable pun, as *'osheq,* the oppressive violence of fools who try to convert others through playful derision, what
is currently called social or peer pressure.

make a sage foolish   K goes deeper into the sense of the
traditional comparison that precedes: granted that the crackling of the
nettles is ineffectual, still the quick fire does warm the pot, perhaps
symbolizing the sage's quick anger.

him   Literally, "his heart," seen as the center of the self and
thus the focus of the sage's (and the fool's aggressive) concerns. Thus, in
wisdom texts the absence of heart, or its perversion or destruction, is
what best describes fools: below 10:3; Prov 10:13, 11:12, 15:21, 19:8.
Alternatively, citing Prov 2:6 ("for the Lord *gives* wisdom") Rashbam
(Japhet and Salters 1985) made the attractive suggestion that the reference
of *leb matanah* is to wisdom, which is a gift from God. The sense would be,
accordingly: foolish derision . . . destroys the understanding heart.

gifts can destroy   Against the background of our text's constant allusiveness to 1 Kgs as a subtext, P may have in mind the juxtaposition of feminine gifts with Solomon (e.g., 1 Kgs 10:2f.) and his turning
away from God and presumable loss of stature as a sage (chap. 11). Or P
may be exclaiming more indignantly against K's complaint against gifts
in general, which would of course include God's gift of wisdom (cf. 1
Kgs 10:24: "his wisdom, which God had given into his heart"; RSV:
"which God had put into his mind").

Alternatively, P may grant that external conditions can make a sage
appear foolish, but this does not actually destroy him.

7:8   Since no agreement can be reached on what constitutes a
sage, perhaps there can be a consensus on what is wise behavior. The
second better-than saying in this verse seems to offer an illustration or an
application of the first. Especially in view of this connection, the evalua-
tions offered here should be precisely grasped. It is not claimed that
beginnings (or haughty spirits) are necessarily bad but rather that they
are "less good" than a higher good.

haughty   Literally, "high" or "heighty" (*gbah*), i.e., chastising or overcritical, in reaction to the implied rebuke.

The question over the value of a "wide" spirit versus a "tall" spirit
seems a bit *précieux,* not that debate over qualities is an unknown occur-
rence in literary texts, but there may be a subtle dig here against the high
station or kingship of the interlocutor as well.

7:9   *do not be quick   'al tebahel beruḥeka*   The reply takes up the
same language of *ruaḥ* ("spirit") and personalizes the broad generaliza-

tions that precede: Though you argue some value in beginnings such as a haughty spirit, "don't be hasty in your own spirit!"

put on an angry face   P has just argued (v. 3) the value of a sage's anger, and Maimonides was to make a distinction between the mere semblance of anger in order to correct another's behavior and actually feeling anger, which is not permissible. K may be suggesting that such a distinction is purely academic and that even wise play-acting may corrupt the sage. Certainly, even Solomon's enormous wisdom was not sufficient to protect him from the world's dangers, which corrupted him even when tried experimentally and on behalf of wisdom.

anger in the bosom of fools abides   The inversion suggests the quotation of a proverb, on the model of its complement: "In the mind of a man of understanding abides wisdom" (Prov 14:33).

7:10   *don't say*   This is a clever tactic of a good debater, to antici-pate the opponent's argument and refute it before it can be stated. Logi-cally, K's projected rejection of the proposition "the end is better than the beginning" can imply one of two possibilities: either that both are the same (thus reverting to the sameness argument of chapter 1) or that the end is worse and thus the beginning is better. This theory of natural decline is the usual conclusion that K's experience leads him to embrace.

such questions   The importance of this statement cannot be exaggerated as definitional of wisdom's enterprise. According to this, wisdom is the right way to ask questions, or, perhaps, ask the right kind of questions. Here it concerns the evaluation of later things and hence both of finality and of life's direction (cf. Introduction 3a).

7:11   Just as K's notion of sages is pessimistic, his idea of wisdom is of the practical sort, and this in two senses. First of all, wisdom can be a help in the acquisition of money; second—and more cynically—wisdom cannot even be enjoyed without money. Rashbam (Japhet and Salters 1985), however, reverses this causality and stresses the inherited nature of this wealth (literally, "inheritance") as opposed to its pursuit. When money comes into one's hands as through an inheritance, wisdom is needed in its preservation.

wealth   naḥalah   Literally, "inheritance." In Solomon's ca-reer as portrayed in such texts as 1 Kgs 10:23, wealth is viewed as totally compatible with wisdom. Here that compatibility is put into a skeptical perspective. To P's argument in favor of the wisdom that comes with age, K observes that the best hope we have from aging is that it increases the chances of inheritance.

those who would enjoy life   Literally, "those who see the sun." "To see" often means "to enjoy" in our text; cf. 2:1n., 6:5, 9:9.

7:12   *protection   tsel*   "Shadow," thus stressing the sharpness of
the retort by the metaphor of contrast with the preceding "sun" (see
preceding n.).

        experience/wisdom   Due to their frequent association (cf.
1:17n.), it seems natural to use these two terms synonymously, especially since for K wisdom is only the sum total of one's experience.
However, P continues the distinction between the two (cf. 1:17–18) and
insists that the present discussion concerns only wisdom. The change of
voice between these two terms is supported by their separation in the
trope of MT, and the dialogic addition "let's conclude this by agreeing"
helps plot the progress of the arguments.

XII   (7:13–29)   More on God's Purposes and Justice

13 *Enjoy God's works . . .*

Yet who can make straight what He has made crooked?

14 *When your fortune is good, enjoy it.*

And, when it is bad, "enjoy"?
God has placed one against the other so that man might not find out anything of His motives.

15 **I have seen everything during the days of my vanity: the righteous destroyed for all his righteousness and the wicked living a long life for all his wickedness.**

16 **Therefore,**
"don't be too righteous
and don't play too much the wise man."
Why should you be destroyed?

17 *Conversely,*
don't be too wicked or a fool!
Why should you die before your time?

18 *It is far better to hold on to this righteousness and not give up on this wisdom. He who fears God will escape from all*

19 *dangers. Wisdom will give more strength to the sage than ten rulers in the city.*

20 **Yet they say that there is no righteous man on earth who does only good and is without sin.**

21 *Yet do not overscrutinize every word that people say, lest, for example, you hear your servant disparaging you (for you*

22 *know in your heart that on many occasions you have disparaged others).*

23 **All of these things I tested for the sake of wisdom. I said: "I shall grow wise, even though it is far from me."**

24 **What has always been is far and deep indeed.**
And what is deep who can find!

25 **(I and my heart turned repetitively to know and explore and seek wisdom and strategies, and to know the wickedness of folly.**
But foolishness is insane!)

26 **For example, I personally find woman more bitter than death, for her heart is full of traps and snares and her hands are chains.**
He who is good in God's eyes will escape from her, but the wicked will be entrapped.

27 *Said Kohelet:*
Look, I have found this, as I set out step by step
28 **to discover a strategy, and anything beyond this I did not find: I found one good man in a thousand, but not even one good woman in the same number.**
29 *Except that I have found this, and note it well: At the outset God made all human beings righteous.*
But they have invented many stratagems.

Commentary

7:13f   The debate continues on the value of wisdom and on how experience diminishes its claims. The real subject of debate comes to center stage here: the value of God's works or creation.

enjoy   re'eh "See, consider," which is the sense understood by K when he later returns to this point in 8:17; cf. also 9:9 and references there. Zer-Kabod (1973) quotes Kimhi's "accept lovingly." This brings us close to P's religious perspective, according to which the world is to be enjoyed *because* it is given by God.

what He has made crooked   The thought is close to Job's reply to Bildad's "Does God pervert (*ye'awet*) justice?" (Job 8:3); "God has put me in the wrong (*'iwtani*)" (19:6). The remark can also be imagined as coming from P's more pious perspective; in which case, cf. Ps 146:9: "But the way of the wicked He makes crooked" (RSV: "brings to ruin"). There is also the suggestion, exploited in 12:9, that what *God* has made crooked cannot be made straight, but what man has made crooked can.

7:14   The thought is less God's power than His freedom, guaranteed by the unpredictable nature of His acts.

when your fortune is good   Literally, "in a good day." In Hebrew Scripture "day" (*yom*) is frequently the time-indicator used for periods of prosperity or adversity.

enjoy it!   Brooding on bad fortune prevents the enjoyment of good fortune.

enjoy   re'eh   K ironically mimics this use in the previous verse.

placed ʿasah Not "made" (RSV) but "set" (Gordis 1968), as in Gen 1:7: "And God set the firmament" (according to Rashi's interpretation).

one against the other I.e., evil against good, since God creates both: "I make weal (literally, "peace") and create woe (literally, 'evil,' " Isa 45:7).

so that ʿal dibrat sh- As in the Aramaic ʿal dibrat di in Dan 2:30; 4:14; see also my last n. to the present verse.

find out Literally, "find," in the sense of "understand, know, discover" (see 3:11; 8:17)

His motives Crenshaw (1987) pertinently remarks that "the bewildering array of good and evil hardly prevents human beings from finding fault with the creator" (139). The point may be, however, that since humans are prevented from finding God's true motives, they are thereby disabled, out of ignorance, from ascribing any fault whatever (human curiosity over God's purposes is of such importance that it closes the work; cf. 12:14). Crenshaw's point is expressed more fully in the following observation, based on the point of view that lack of final truths does not infirm the truths of personal experience.

Alternatively, ʿal dibrat sh- may be rendered as follows: "As they say: 'man will not achieve anything after himself.' " When he's dead, he's dead! Here ʿal dibrat retains its meaning (3:18, 8:2) of "concerning," but serves the more literary function of introducing a quotation, as it can also be so construed in these other two passages, especially in 8:2. In this reading 'aḥaraw refers not to God but to man himself (also Gordis 1968). Such a reply would perhaps be more appropriate to K and would form a transition to the theme of death that follows. Also, yimtsaʾ would then have the meaning of "achieve" (cf. Prov 16:31).

7:15 K returns to the subject of 3:16, again expressed as a conclusion based on personal experience and observation and thus in deliberate contradiction to official wisdom. Here K calls into question such doctrines as expressed in Prov 16:31, which promised long life for righteous living: "Grey hair is a crown of glory; it is found in a righteous life." Dialogically, K is ironic about P's claim that God has placed "one against the other" since, by treating the good as the wicked and vice versa, "He has made good and evil correspond to each other" (Barton).

everything According to Zer-Kabod (1973) this refers to the two cases previously cited, and he adduces also 2:14 and 3:19 as further examples of how "all" in Kohelet is often the minimum plural, referring only to *two* things. One must add, however, that in such cases these two things are opposites (complementary or opposing binaries) and are therefore intended to exclude all competing possibilities. In the present context the totalizing "everything" thus excludes precisely those elements uncongenial to K's argument: cases in which the righteous are rewarded and the wicked punished. Such cases are not important for K, however, as even a single contradiction signals a lack of perfection in the original creation. Recall, too, that for K "all" or "*everything*" is decidedly negative, a catch-all phrase expressive of his despondency and pessimism.

7:16–17   The formulaic nature of these verses suggests not only "wisdom sayings" but also, given their antithetical character, contradictory proverbs (cf. Introduction 2a).

7:16   *too righteous   harbeh*   As often, indicates what goes beyond the appropriate mean; cf. 5:6, 19.
          don't play . . . the wise man   'al tithakam   The *hitpa'el* here has the meaning of "pretend," as in 1 Sam 21:14, *veyithalel,* "he played the madman"; also Prov 13:7: "One man pretends to be rich *(mit'asher)*, yet has nothing; another pretends *(mitroshesh)* to be poor, yet has great wealth"; see Menachem ha-Meiri on Prov 10:2. Such a meaning is perfectly expressive of K's view, for, while cynically admitting above (7:12) that wisdom can increase earnings and therefore longevity, he again suggests that the sages are pretentious (cf. 7:4ff. and nn.).
          be destroyed   In the case of the sage's pretense or hypocrisy, this may refer to destruction by other humans. If the reference is primarily to righteousness, K may be thinking of such views as that of the Rabbis, according to which humans are judged according to their level: "the Holy One is strict with the righteous even to a hair's breadth" (BT Baba Kamma 20b–21a and Rashi on Num 20:13). In the latter case, K is commenting sarcastically on P's warning in 5:5 concerning God's destructiveness because of imprudent speech: If you are worried about that, then there are dangers greater than words!

7:17   The repetition of formulaic structure with contradictory meaning is deeply ironic. Thus, one shouldn't be "too" wicked because one shouldn't be wicked at all! For P there is no middle ground, at least for the sage, since any diminution in wisdom and righteousness signifies a proportionate increase in their opposite, and such conscious withdrawal renders one liable. For the thought, cf. Deut 30:15f and Prov 10:27.

7:18   *this righteousness/this wisdom*   These are interpretative, and the text simply indicates "this" and "this."
          all dangers   Literally, "all," i.e., "both" (cf. 7:15n), referring to self-destruction and premature death, but perhaps rather to the foolishness and wickedness mentioned in the previous verse.

7:19   The strength that flows from wisdom and, in the previous verse, from fear of God (for P, fear and wisdom are synonymous) is expressed in such texts as Ps 147:10–11: "He delights not in the strength of the horse, nor does He take pleasure in the legs of a man. The Lord takes pleasure in those who fear him. . . ." The thought recurs below in 9:15 and in Prov 21:22: "A wise man scales the city of the mighty . . ."

7:20   *they say that*   The formulaic ring of this saying gives it the sound of a traditional view; for example, cf. 1 Kgs 8:46: "for there is no man who does not sin," reinforced perhaps by Gen 8:21. K quotes Solomon (!) perhaps apologetically but also to assert that, since *no* person is guiltless, the sage's strength is purely hypothetical.

7:21   Words (e.g., *debarim,* wisdom sayings) need room for interpretation, just as servants need space to do their own work. Too close scrutiny spoils the one and corrupts the other. In context, P is objecting to the leveling inference that, since everyone sins, therefore everyone is the same and no meaningful distinctions can be made among human beings.
    yet   gam   Used adversatively to change speaker; cf. above 2:14 and Gordis (1968, 222); note also that the dialogic rejoinder is strengthened by the personal address: you, your.
    lest   'asher lo'   See Gordis (1968). Alternatively, *'asher* can be taken as "for example, seeing that" (see Gordis 1968 on 8:11), almost the equivalent of our colon.
    your servant   Rather than indirect proof that the sages belonged to the slave-owning class (Crenshaw 1987), this expression has a contextual reference: either to the king (again the royal fiction) or, dialogically, to the speaker himself ("your humble servant").
    disparaging   qalal   Is better understood here and in the following verse as "revile" (Gordis 1968) or "disparage" (Zer-Kabod 1973) rather than "curse" (RSV); Zer-Kabod cites 1 Sam 2:30: "those who honor me I will honor, and those who despise me shall be lightly esteemed (*yeqallu*)."

7:22   *in your heart*   P taunts K that experiential knowledge includes self-knowledge and that the behavior of others is often similar to one's own.

7:23   *all*   K returns to his favorite term of inclusive complaint, the one that allows him to generalize his limited experience.
    tested   nisiti   As in 2:1.
    for the sake of wisdom   ba-ḥokmah   As in 1:13 the preposition *b-* indicates not agency but rather purpose. This gives better motivation

to his decision to be wise, since wisdom is his pursuit as well as his method.

       I said   Not necessarily to myself; perhaps "I boasted to others."

7:24   *what has always been*   The focus is not on the present (RSV: "that which is"), which is all that is available for enjoyment, nor on the past for its own sake, but rather on the past as constitutive of this and every present; K claims to have sought eternally valid patterns of behavior, whether of the universe (cf. 1:4–10) or of humans (1:11). The word "always" is added to make this clear.

       far and deep   In K's usage these seem to be synonymous, a repetition that emphasizes his lamentative tone.

       what is deep   This may refer to God's deep and therefore inscrutable thoughts (Ps 92:6) or, more likely here, to the wisdom tradition of viewing a person's speech as deep (Prov 18:4). The repetition signals a change of voice and perhaps also an ironic allusion to this more traditional association of the term, which in this case allows P to cut short the complaints by departing from generalities and returning to the topic at hand.

       who can find   In Prov 31:10 the subject of the "worthy woman" is introduced as follows: "A good wife who can find (*mi yimtsa*)? She is far more precious (*raḥoq*) than jewels." The repetition of these key words leads into a discussion of the possibility of finding a good woman in v. 26. The allusion is strengthened by the fact that in the Prov text the question is purely rhetorical. Indeed, in 31:29 it is stated that "*many* women have done excellently," and traditional Jewish practice encourages the husband's recitation of the entire passage (Prov 31:10–31) on the Sabbath in the presence of his wife. This intertextual situation may explain why P repeats only "deep" but not "far," since the opposite is asserted in Prov 31:10f (i.e., she is far above jewels but not far away). Significantly (cf. 7:28n. *a thousand*), this rhetoric of impossibility is elsewhere applied to wisdom itself (cf. below, 8:17): "where shall wisdom be found?" (Job 28:12), in spite of implications to the contrary such as "Happy is the man who finds wisdom" (Prov 3:13). In short, P is asserting the possibility of finding "what is deep," or at least the necessity of looking.

7:25   This parenthetical verse allows K to return to the language of personal search and to stress the experimental and experiential nature of his approach. The heaping up of terms that have now become synonymous strikes one as purely rhetorical and somewhat humorous, but by now it is apparent that K occasionally allows his language and rhetorical skills, which are considerable, to do his thinking.

I and my heart   One should resist the emendation *be-libi*, "in my heart," since this removes the important literary and Toranic distinction between the heart and the self (see 2:1n.). This *précieux* phrase thus emphasizes that wisdom is itself a mutual or dialogic adventure *with* his heart.

    turned repetitively   saboti   Cf. 2:20n.

    explore   Cf. 1:13n. Here too the verb is attached to a negative conclusion.

    strategies   ḥeshbon   The usual understanding of this important term (RSV: "the sum of things," based apparently on the later Hebrew *ḥeshbon*) is tempting, as K's ambition is to arrive at wisdom by totaling up his experiences. It is thus in accord with his experiment of "adding to" his possessions, as it is with its immediate context here, coming as a conclusion to three almost synonymous verbs ("know and explore and seek"), thus "arriving at a conclusion" (Gordis 1968). This would also be appropriate to 7:27, with its association with counting ("step by step").

However, another possibility is suggested in the other three uses of the term in Hebrew Scripture: 9:10 below, and the alternative form *ḥishbonot* (see Gordis 1968) in 7:29 below and 2 Chr 26:15: "He made engines (*ḥishbonot*), invented by skillful men," which Rashi glosses by quoting Prov 24:6: "By wise guidance (*taḥbulot*) you can wage your war." See further Prov 20:18: "Plans (*maḥshabot*) are established by counsel; by wise guidance (*taḥbulot*) wage war." The semantic picture can be completed by Prov 24:18: "He who plans (*meḥasheb*) to do evil will be called a mischief-maker (*baʿal mezimot*)." The chain of synonymy exists, then, whereby the root *ḥshb* is related with *taḥbulot* and *mezimot*, and these can be referred to the programmatic prologue to Proverbs (1:4–5): "To give cleverness to the credulous, experience and shrewdness (*mezimah*) to the inexperienced . . . , that the man of understanding may acquire planning skill (*taḥbulot*)." Such knowledge is practical in that it is goal-oriented, but its more important wisdom function is that it helps plan the future and avoid danger by knowing what to expect. Thus, fools will come to naught because they do not know (Prov 1:17), either because they have no experience of evil or because they do not believe their wiser teachers.

    foolishness   Cf. 10:13 and nn. This is P's final and strongest judgment of that aspect of K's experiment with excess.

7:26   *For example*   These words are added. The discussion of women is actually hinted in the allusions to Prov in vv. 23–24 (cf. 7:24n. *who can find*). It is even possible that K's announced desire to grow wise in 7:23 is now reread in this sense: "I shall grow wise, even though it . . . ," literally "she" (*hi'*), a feminine gender possibly referring to the common feminization of Wisdom in such texts as Prov 1–9.

    personally   This is added in translation, since by this point K's opinion seems less a matter of intellectual discovery than of personal taste, humorously projected by the emphatic pronoun and the overly dramatic comparison "more bitter than death."

    woman   From the identical vocabulary with chapter 2, K seems to be referring to the emptiness of pleasure, and he takes woman as an example. This seems a better explanation than any antifeminism of the text. So, too, the wiles of the "foreign woman" as described in Prov 1–9 are balanced by the virtues of Dame Wisdom, showing that both are but figures of speech.

7:27   *said Kohelet*   *'amrah Kohelet*   This unique feminine use of the verb form (contrast the masculine form in 1:2, 12:8, 12:10) may have a contextual solution. This pessimistic passage, presented as based on personal experience rather than "the nature of things," is even less favorable toward women than toward men (one in a thousand as opposed to not even one in a thousand). By compensation or identification, Kohelet feminizes his name, as if to say: I am not more reliable than women are. This essayistic posture of self-diminution and self-defense was well known to Montaigne, who consistently identified himself with women and commoners (e.g., *Essais* 1:1). For further comment on a possibly female persona, see 1:1n. *Kohelet.*★

7:28   *I found*   I.e., I had the good fortune to find. On the rhetoric of finding, see 7:24nn.

    a thousand   This seems an allusion to Solomon's harem of that number (1 Kgs 11:3). Here, however, the adventure is ascribed as much to the experiment on behalf of wisdom as to the wiles of women ("his wives turned away his heart after other gods," 1 Kgs 11:4). See also 9:9n.

7:29   *I have found this, and note it well*   The repetition of *re'eh zeh matsati* signals an emphatic contradiction.

    God made . . .   This is at the heart of the discussion, for P continues to assert the goodness of creation, a point that K will only question indirectly.

    stratagems   *hishbonot*   A synonymous variant of *heshbon* (v. 7:25). The word here is perhaps an ironic calque, intended to debunk the nobler wisdom-uses of the semantic nexus studied in 7:25n.: *mezimah, tahbulot, mahshabah*. The point is that if humans have been able to disfigure the goodness of God's creation, this change may be no more visible than the distinction between the prudent planning of *ḥeshbon* and the trickery of *ḥishbon*.

    many stratagems   This seems to echo Ps 19:21: "Many are the plans (*rabot maḥshabot*) in the mind of a man." Here the root *rab* may imply a departure from the mean, thus "*too* many," as often (cf. 1:18n.).

XIII   (8:1–7)   Reacting to Absolute Power:
                     Obedience or Wisdom

8:1   *Who is like the sage?*
      But who can know the interpretation of a thing?

      A person's wisdom lights up his face.
      But is the arrogance of his face also changed?
2   **As for me: keep the king's commands!**

      But only because of his oath of loyalty to God.
3   *As they say,*
            "don't hasten to leave the King's presence."
      As they also say,
            "don't remain before him during a bad
      affair," for he can do whatever he wishes.

4   *Inasmuch as a King's word is Law,*
            "who will say to Him 'what doest Thou?' "
5   **He who obeys commands will know no evil.**

      Yet the sage's heart judges the proper time of things.
6   **If all things have their proper time of judgment,**
      this is because of the enormous evil that is upon
7   **man. For man does not know what will be, for**
      who can tell him how things will be?

Commentary

8:1   P returns to the excellence of true wisdom, perhaps in reply
to the leveling criticism of the previous remark (*all* men seek mischief).
From this point of view, the sage represents the goal of humanity, perhaps because the sage best preserves the original rectitude of human
beings.
          who can know?   I.e., can even the sage solve the real prob-
lems? The question is rhetorical.
          lights up his face   P claims that wisdom is visible; one has
only to look upon the sage's face, presumably its gentleness. In Scripture
the light of the face is usually that of God (in Prov 16:15, however, it
refers to the king), and in fact P always has in mind the sage's godly
qualities. Here the sage's gracious countenance may be seen as emble-
matic of God's tolerance of humanity.
          arrogance of his face   K sees other signs in the faces of those

who are known in the world as sages. K's two replies, focusing both on the question *mi yodeʿa?* and the *ʿoz panaw,* seem to recall Ps 90:11: "Who can know the power of thy anger" (*mi yodeʿa ʿoz ʾapeka*). If so, it is a veiled allusion to God. Or, this may allude to P's praise of the sage's strength in 7:19.

8:2   *as for me, keep*   ʾani . . . *shmor*   The combined emphatic pronoun and the imperative both stress the dialogic and combative nature of the text. K will have nothing to do with such sages and opts to rest his hopes on obedience to authority. As often, the attribution of our text to the "king in Jerusalem" encourages reflection on royal power.

    only because   ʿal dibrat   Perhaps "concerning what people say" and introducing a quotation (see 7:14, final n.). There seems to be a debate here on the sources of power, whether it originates with the king (K), or whether it derives from God, as P argues.

    oath of loyalty   This sacred oath refers neither to God's oath regarding kingship nor to an oath of loyalty to the king. The reference, rather, is to the king's oath to God such as the one made when Jehoʾash was consecrated: "And Jehoiʾada made a covenant between the Lord and the king" (2 Kgs 11:17).

8:3   The formulaic style of these two sayings suggests quotation of well-known proverbs, and in fact this seems to be another instance of proverb-debate, of squaring-off by countering one authority with another.

    don't hasten   I.e., stay before Him at all times, as recommended by King David: "I keep the Lord always before me" (Ps 16:8). Here P continues the play on the obvious double-meaning of king (political and divine). By suggesting that royal power ultimately derives from God, he thus implies that one should not attempt to escape the scrutiny of Judgment.

    don't remain before him . . .   K's observations on the nature of royal power are also, in this dialogic context, exquisite examples of the language of indirection: "Watch what you say, or get out while the getting is good!"

8:4   *what doest thou*   This is a direct quote of Job 9:12: "who will say to Him 'what doest Thou?' " By this well-known citation P continues to allude to God while speaking of and to the king.

8:5   *commands mitswah*   Singular for plural, as in Ps 19:9, parallel with the plural *pequdei.* In Scripture *mitswah* can refer to commands of both a king (2 Kgs 18:36) and God (Jos 22:3) and thus lends itself to the ambivalence of this passage.

the sage's heart   leb ḥakam   This refers to the heart or mind of the sage, but in the background K is reminded of Solomon's request to have a wise heart (1 Kgs 3:12).

judges the proper time of things   "Knows the time and measure" (*mishpat;* cf. 1 Kgs 5:8) and therefore judges what is appropriate and fitting. The suggestion, with respect to earthly kings, is that the sage responds less to commands than to what is appropriate. The quality being emphasized here is thus not obedience or even caution but rather discernment.

8:6   *time of judgment*   K puns on *mishpat,* which of course usually means "judgment." This passage seems to review the arguments of 3:17–18 above. This phrase is often taken as a hendiadys: *ʿet u-mishpat,* "proper time and judgment," that is to say, the proper time for judgment to occur. The phrase thus anticipates 9:11: *ʿet wa-pegaʿ,* "time and accident."

enormous evil   This stich may be attached to what precedes or to what follows. In the first and more likely instance and continuing the parallel with 3:17–18, K returns to the theme of man's wickedness, the evil that man does (cf. 7:29 and n., both passages emphasizing the *rab* or great extent of the evil); it thus prefigures divine judgment, as in Gen 6:5: "the wickedness of man was *great* in the earth." Alternatively, this stich describes what follows: not the evil that he does but rather the one which he has from other sources and which can visit him at unknown times.

8:7   *what will be/who can tell?*   Here K returns to his basic skepticism, cf. 6:12. The question "who can . . . ?" is a typical formula of skeptical wisdom writing, cf. Sirach "who can count?" (1:2); "who can inquire?" (1:3); "who can know?" (1:6). In this verse it is synonymous with "no man knows" (cf. 10:14 below).

XIV   (8:8–9:3)   On Wickedness and Retribution

8   **"Man has no power over the wind!"**
         . . . to hold the "wind" back, since
         "There is no dominion on the day of death."
But
         **There is no escape even from the dangers of
war.**
But
         Wickedness cannot save its perpetrators.

9   **All this I have seen and considered all things done
     under the sun: whenever man rules over another**
10   **man to the latter's hurt. Indeed, I have seen the
     wicked buried and come to their rest even as they
     were coming from a holy place . . .**
     *They were promptly forgotten in the very city where they
     acted in this way.*

11   **This too is vanity: It is because judgment is not
     quickly brought against evil that the hearts of
     human beings are full of wrongdoing.**
12   **For a sinner does a hundred wrongs, and yet his
     life is prolonged.**
     Yet I also know that it will be good to the God-fearing who
13   *constantly fear Him, but that good will not come to the
     wicked nor, like a shadow, will he live long because he does
     not fear God.*

14   **Yet here is a vanity perpetrated upon the earth,
     when the righteous are rewarded as the wicked
     and the wicked are rewarded as the righteous. I
     say that this too is vanity.**
15   *As for me I recommend contentedness, for there is nothing
     better for man under the sun than to eat and drink and be
     content, and this contentedness should accompany his labor all
     the days of his life that God has given him under the sun.*

16   **When I set my whole mind to experience wisdom
     and to really see what was happening upon the
     earth . . .**
     *Surely, either by day or by night one does not see sleep with
     one's own eyes!*

17 **I considered all of God's works . . .**
    But a mere human being cannot discover the things that are
    done under the sun. No matter how much one tries, one will
    not find out . . .
    And even if the sage says that he knows, he will be
    unable to find out.

9:1 *I have set my mind to this entire matter and I have decided*
     that the righteous and the wise and their deeds are in the hand
     of God.
     But man does not know whether it is in love or
2   **hatred. It is all preordained: The All never**
     changes. A common lot befalls the righteous and
     the wicked, the goodly pure and the impure, the
     one who sacrifices and the one who does not sacri-
     fice. The good person is like the sinner, and one
     who swears is like one who fears to make an oath.
3   **This is the worst of all the evils that happen under**
     the sun: that one fate awaits all, and this is why
     men's minds are full of evil and their hearts full of
     vanity throughout their lives, for after they
     die . . .

Commentary

8:8   This verse is composed of four statements of similar rhythm
and structure: *'ein . . . , we-'ein,* "there is no . . . ," with a slight varia-
tion on the last member (*we-lo'*) to indicate closure. Whybray (1989) has
noted the structural similarity with wisdom numerical formulas, but it
seems more likely that this is but another example of a debate in proverbs similar to the one in 9:11 (cf. n.). In their generality these four
assertions are difficult to assign to a particular point of view, and my
attempts to do so, though tentative, try to account for verbal ambiguities and dialogic reactions. In these clipped exchanges, K focuses on the
limitations of human power in the outside world, whereas P always
directs attention to the underlying factors, here God's control over death
and justice.
          man has no power over the wind   K's point here seems to be
that man's misery is less that he lacks knowledge than that he lacks
power. His additional point may be that man has no power over the
wind but God has (cf. Jer 10:13; Ps 135:7), and He should therefore be
held responsible for the state of the world's affairs.
          to hold the "wind" back   From the same speaker one would

expect a pronoun rather than a repetition of "wind." However, here the second usage interprets the term differently, in the sense of life-spirit (cf. 3:19, 21).

    escape   mishlaḥat   Perhaps "weapon" (Ibn Ezra) or adequate protection against war. The meaning is unsure and is derived contextually.

    even from the dangers of war   Literally, "there is no weapon in war." Dialogically, K goes one better by pointing out that death is not the only danger.

    wickedness cannot save . . .   Despite the war-zone view of human existence just expressed, P insists that humans still do not live in a jungle and that one remains accountable for one's actions.

8:9   From the preceding remark, one might conclude that the wicked are powerless. Not so, observes K; although they cannot save themselves, they surely can work harm upon others. K is overwhelmed by the power in the hands of the wicked, even to the extent that "one fool can destroy much good" (9:18). He goes on to argue that wickedness derives its strength from the failures of human and especially divine justice. Note, however, that K (the king) does not argue that power is intrinsically evil.

    whenever   ʿet   The "appropriate" time. In the previous section P had argued that justice will have its appointed time. Here this argument is ironically treated by noting that what seems appointed is not justice but rather the occasions for man's ruling over his fellow. The continuity and irony is conveyed also through repetition of the verb *shalat* from *shilton* (8:4, 8:8).

8:10   *buried*   Perhaps "even with a proper burial" (cf. 6:3), to emphasize the irony that the wicked do not suffer injustice even after death; indeed, that even those that they may have injured give them a dignified burial.

    come to their rest   wa-baʾu   This verse returns to the semantics of *halak* and *baʾ*, "to go forth" and "to come to rest"; see 1:4n and Introduction 2a, 3a.

    even as   "And yet." This is the *waw* expressing the circumstances or concomitant conditions (BDB, 253, sec. 1k).

    coming from a holy place   Even if you argue that the townspeople were deceived by such hypocritical behavior, can such an argument be applied to God?

    They were promptly forgotten   Don't make too much of the fame of the wicked after death!

    where they acted in this way   ʾasher ken ʿasu   Where the wicked acted as mentioned in the previous statement.

this too is vanity   I.e., that they were allowed (by God) to do
evil with impunity in the first place.

8:11f   K now launches into a familiar question: "where is justice,"
and especially "where is the God of justice?" His complaint seems to be
Jonah's (4:2), that God is *too* merciful and long-suffering.

8:12   *hundred*   I.e., a large number, cf. 6:3.
            his life is prolonged   *u-ma'arik lo*   Perhaps "(God) prolongs
(His anger) for him," thus "God is patient with him," with the common
suppression of God as grammatical subject in wisdom texts (cf. 2:21n.
He will give). However, it is more likely that the subject is the wicked
person and that the omitted object is *yamim,* "days," as in 7:15 above and
immediately in 8:13. The dual reference of this traditional expression is
important, however, since it allows P to apply it *a lo divino.*
            Yet   *ki*   Used to indicate change of speaker, as often.
            good   I.e., in the long run and despite the evidence of experi-
ence. Cf. 11:1 and also Perry (1993a, III.3.d and Conclusions).
            the God-fearing   From other contexts in wisdom literature
(e.g., Sirach 8:7–9), the *yir'ei h'* or fearers of God seem to constitute a
distinct category of religious observance. Such seems to be the situation also in this passage, in which case the apparent tautology (literally,
"the fearers of God who fear Him") is really definitional: the "god-
fearing" are those who are constantly in fear of Him. Note the plural
and its contrast with the wicked in the singular, perhaps to stress that
the latter are only incidental cases as against a universal fear of God
among humans.
            who constantly fear Him   *'asher yir'u milpanaw*   The prefix
mi- is due to the verb (cf. 12:5 below); the additional prefix *lipnei* means
"before, in the presence of" and acquired honorific status. The expression thus means "to fear God's presence," which could refer to the
Temple (and later the Synagogue) but also to the entire universe. V. 5:1
above could refer to either dwelling, either to God's house (4:17) or to
the heavens, as the rest of the verse implies. In the latter case, God's
presence is everywhere and constant.

8:13   *good*   Perhaps this is defined by the synonymous second
clause: he will not live long. This would then recall 7:17: "Don't be too
wicked or a fool! Why should you die before your time?"
            like a shadow   The comparison is surely not of a positive
thing ("a lengthening shadow as the sun goes down," Crenshaw 1987)
denied to the wicked and thus cannot be rendered "the wicked . . . will
not prolong their days like a shadow." Rather, in Scripture the image is
negative (cf. 6:12); it refers to what quickly passes and leaves no trace

(Ps 102:12; Job 8:9; and especially Ps 144:4): "Man is like a breath, his days are like a passing shadow."

  because   It has become customary to place a comma before this word in English translations, thus advancing the argument that the wicked will not live long *because* they do not fear God. However, this departs from the more general hope in an unspecified good and evil that awaits the righteous and wicked in the long run. It seems, rather, that here P wishes to avoid the extreme implications of K's previous remark, namely that the wicked live long lives precisely because of their wickedness.

8:14   *upon the earth*   I.e., in this life. K thinks that reward and punishment should not be deferred to other worlds and times, perhaps because we only live in the present. This thought leads directly to the imperative to enjoy.

8:15   *As for me*   Note the inversion of subject and verb, or perhaps the pleonastic repetition of the pronoun subject (cf. 4:4n) to indicate change of speaker.

  contentedness   ha-simḥah   Cf. 2:26.

  under the sun   The repetition of the stereotypical formula is polemical and ironic (it is twice repeated), indicating that there is indeed something that escapes vanity.

  eat and drink and be content   Not "and be merry," which is K's position, whereas P always attaches sensual enjoyment to the thought that it is a gift of God, as he is careful to state at the end of this verse. For the idea, see also 9:7 below. The order of thought is that of Deut 8:10: "And you shall eat and be full, and you shall bless the Lord your God for the good land *he has given you*." P argues that this positive and active acceptance from God is the true reward, and it occurs in the present.

  Alternatively, the three concepts occur together in 1 Kgs 4:20, where the context is one of security from harm.

  should accompany his labor   What a human being contributes is his or her labor, and though one never knows whether one's labor is effective, for that very reason one must make an effort, if only to avoid the charge of laziness. In other words, one is not encouraged to depend entirely on God's gifts.

  all the days of his life   Literally, "the days of one's life." One recalls Ben Zoma's distinction in the Passover Haggadah between this expression and the addition of *kol* ("all"; cf. Gen 3:14), which according to this interpretation includes nighttime. If this is the case, then the present verse is precisely stated, since labor would occur only during the days but not at night.

8:16   *to experience . . . and to really see*   K's repetitious focus on his methodology is a bit tedious by this point, and this leads to the sarcastic observation that is soon injected.

(not) by day or by night   That is to say, never. For this use of opposites to express totality, see also 2:23 above. The sense seems to be that of continuous effort and anxiety, as expressed above in 2:23.

one does not see sleep with one's own eyes   The change of speaker is signaled not only by *ki* but also by the switch from the first- to the third-person subject. The expression idiomatically means "one never sleeps," as in later Rabbinic literature (cf. BT Megillah 13b; Sukkah 53a), but P seems to be insisting on the literal meaning: of course one cannot "see" sleep since the eyes are closed, and that's the point of the sarcastic comparison. How can one claim to see or understand something when one is within it and thus lacks any perspective whatever! P here reacts to more talk about the world's vanity by the comparison with sleep, which is also fleeting and without substance: "Thou dost sweep men away, they are like sleep (RSV: "a dream")" (Ps 90:5). In the same way, some things may be naturally beyond the mind's perception.

8:17   *God's works*   K compulsively returns to his favorite topic, not only all that "happens" but especially God's responsibility in all this. Here, however, he is also addressing (in a different sense, to be sure) P's admonition to "enjoy God's works" (7:13), which he now understands as "consider."

all of . . .   Note again K's characteristic argument of totality. However, it is possible that the sense is not that of a totality but rather of a listing of single instances: "I considered each one of God's works." His argument would then be that his conclusions can be derived from any one of the cases cited, as well as, of course, from the totality of such cases. This sense of "all" (*kol*) is seen in such texts as Job 1:11: "But put forth thy hand now, and touch even a single thing that he has" (RSV: all that he has); "touch nothing (*kol*) of theirs" (Num 16:26).

But a mere human being   ki ha-'adam   The change of speakers is again marked by *ki,* which is surely not causative here. P wishes to stress the distance between God and humans; in his response K will insist on a similar distinction, or lack thereof, among humans and particularly between humans and sages.

the things that are done under the sun   P is willing to use the concept "under the sun" for the sake of argument, but keep God out of the issue!

unable to find out   On the impossibility of finding wisdom in K's view, see 7:24 and nn.

9:1   *and I have decided   we-la-bur*   See 3:18n. *I have observed that.*

and their deeds   The sages and the righteous thus do have leeway for their own independent actions.

love or hatred   This seems an echo of 3:8 above: "a time to love and a time to hate," with the order again expressing the pessimism typical of K.

it is all preordained   Literally, "all is before them," in the sense that there is a preordained time for everything. Alternatively, this can refer to the righteous, meaning that they are subject to all the misfortunes that happen to everyone (Rashbam).

9:2   *the All never changes*   Literally, "the all (happens) alike to the all." Ibn Ezra takes this to mean that chance will happen to all men as it happens to all events in nature. Gordis's (1968) citation of the divine self-revelation in Exod 3:14 ("I am whatever I am") is not only a vague grammatical and rhythmic parallel but, through these resemblances, suggests that K's formulation is intended as descriptive of the very constitution or structure of Being.

the goodly pure and the impure   Literally, "the good and the pure and the impure." Since the opposite of good is absent, apparently because the ethical category is covered in the previous pair "just and wicked," this "good" seems to refer to goodness toward one's self as opposed to goodness toward another and therefore qualifies purity.

one who sacrifices   K never departs from the theological focus of his argument.

9:3   *this is why*   This seems to continue the thought of 8:11. Thus, *we-gam* does not indicate a simple sequence ("and also") but rather the cause (cf. 6:7): it is because all are subjected to one fate that man's thoughts are full of evil: "they say to themselves: 'What does the evil-doer lose, for all have one fate, the one like the other . . . ?' Therefore wicked men hold to their wickedness" (Rashbam, in Japhet and Salters 1985).

minds . . . hearts   leb . . . lebab   Literally, "the heart." The stress on the psychological locus here may be due to K's wish to pursue the theological point introduced in 3:11, namely, that such thoughts too come from God.

XV   (9:4–10)   To Life!

4   *Then he who is still attached to the living has hope!*
      Indeed, they say that
          "a living dog is better than a dead lion!"
5   *Yes, the "living" know that they will die . . .*

      But the dead know nothing . . .
      Surely they have no longer any hope of reward.

      Their very memory is forgotten!
6   **Their love and hatred . . .**
      . . . and their envy!

      **. . . has already perished, and they have no further
      portion ever again in all that happens under the
      sun.**
7   *Then go, eat your food in contentment and drink your wine
      with a glad heart because God has already approved your*
8   *actions. At all times let your clothes be white, and let*
9   *not fine oil be wanting for your head. Enjoy life with a
      woman you love "all the days of your vain life" (as you put
      it) which He has given you "all the days of your vanity
      under the sun." For this is your portion in this life and in the*
10   *toil that you undertake "under the sun." All that your
      strength is able to do, do it with strength . . .*
      **Surely, in the grave toward which you are going
      there is neither deed nor thought nor knowledge
      nor wisdom.**

Commentary

9:4–5   In these two verses the rapid exchange of dialogue is punctu-
ated four times by the marker *ki,* which does not have "because" as its
primary meaning; or rather, these frequent interjections have as their real
point not the relentless argument of causality but rather the nervous shift
of point of view.

9:5   *the "living"*   It is pointless to see here the basis for the
distinctiveness of the human species, much like Pascal's "roseau pen-
sant," the idea that humans are superior to nature because they have
knowledge, even though only of their own mortality. Nor is this a
simple repetition of the preceding point, the assertion that a dog is

superior to a lion only when it is alive. Nor can this be a simple observation, since the point has been repeatedly and forcefully made that the living do not think about anything, certainly not about their end or mortality! The point, rather, is that this is a wisdom saying, one in which the sage uses the words of the tribe in a purer or wiser or more original sense. Here the "living" are they who truly live, the sages, who have the thought of their mortality constantly before their mind (see 7:3–4) and therefore avoid sin.

no longer   This important qualification shows that it is probably uttered by P, since it implies that there is hope of reward before death, perhaps in the form of those joys and pleasures admitted by K, but more likely in one's feelings of gratitude and contentment over whatever has been given.

their very memory   The memory of them, since no one remembers them or their deeds. Despite the Toranic commands to remember (e.g., Deut 25:6 concerning levirate marriage) and the living memory of the righteous dead as distinct from the "name" of the wicked (Prov 10:7), K is thinking here of what Camus euphemistically called the "tender indifference of the world," which occurs with greatest finality after death but which is also seen as common during lifetime. Alternatively but less likely, this can be taken as a subjective genitive: their very memory or consciousness (see 11:8, where *yizkor* means "remember" in the sense of "being aware or conscious") has vanished.

reward . . . memory   This untranslatable wordplay *sakar . . . zeker* is again a sign of the contentiousness of the debate.

9:6   *love and hatred . . . and envy*   Each member of this series is preceded by *gam,* "also," but the different functions of this connective must be clearly distinguished; in the first two cases *gam* is conjunctive whereas in the third it indicates a change of speaker, as frequently in Kohelet. The unusual (but not unique; cf. Isa 48:8) recurrence of three such particles in proximity should provide a clue. I propose that the first two cases, "also their love, also their hatred," again renders K's pessimistic dramatization of the human condition (cf. 9:1), intensified here by the remarkable rhyming of all four words: *gam 'ahabatam gam sin'atam.* At this point P interrupts with a sarcastic mimicking, using the same rhyme and particle, which also indicates a change of speaker and a distancing of point of view: *gam qin'atam.* That this interjection is totally disregarded by K is indicated by the singular verb *'abadah,* since his two subjects are conceived by him as a single topic.

love and hatred   The order is the same as 3:8 and 9:1, which is the pessimistic view preferred by K, as, according to him, all love ends in hatred.

and envy   Rashi refers this to jealousy toward the Creator ("they were envious of God in the works of their hands"), in which case this is a gibe about K's or Solomon's overambitious activities. However, in 4:4 K states the view that all human behavior can be explained by this motive, and there the meaning is clearly interpersonal: "envy *of one's neighbor.*"

portion   This refers to reward (9:5); see 2:10n. *my only portion.* As spoken by K the word may be an ironic quotation of P's view, as if to say: A portion indeed, stressing not that it is given (*ḥilleq*) but rather that it is only a piece of an unknown and unmanageable whole.

ever again   le-'olam   This semantically redundant adverb is but another instance of the dramatic intensification so typical of K's discourse.

9:7–10   P's exhortation to enjoyment differs from K's, as previously noted, in that it stresses contentment, being satisfied with what one has, and precisely *because* this comes from God by way of a gift. When addressed to a fictitious Solomon, who had everything one could desire, its tone is marked by irony and impatience: you have everything anyone could desire; now enjoy it! Note carefully the direct address.

9:7   Crenshaw (1987, 162) appropriately notes that until this point the call to enjoyment has been in the form of advice; now it is proclaimed in the imperative. Such a tone is more befitting P, who may simply be drawing a forceful conclusion based on K's observations.

your food   laḥmeka   "Bread," often used for food in general.

contentment   simḥah   Cf. 8:15. The word's emphatic purpose is also underscored by the encouraging *lek,* "go," and by reinforcement with the synonymous "with a glad heart," as if to say: Do not do so out of folly or absent-mindedness (Zer-Kabod 1973).

because God . . .   The point expresses not only the permission to enjoy but also the source of enjoyment, which is not the food or drink itself but rather the spiritual contentment derived from the awareness of the divine gift. Thus, the word *ki* ("because") does not gloss "eat and drink" but rather "in contentment" and "with a glad heart."

9:9   *enjoy   re'eh*   See 2:1, 6:5, 11:7–8.

a woman you love   The word neither stresses, nor excludes, marriage. The point, rather, is that K's approach has once again been defective in that it stressed (as did Solomon) the accumulation and abundance of erotic adventures (2:7 and especially 2:8 above), and this may be the explanation of the misogyny expressed with such vehemence in 7:26–28. In other words, K had complained that he could not find even one good woman. It is now suggested that this is because he did not try it with only one. The stress on erotic experience as a *loving* relationship seems quite modern; it is, however, already present in the Canticles (e.g., 8:7).

all the days of your vain life, etc. The quotations of K's florid rhetoric of vanity are deeply sarcastic (all the more so in that they are addressed to him), making the point that a person of such wealth and achievement has no basis for bemoaning the world's vanity.

which He has given you 'asher natan leka referring to the days. It may, however, refer to the woman, as in Gen 3:12: "The woman whom You gave." The thought of God's gift repeats 3:22 and 5:17. Note that the grammatical subject is carried forward from v. 7 or is not stated (cf. 2:21n. *He will give*).

9:10 *your strength* Literally, "your hand," synonymous with strength (*yad/koah;* cf. Zer-Kabod 1973 and Exod 32:11).

with strength "With all your strength" (Targum), that is to say, with conviction and confidence, as if it mattered very much, thus anticipating the affirmation of human activity of 11:1f.

surely ki Indicating both change of speaker and dissent. K returns to his radical rejection of all of existence before the absolute cessation of the grave. His rejection is ironic, as he uses precisely P's argument for activism ("while you are yet alive") as the basis for its rejection: what does it all matter?

the grave she'ol Cf. 3:17n.

toward which shammah "Toward there," equated with she-'ol; see the previous n.

deed/thought/knowledge/wisdom This is another instance of K's penchant for rhetorical accumulation, of his wish to steal the argument through overdramatization.

XVI   (9:11–10:7)   More on Sages and Fools

11 **Again, I have observed under the sun that
the race is not to the light-footed . . .**
. . . and the war is not to the brave . . .

. . . nor are wares to the wise . . .
. . . nor are monies to the clever . . .

**. . . nor graciousness to the learned!
Indeed, time and accident overtake them all.**
12 *To be sure, no man knows his time.*

**Like fish caught in an evil net or like birds caught
in a snare, men are trapped in a bad time, when it
falls upon them suddenly.**
13 *Yet I saw this example of wisdom "under the sun," and I*
14 *found it impressive. There was a small city with few inhabitants, and a great king came upon it and surrounded it with a*
15 *powerful siege. There happened to be there a lowly sage and*
16 *he saved the city through his wisdom. And though nobody
remembered this poor man, I still say that*
"Wisdom is better than strength."

**Yet a poor man's wisdom is scorned and his words
go unheeded!**
17 *The quiet words of the sages are heard better than the screaming of the king of fools:*
18   *"Wisdom is better than weapons."*

Yet,
"One fool can destroy much good."
10:1 **Dead flies can spoil an entire container of per-
fumer's ointment, causing it to stink.**
*Then shall we say that "a little foolishness is weightier than
wisdom, than honor"!*
2   *Rather, the mind of a sage inclines to the right way . . .*

. . . but the mind of a fool inclines to disaster.
3   **The very way upon which the fool walks shows
that he lacks sense . . .**
(Yet he has said about everything: "It is all foolish!")

4   **If the anger of a ruler is kindled against you, do
not retreat.**
Indeed, healing words can set aside great acts of folly.

5 **There is an evil I have observed under the sun,**
6 **when error issues from the ruler himself.**
   Fools often sit in high places . . .
   . . . while the rich sit among the humbled.
7 **I have seen servants ride upon horses and lords**
   walk on the ground like servants.

Commentary

9:11   At this point the topic reverts to the value of human effort (already present, however, in the "strength" of the preceding verse) and especially of wisdom and sages. K rhapsodically launches into another tirade on conditions "under the sun," this time against chance and fate; in so doing he affords P the occasion for undercutting. Indeed, in this verse the debate in proverbs rages in its most palpable form, as each stylistic formula is immediately undercut by its mirror image.

the race is not to the light-footed   This is once more a typical exaggeration regarding *all* things under the sun, for P might agree that the race is not *always* to the light-footed.

and the war . . .   This seems to be an ironic recall of K's point in 8:8. P seems ready to tell his illustrative tale (9:13–16) but is interrupted by K.

nor/nor/nor   we-gam lo'/we-gam lo'/we-gam lo'   P again parodies the formula, perhaps at his own expense.

wares   Literally, "bread, food." This is an attempt to reproduce the wordplay that occasions the exchange: *milḥamah* (war) and *leḥem* (food).

nor graciousness   That is to say, "don't interrupt!" On this topic see especially 10:12nn.

time and accident   'et wa-pega'   I.e., the time of the accident, cf. 8:6n.

9:12   *no man*   I.e., not even the wise, and to this degree P agrees with K.

his time   The moment of his death. Later in the verse K gives the term a negative twist by referring to it as his "bad time."

fish . . . birds   Perhaps from their joint creation on the fifth day (Gen 1:20–23), it was natural to associate the two (e.g., Zeph 1:3; Ps 8:9). The proximity of their creation to the creation of man on the sixth day adds to the appropriateness of the comparison. The particular violence of the comparison and its unfavorable implications for the Creator also appear in Hab 1:14–15: "For You have made men like the fish of the sea. . . . He drags them out with His net."

birds caught in a snare   Comparison with such a passage as
Prov 7:22–23 adds a frightening aspect to the discussion (I italicize the
verbal parallels): "*All at once (pit'om)* he follows her . . . *as a bird rushes
into a snare; he does not know* that it will cost him his life." Until this point
K has argued that external fate is indifferent. He now takes the summary
of that point ("no man knows his time") as also directed to human
complicity.

   suddenly   This restates the preceding "no man knows his
time," but it does so dramatically, stressing (again against the sages) that
all of human prudence is of no avail against our common fate and
chance. The theme of suddenness was prevalent in wisdom literature
(Prov 3:25; 6:15) and for the Stoics constituted a major challenge to the
sage. See also the preceding n.

9:13   *wisdom under the sun*   This is a contradiction to K's argument that all is vanity, and its provocative intent is evident in the in-
verted style: *gam zoh ra'iti hokmah tahat ha-shemesh*, "this too did I see:
wisdom under the sun." Further, the repetition of the verb from 9:11
also accentuates the contradiction: "You have seen . . . ; well, this is
what *I* have seen." The complement to this situation is stated in Prov
21:22, with the same moral (the superior strength of the sage over the
mighty of war): "A wise man scaled (RSV: "scales") the city of the
mighty . . ." In that passage also the past tense of the verb suggests the
recollection of an anecdote.

9:14   *siege   metsodim*   Thus forming an explicit verbal connection with what precedes (net, *metsodah* 9:12) and making the point that
not all evil "nets" are successful.

9:15   *lowly   misqen*   Either in social status (above 4:15) or in
wealth and power, in either case meant as a contrast to the kingly qualities of the invader.

   though nobody remembered   This could be an objection voiced
by K, based on his complaint that the very memory of the dead is forgotten (9:5), in which case P's rejoinder ("Yet I still say that wisdom is better
than strength") would be a simple insistence in the face of this unfortunate
circumstance. However, P's argumentation is stronger in its allowance
that, even though from the point of view of the sage there is no recollection, *from the point of view of the victims* wisdom is preferable. This gives
better motivation to K's reply: that such victims will not even listen to
good advice, if it comes from someone who happens to be lowly.

9:16   *wisdom is better than strength*   I.e., the wisdom of the sage is
better than the strength of the invading king. See the reformulation of
this proverb in 9:18.

a poor man's wisdom is scorned K the realist challenges the generality of the proverb: wisdom is better for whom? Surely not for the victims and potential beneficiaries, since in this world advice is not even heard unless properly packaged.

and his words go unheeded This is an additional objection: if even the sage's words are unheeded and forgotten, how much more so those of others. The thought has already been expressed in 1:11 and 2:16. There may also be skepticism here concerning the authenticity of the personal anecdote recounted by P; and, indeed, the very fact that it is only a personal anecdote proves the point that such momentous events can be forgotten even in the very generation in which they occurred. This point goes far beyond P's assertion that the wicked are forgotten (8:10), as he now gives the example of the same happening to a sage.

9:17   *quiet words* Words spoken in quiet; cf. 10:12.

screaming of the king of fools Beyond the topic of folly among kings and rulers, this remark has a dramatic and dialogic intent when addressed to the (fictitious) king: Power, whether political or vocal, is less effective than reason; therefore, "stop screaming!"

9:18   *Wisdom is better than weapons* Rashbam (Japhet and Salters 1985) and others understand the weapons as those of the invading army, in which case this proverb would be synonymous with the previous one in 9:16. However, it seems that this is a reformulation of the earlier proverb (9:16), this time focused not on the sage (or anti-sage, the king) but rather on the victims, the inhabitants of the small city. From their point of view, wisdom, though unarmed, is better than armed foolishness since it has saved their lives.

Yet one fool If P is arguing for the special status of sages, then of much greater moment is the weight or negative influence of their opposite, the fools. Awareness of the strength of evil (see above 8:9) and the necessity of its removal became the basis for many sayings in the wisdom tradition, and Santob de Carrión's (fourteenth century) is especially dramatic: "It is worse when an evil man rises up among the people, much worse than when ten righteous men perish" (Perry 1987, 34).

10:1   *foolishness is weightier than wisdom* But not "better-than" or of greater value than wisdom. The point is that abstract value is one thing but that in daily living it can be more important to remove negative things than promote positive ones; cf. Perry 1993b.

than honor This should not be seen as tacked on as an afterthought; although the main topic is the value of wisdom, reputation is also very much on the agenda (9:5, 9:15). Further, the accumulation of points of comparison may be due in part to structural reasons, since such "better-than" proverbs tend to emphasize paradox. Thus, "even a *little bit* of foolishness is weightier than even *a lot* of good, i.e., wisdom *and* honor."

      than wisdom, than honor   Without the connective, one can imagine this sentence as spoken by P, expressing his breathless sense of incredulity and outrage at such a view. That honor follows from wisdom was a tenet of the sages: "The wise will inherit honor" (Prov 3:35); and thus "honor is not fitting for a fool" (Prov 26:1).

10:2   *mind of a sage*   According to P such foolishness could not originate from a sage.

      the right way   Literally, "the right."

      disaster   Literally, "the left," perhaps indicating bad luck, what K would call his fate, hence "unlucky star, disaster." What is stressed here, however, is the disaster of others.

10:3   *he has said about everything*   "The All" (*ha-kol hebel*) is K's slogan; here a patent variant (see the next n.) is used ironically against him. There is also the suggestion that, if all is foolishness, then any attempt to distinguish the term is invalid, foolish even. Here, in an aside to the audience, P distances himself from K by referring to him in the third person, and it may be this that occasions K's angry response.

      it is all foolish   I.e., foolishness, following the Septuagint, because in calling everything vanity and denying wisdom he himself is a fool. This direct attack provokes the ensuing angry threat.

10:4   This returns to a previous dialogic situation (cf. 8:2, 8:3) concerning the counselor's need to leave his master's presence when the latter is angry. The argument seeks to demonstrate that, just as one fool can destroy much good, one sage can prevent much evil. In the development of the dialogue, K seems to soften his anger in the middle of his sentence and appeals to his interlocutor to stay.

      healing words   I.e., those just spoken in a conciliatory tone: "do not retreat."

      great acts of folly   I.e., angry revenge against a counselor who is only speaking his mind and defending the sages.

10:5–7   Here K continues his appeasement of P by admitting that folly has no regard for greatness, especially since this further illustrates his more general point that this world is upside-down and that the merit system has broken down. The possibility that here K is offering a further veiled critique of Providence (see the next n.) is increased by parallel texts that ascribe such reversals as those described in vv. 6–7 uniquely to God (e.g., 1 Sam 2:4–7).

10:5   *the ruler   ha-shalit*   The primary sense here is political, but our text has already used this term as a prime instance of the language of indirection; cf. *shilton* in 8:4 and *shalit* in 8:8 and nn. there. This would further extend K's complaints against the Creator and Ruler of the universe (see the preceding n.). Note also that when the reference is to a political ruler in the previous section (10:4), the term used is *ha-moshel.*

10:6   *in high places*   I.e., next to the ruler, where they dispense their foolish advice and wisdom. Dialogically, this can be taken as indirect criticism from a king to an adviser.

        the rich   K and P are sharply divided on the question of wealth. The former holds that it is money (and power) that makes the world go around, so to speak (cf. 10:19n. *it is money* . . .), and the rich are therefore to be feared ("do not curse the rich," 10:20). By contrast, P is delighted to observe the lowliness of the rich.

        the humbled   ba-shepel   The term is to be related not to *shapelah,* the lowland as opposed to the mountain (e.g., Jos 9:1), but rather to the consequences of a moral quality: "The man of haughty looks shall be humbled" (*shapel,* Isa 2:11). Perhaps the retort is no more than an elegant rejoinder: "I am humbled by your remark, and it is gracious of the likes of you, a rich man, to sit with me."

10:7   *and lords . . .*   There may be a tinge of self-complaint here, if indeed K is no longer king; cf. 1:12 and n. It is more likely, however, that here the initial "servants" is synonymous with "lords" rather than oppositional, as in Esth 5:11: "he had advanced him above all the princes and the servants (*ha-sarim we-'abdei ha-melek*) of the king." K's point is that all are alike before the king's power.

XVII   (10:8–11:10)   A Debate in Proverbs

8   *"Who digs a pit*
          will fall into it."
     And
          "Who through a fence breaks
          will be bitten by snakes!"

9   *He who quarries stones is crushed by them.*
     He who splits trees will "warm" himself with
     them.

10   *If the iron is dull and a man does not sharpen it beforehand,*
          then he will have to exert more energy.
     Then let's say that wisdom is the advantage af-
     forded by prudence.

11   *"If the snake bites before it is charmed,*
          the charmer's wail is to no avail."

12   **"The words of a sage's mouth are gracious-**
     ness . . . !"

          . . . But the lips of a fool will trip him up.
13   *The first words of his mouth are foolishness, and their*
14   *end evil madness. The fool multiplies words to no avail.*
     No man knows what will be; and as to what will
     come after him, who can tell him? We are all
     fools!

15   *The efforts of fools are wearisome only to one who can't even*
          find his way home!

16   *Woe unto you, Land whose king is a foolish youth and*
          whose lords feast in the morning!

17   **Happy are you, Land whose king is well-born and**
     whose lords feast in due season, in strength and
     not in drunkenness.

18   *It is through sloth that the roof caves in and because of slack*
          hands that the house leaks.

19   **Yet it is for pleasure that men make banquets . . .**

          And wine gladdens human life.
          . . . and it is money that answers everything.

20   **Do not curse the king even in your thoughts, and**
     do not curse the rich even in the privacy of your
     bedroom. For a bird of the air may transmit your

voice and a winged creature may reveal the matter.

11:1 *"Cast your bread upon the face of the waters,*
for in the abundance of the waters you will recover it."

2 **But divide it up into seven or eight portions, for you cannot know what disaster will fall upon the earth.**

3 *Surely if the clouds fill up with rain, "upon the earth" they will empty it. If seed falls in the south or the north, where it falls it will remain and sprout.*

4 **"He who watches the 'wind' will never sow."**
And
"he who observes the clouds will never reap."

5 *Just as you do not know the ways of the wind, like the powers hidden in a pregnant womb you cannot know the workings of God, Who makes everything.*

6 *Therefore, in the morning plant your seed.*

But don't let up your effort even by evening! For you have no way of knowing which will succeed, this one or that one.
Perhaps both will succeed . . .

7 *Certainly, the light is sweet . . .*
. . . and it is good for the eyes to see the sun!

8 *And if a man lives for many years, let him be contented with them all!*
But let him also remember that the days of darkness will be many. All that dies is vanity.

9 *Young man, even in your youth be contented, and let your heart bring cheer to the days of your youth.*
And follow the desires of your heart and the wishes of your eyes.

And know that for all these things God will call you to
10 *justice. Therefore, remove anger from your heart!*
And dismiss sadness from your flesh, for
"youth and morning pass like a breath."

Commentary

10:8–11   This lively debate takes the traditional form of a rapid exchange of well-known proverbs, or perhaps merely sayings which, through their paradigmatic style, have a traditional ring. The topic continues to be the importance of sages and fools, but the underlying question of the dialogue remains the role of criticism with respect to the ruling power: K's and, by implication, the Creator, and P's criticism of K, his king and master. However, in such highly allusive and metaphorical exchanges the precise meaning is often conjectural, except to the expert participants themselves. What does seem clear is that these are superb examples of the language of indirection necessitated by the unequal power between the two debaters.

10:8   *Who digs a pit*   Apparently quoting a well-known saying (for very similar formulations see Sirach 27:26–27; Prov 26:27), P suggests that fate follows from one's actions and that the king's fall is like falling into a hole that he himself dug. In other words, P rejects the tendency of placing the blame on the structure of things and insists on personal responsibility.

   who through a fence breaks   This seems a veiled threat of the danger of breaking through the fence of propriety surrounding the ruling power: "watch your words!"

   bitten by snakes   yishkenu nahash   Perhaps too tempting a wordplay (cf. Num 21:6: *ha-nehashim . . . wa-yenakshu*). The snake symbolizes worldly power in Isa 27:1, and the warning not to fool with snakes is again alluded to in 10:11. I alter the word order and use the plural "snakes" in the rhyming position in order to evoke the elegant formulaic game being played by the contestants here.

10:9   *quarries stones   masi'a 'abanim*   This image follows naturally from the preceding, as fences were normally made from stones (cf. Prov 24:31). However, this may also be another gibe in the continuing critical appraisal of Solomon's reign. It is stated of King Solomon (1 Kgs 5:31 17E) that "at the king's command they quarried out great, costly stones (*wa-yasi'u 'abanim*)" raised from a levy of forced labor, and it is this yoke of service that led to troubles later (1 Kgs 12:4). The sexual connotations of stones (cf. 3:5 and nn.) will be exploited in the following response.

   will "warm" himself with them   yissaken bam   Usually related to later Hebrew *sakanah*, "danger," thus "will endanger himself," agreeing with the preceding saying. However, Rashi and Rashbam (Japhet and Salters 1985) relate the term to *sokenet* (1 Kgs 1:2), which in context they take as synonymous with *ham*, thus "to warm." This ambiguity or wordplay allows K to add another saying to the series, again with the meaning that fools exercise no caution and that humans are victims of their actions, thus "warm" in the sense of "overwarm and endanger." But the second meaning allows a break in meaning of the proverb chain, so that metaphorical reading is short–circuited and the plain meaning emerges: productive work like tree-cutting brings not only danger but also productive results!

10:10   *the iron   ha-barzel*   Referring to the axe but also to the weapons of war mentioned above in v. 9:18 (cf. Deut 19:5).

   wisdom . . . prudence   This summarizes the implications of the two preceding images, that of cutting trees to warm one's self and of sharpening the iron in order to save energy. It also explicitly introduces the topic of the discussion through 11:6, which is the value of prudence, here equated with wisdom. In terms of the ongoing personal exchange, the sense seems to be: "If the wise know prudence, watch your words!"

10:11   This continues the thought of the previous verse on the value of prudence, and it also refers to 10:8 (see n.). P observes that if the snake (i.e., K, the king) is too quick to react, then his own words are of no avail. A king has to be willing to accept harsh advice.

   charmer's wail/no avail   This is an attempt to render the double rhyme of the original: *we-'ein yitron le-ba'al ha-lashon* and also *nahash/lahash,* which gives it the ring of a popular saying.

10:12   *graciousness*   And should therefore be heeded; the subject was introduced in 9:11 and is one of the standards by which K judges the presence or absence of wisdom.

   graciousness . . . lips   hen we-siptot . . .   The connection or transition between the two stichs of this verse affords a good example of what Scott (1965) has called the instructional method "in which a teacher spoke the first line and was answered by . . . an individual pupil" (9). This likelihood is increased in the present case if one assumes that the phrase "the graciousness of his lips" (*hen sepataw,* Prov 22:11) was a well-known tag. Thus, the first speaker's pause on the word *hen* would provoke a response on the same subject beginning with "lips." Also, the two scriptural uses of the phrase are highly relevant to the present context of a debate between an adviser and his king: "He . . . whose speech is gracious will have the king as his friend" (Prov 22:11); in Ps 45:2–3 1–2E such graciousness is a quality of the king himself ("I address my works to a king . . . grace is poured upon your lips").

   trip him up   tebal'ennu   Can mean either "confuse" or "devour" (cf. Ps 55:10 9E). Both are possible in terms of the next verse: the fool's foolishness would confuse him and his ensuing madness would destroy him. The singular verb can be explained by the fact that this stich is a response to the preceding singular subject (*pihu,* "his mouth"). The attached direct object is referred by Sforno to *hen:* "But that graciousness the lips of the fool will devour."

10:13   *foolishness*   This perhaps refers to K's original project to "take hold of foolishness" (2:3), or it may be an evaluation of K's conclusion, announced at the start, that all is vanity.

foolishness/madness   The same sequence occurs in 2:12 (but not in 1:17, see n.). P's point is that such a project could only have been undertaken by a fool.

evil madness   One may ask whether there is a madness that is not evil! In fact there is, since in the presentation of his project (2:12) K gives a positive valuation to madness, or at least keeps the question open as to its value.

10:14   *the fool multiplies words*   (*debarim*)   Such impersonal talk disguises yet another attack, since K, who has confessed his love of abundance, of multiplying things, is also loquacious. This reverts to the opening criticism that K has spoken many vanities (1:2). "To no avail" is added to the translation.

no man knows   Not even the sages. This skeptical attitude is typical (cf. 8:7, 8:17) and is intended specifically to counter P's ongoing defense of the sages and their wisdom.

what will be   For him during his lifetime.

after him   After he dies.

who can tell?   Cf. 8:7n.

we are all fools   K holds that humans are equal in their fate and in their foolishness; the only real distinctions, according to this point of view, have to do with money and power. These words are added in the translation to make this point clear.

10:15   As a partial solution to this highly allusive and grammatically difficult verse I propose that the second stich be considered as a recapitulation of the direct object: "The efforts of the fool exhaust him who doesn't know how to go to the city." That is to say, the actions of fools are not so "weighty" as proposed (cf. 10:1), and the person who is affected by them is already in a state of disorientation.

efforts   *'amal*   "Labor," perhaps with a change of emphasis so as to focus on actions rather than words. This would be consonant with the gradual shift in the discussion toward things practical: concrete actions and prudence.

10:16   *Land whose king*   P minimizes the danger of fools but does not deny it, and of fools the most dangerous is a foolish king, because of his position of power and leadership.

foolish youth   *na'ar*   I.e., and therefore he has no wisdom. *na'ar* has two basic meanings: youth (Exod 2:6) and servant (2 Kgs 8:4), each of which developed its own negative connotations. Thus, a "youth" is one inexperienced: it is parallel to "simple" in Prov 1:4 and 7:7, thus one who through inexperience "does not know" (Prov 7:23) and therefore stands to learn a great deal from wisdom's teachings. Interestingly, Solomon notes this very characteristic in himself: "I am but a little *child (na'ar)*, *I do not know* how to go out or come in" (1 Kgs 3:7). In wisdom literature the pejorative aspect of inexperience became standard: "Folly is bound up in the heart of a child (*na'ar*)" (Prov 22:15). The example of the "youthful" king thus exemplifies the ongoing discussion of foolishness; it appears in fact that this meaning is highlighted, even provoked, by the previous remark: "man does not know" (10:14).

To render *na'ar* here as "slave" (e.g., Zer-Kabod 1973) because it is required by opposition to the ensuing "well-born" is to injure the dialogic progress of the discussion. What occurs, rather, is that P, to counter the argument that there is no distinction among humans in their foolishness, asks what would happen in the extreme situation in which the leadership is inexperienced, when the king is foolish and the lords lazy and pleasure-seeking. In response, K misreads *na'ar* as "slave," perhaps intentionally, since he does not wish to consider the prospect of such a king.

whose lords feast They eat at an inappropriate time and thus destroy the land because they do nothing constructive (Rashbam [Japhet and Salters 1985], thus anticipating v. 18).

10:17   *well-born* And not a slave (cf. 10:16n. *foolish youth*). Or, the reply is that a person may be a *na'ar* and still worthy because chosen by God, as were Solomon and Jeremiah (Jer 1:6–7). According to such a view, the main requirement seems to be noble birth, which is seen as guaranteeing proper comportment.

10:18   Dialogically, the remark is motivated by the previous suggestion that proper behavior depends on one's birth. P observes that constructive behavior is due not to birth but rather, for example, to the simple circumstance of owning a house and the necessity of avoiding the disrepair occasioned by natural causes.

the house leaks   yidlop ha-bayit It is traditional to regard the second half of this verse as but a parallel or semantic repetition of the first half, but this is not likely. Gordis (1968) rejects the interpretation that sees the house as a figure for the state, but in such a highly allusive text as Kohelet one can object only to the identification but not to the procedure. As an alternative I propose that "house" refers to one's wife, as often in Rabbinic literature (see Mishnah Yoma 1:1). A "leaking" house would therefore refer to a cantankerous wife, one out of control and harmony with her husband, and this is the usual context of the root in Proverbs: "a wife's quarreling is a continual dripping of rain (*delep*)"

(19:13; also 27:15). The precise circumstances are here speculative, but the cause of "slack hands" seems to point to sexual withdrawal. In 9:10 hand is synonymous with strength, and the dual *yadayim* here may be due simply to an echo repetition of the dual *'atsaltayim* in the first stich. P would then be saying that K's complaints about women may be due to simple sexual neglect or present withdrawal.

10:19   *yet it is for pleasure   li-seḥok*   Cf. also 2:2. K will have none of this negative morality wherein behavior is explained by what one wishes to avoid. Rather, he argues that pleasure is the true human motivation, and that pleasure is achieved not by avoidance but by pursuing the occasion, such as a feast. In the debate context, K is retorting that one does not grant sexual contact out of marital duty but rather out of pleasure.

      banquets   leḥem   Meaning "feasts" with many people; cf. 2 Kgs 5:2. On possible sexual connotations see the two preceding nn. and also 11:1n. *cast your bread.*

      and wine gladdens human life   The thought seems similar to "wine to gladden the heart of man" (Ps 104:15), a parallel text that emphasizes the goodness of God's gifts and thus consistent with P's argumentation.

      wine   In 2:3 wine was associated with foolishness, but in 9:7 it is drunk with a glad heart. Here, through allusion to a well-known parallel text, P makes the clarification that wine is not the source of gladness but merely its occasion.

      gladdens   The root *smḥ* has the meaning of contentment in our text (cf. 2:26; 8:15).

      it is money that answers everything   The sharp debate on money began in 5:9 ("he who loves money will never be satisfied") and was continued in 7:12, where K retorted that wisdom is effective only when backed by money, which, by extension, means power. Here K continues the rebuttal by alluding again to one of P's favorite arguments, namely that true happiness arises from inner contentment with God's gifts. K takes the matter head on by quoting P's *God answers him* (5:19): from experience it seems that it is not God that answers but money and power.

10:20   *the king/the rich*   The parallel examples specify the intended senses: the king is the richest in the kingdom, and the rich have kingly powers.

      bird of the air   For ancient and medieval parallels of this traditional theme of "a little bird told me," see "The Cranes of Ibycus" in Perry (1993a); also below, 12:4n. The figure allows K to allude to retribution without its frequent theological implications.

your voice   I.e., "the voice (*qol*) of your curse, that you will curse (*teqallel*)," apparently an irresistible pun; cf. also Prov 27:14: "He who blesses his neighbor with a loud voice (*be-qol gadol*) . . . will be counted as cursing (*qelalah tehasheb lo*)."

11:1–6   In this section the debate in proverbs becomes so highly allusive as to defy interpretation, although the general drift is clear enough.

11:1   *cast your bread*   The allusion of the metaphor may be the following: "Release, direct your sexual energies to procreation!" In the previous section there were allusions to "making banquets (literally, bread)" and to the privacy of one's bedroom. The conversation now quite naturally pursues the subject of sexuality (cf. 10:19n.). In 3:5 the verb *shlh* was used (in the *hif'il* and in combination with "stones"; cf. n.) to suggest sexual congress. Here it is allied with *lehem* to the same purpose, since "eating" can hint at sexual union (Prov 30:20), as can "bread" (*lehem*, Prov 20:17; 9:17).★

   upon the face of the waters   *'al penei ha-mayim*   To be distinguished from *'al penei mayim* (Isa 18:2), the inclusion of the article signals a deliberate allusion to Gen 1:2—indeed, this seems to be the subtext of vv. 1–6: "And the spirit [*ruah 'elohim*, the 'wind of God'] was hovering upon the face of the waters." Again, this time through direct literary reference, the debate continues over God's relation with the world, and the reader is thus encouraged to relate the workings of the wind or *ruah* in 11:1–6 to the larger debate. The context of Gen 1:2 is to be noted, as this verse immediately precedes God's first act of creation.

   in the abundance of the waters   Cf. ★. According to the usual rendering "with the passing of time," P does not deny that things can get worse but he also insists that this trend is not unique and irreversible, except that in such cases patience is often required (cf. 8:12n. *good*).

11:2   *seven or eight*   In keeping with the subtext of Genesis 1, v. 11:7 will summarize the debate on creation by the biblical evaluation that it is (or is not) "good." Here the point is anticipated by allusion to the seven days of creation. "Seven or eight" is of course a typical formula of numerical heightening, but this formulaic usage should not prevent us from seeing its role in the debate. K's deeper question seems to be why the Creator had to spend seven days when only one would have sufficed ("could not the world have been created by a single Saying?" Abot 5:1). This likelihood is increased when one considers the usage of "good" in the creation text: 1:4, 10, 12, 18, 21, 25, 31. This amounts to seven; however, in the final example (1:31) it is asserted that it is "very good," thus doubling the latter number and amounting to a seven that is eight.

you cannot know   K repeats the point of man's basic ignorance (cf. 6:12, 8:7, 10:14) but, according to his method, he again tries to
force a pessimistic conclusion.

11:3   *fill up . . . empty*   The dialectic of fullness/emptiness is continued in 11:5. The figure implies that God empties his fullness upon the
earth, thus justifying the claim, as it were, that "the earth is the Lord's
and the fullness thereof" (Ps 24:1).
          upon the earth   The sequence with the previous verse seems
to be the repetition or quotation of this phrase: "You always anticipate
that disaster will fall upon the earth; well, rain falls 'upon the earth,' and
it is beneficial!"
          seed 'ets   Literally, "tree, wood." Zer-Kabod (1973) cites
an opinion that understands this as "the *seed* of the tree," and this possibility is enhanced by the productivity of trees in Gen 1:11: "plants yielding
seed: fruit trees . . ." This would then motivate the immediate reference
to sowing.
          north or south   This is the dimension of the wind's move-
ment (see 1:6), thus increasing the likelihood that this saying is also
intended as applying to the wind. The point is that the wind does not
upset or interfere with the earth's natural productivity.
          it will remain and sprout   Interpreting *sham hu'*, "there it is."

11:4   *he who watches the wind . . .*   Here K apparently uses a popular proverb, along with its highly metaphorical allusiveness, to indicate a
low point in his pessimism. If I am right that the subtext to the debate
here is Gen 1:2 in which God's *ruaḥ* (wind, spirit) precedes the first act of
creation, then K is insinuating that man's creativity can derive no com-
fort or inspiration from the divine act; indeed, he who does observe the
actions of that creative wind will never himself sow.
          will never reap   P retorts with a parallel popular-sounding
proverb, the point of which seems to be less its metaphor of clouds than
its parallel form (thus making it an appropriate retort in a debate) and its
message: whoever does not sow does not reap. P will reply still less
metaphorically in 11:6a.

11:5   *as you do not know*   Whereas K would argue negative conclusions from human lack of knowledge, P uses that same ignorance
as an indication that good as well as evil is possible (cf. 11:6n.
perhaps . . .).
          pregnant mele'ah   "Full."
          God, Who makes everything   The indeterminacy of things is
thus only a reflection of their Maker, and one should not expect otherwise. The God referred to here is again *'elohim,* the creator of Genesis 1.

The clause can also be rendered "Who makes the all," thus provoking and challenging K's main thesis of the vanity of "the all."

11:6   *plant your seed*   The Rabbis stressed the connection with the preceding image of the pregnant woman and understood this as referring to procreation. If so, it seems more natural to interpret the advice as referring to young adulthood, the "morning" of one's life, rather than to mornings as opposed to evenings or nights.

        perhaps both will succeed   This is a moving and glorious moment in the debate. P now uses K's skepticism against him: since man does not know the future, then why not hope for the best and trust in God! Zer-Kabod (1973) cites the example of Jacob, who prepared to meet his brother Esau by dividing into two camps (Gen 32:9 8E): "If Esau comes to the one camp and destroys it, then the camp which is left will escape." And in the end *both* camps escape.

11:7   *the light is sweet*   This is an effort to summarize the debate on creation by putting into a favorable perspective the first element of creation. This provokes K's rather violent reply.

        and it is good   This is a direct quotation of Genesis's judgment of creation. K says that it all depends: does the eye find the sun good when it looks directly at it (perhaps, metaphorically: how does man find God in His appearance as Creator)?

        to see the sun   Comparing the two other allusions to "seeing the light" in 6:4 and 7:11, one is tempted to translate: "and it is good to be alive." The problem arises from the very precise focus on "for the eyes," and it would be silly to assert that being alive is good for the eyes. Despite this dialogic displacement, the usual meaning for "seeing the sun" in our text is "to enjoy" (cf. 6:5, 7:11, 2:1n.).

11:8   *let him be contented*   Even if the "objective" facts of creation do not correspond to one's desires, one still has the obligation to see things in a "good light."

        let him also remember   Let even the person who lives a long life remember; cf. 5:19n. *he should . . .*

        All that dies   kol she-ba'   The verb has the strong meaning here (see Introduction 3a). Thus, "all that comes in [in its last phase] is vanity," implying, P would insist, that whatever in some sense incorporates decline and negativity will prosper in the end. I admit that this is a strong reading, hence not to everyone's liking, but I would defend the possibility of such a reading.

11:9   *heart/eyes*   See 1:13n. *explore.*

        and know that   In contradiction to K's frequent complaint that nothing can be known, P is emphatic that there is a form of certainty or knowing as secure as experiential knowledge. Gordis's (1968) insistence on reading a consecutive "and" here rather than the usual adversative "but" receives support from the fact that parallel invitations to enjoyment throughout the book (2:24–26, 3:12–13, 3:22, 5:17–19 [E18–20], 7:14, 8:15, 9:7–10, 11:8–10; cf. Rousseau 1981, 210–11) are invariably followed by an insistence that such enjoyment is a gift of God. But one must go on to distinguish this religious argument from K's more epicurean emphasis; in P's counterview it is not pleasure that is perilous but rather the denial of its divine sanction.

God   ha-'elohim   The God of creation of Genesis 1 is also the God of justice.

11:10   therefore   This seems to explain the preceding. Humans can avoid pain and anxiety because the outcome is known and can be anticipated or avoided.

remove anger   Be hopeful and grateful! Dialogically, one can attribute this remark to K, who has an ongoing diatribe against the sages' anger (7:3, 9nn.).

for youth and morning   K gives a different reason for avoiding anxiety and pain, namely, the fleeting quality of existence.

pass like a breath   Literally, "are vanity."

XVIII   (12:1–7)   An Allegory on Old Age and Death

12:1 *In the days of your youth remember your Creator, before*
"bad days" come upon you, years of which you will say: "I
have no pleasure in them."

2 **Before the light darkens,**
the sun and the moon and the stars . . .
Do the clouds remain after the rain?!

3 **In the day when the watchmen of the house trem-**
ble . . .
And men of power and influence have been corrupted!

And the grinders cease their work . . .
Indeed, they are become few, and the women watching at the
windows grow gloomy.

4 **And the portals to the market are shut because the**
sound of the mill is low . . .
But he will rise up at the sound of a "little bird."
But for him all the songbirds will be silenced!

5 *They are afraid of a higher One . . .*
But there are dangers right in front of them!

But the almond tree will blossom . . .
And the locust shall fatten itself on it until its de-
sire fails . . .
. . . and man shall go to his eternal dwelling. And the mourn-
ers shall go about the streets.

6 *Thus, before the inheritance of silver is distant . . .*
. . . and the pot of gold is broken,
and the pitcher is smashed at the fountain,
and the dung descends to the pit,
7 **and the dust returns to the earth as it was . . .**
And the spirit returns to God, who gave it . . .

Commentary

12:1–7   The advice to remember your Creator is here cast in a dual
perspective. On the one hand, it is advanced as a vital activity appropriate to one's youth, as against the assertion of youth's vanity in the
previous verse; on the other hand, it is recommended as appropriate to

the period preceding old age and death, as described in the seven verses that follow.

Three stages or aspects of this challenge to youth are distinguished: old age, communal turmoil, and the demise of the desires of the individual. These three aspects are marked stylistically by the three appearances of *'ad asher lo'* ("before") in vv. 1, 2, 6.

12:1   *your Creator*   Hardly an unfitting allusion, as some have maintained, this call to remember creation harks back to the initial and central claim of K, that the world of creation is vanity. Here the point is personalized: the Creator of the universe is also *your* Creator. The plural *bor'eka* is the plural of majesty.

those bad days   As distinct from the day in the singular of v. 3f., these days are the years of old age. The speaker does not assert their evil but rather quotes this as the opinion of his interlocutor. K's negative view of ends as opposed to beginnings was already expressed at the start of chapter 7 and, indeed, in the Prologue on the Nature of Things that opens the book.

12:2–5   The allegorical reading of this much-discussed passage (signifying the decline associated with aging) has received a fair hearing and has adherents from the most diverse schools of criticism. Suffice it to say here that it derives its cogency from K's rhetoric of power, his love of dramatization and appeal to myth and poetry and proverbial authority already evidenced in the opening Prologue on the Nature of Things. His allegory is merely an extension of self-pity, a monologic and self-indulgent lament on his personal losses, expanded to universal proportions. Unfortunately, this reading has been so dominant as to exclude from consideration the passage's contribution to the ongoing debate. At any rate, K's vague and emotional rhetoric is placed in counterpoint to P's ironic undercutting, and the exchange resembles the stichomythia of the classical theater.

12:2   *the light darkens*   It is unclear whether the individual's light (either his vision or his life) is meant, or whether the allusion is to a universal destruction, the undoing of the works of creation.

the clouds remain   Literally, "the clouds return." P observes that the only real conditions that would allow the hyperbolic darkening of all light would be the rainy season, which soon passes. K's claim that winter lasts forever is absurd.

the rain   The reference is apparently to the rainy season, which eventually yields to another spring.

12:3   This verse seems to view the death of the king as a communal disaster, mainly in the disarray of the defenses and the consequences of military defeat. Its motto would be "there is no dominion on the day of death" (8:8), which refers explicitly to 8:4 and hence to the king.

men of power and influence '*anshey he-ḥayil* Referring to social and moral status rather than military strength. However, the ambivalence allows P to give the military allusion a moral interpretation and to assert that defeat has moral rather than natural causes.

corrupted "Twisted, perverted," in the moral sense of perverting justice (e.g., Job 8:3, 34:12). However, the secondary sense of "bent over" allows this response to be applied to the previous remark: the men of valor are bent over in defeat.

the grinders Probably the teeth, as K pursues his vague allegory of individual death.

they are few P again forces the interpretation back to the literal level. Here he refers to the women who grind; they may be few because the poor security situation has diminished the food supply or because they (wives, slaves) have been carried off as spoil. Alternatively, the subject is the keepers of the house, again because of poor security and diminished food supply.

women watching at the windows The closest parallel situation in Hebrew Scripture is the scene at the end of Deborah's song (Judg 5:28): "Through the window peered Sisera's mother, Behind the lattice she whined: 'Why is his chariot so long in coming . . .' " The meaning is that, here too, the heroes have failed to return (the men of valor are therefore bent over in earnest) and disaster is about to descend upon the unprotected community.

12:4   *because the sound is low* *bi-shepal qol* See BDB. The stich comes to spell out the results of the diminished food supply (the silencing of the grinders); namely, that all normal commercial and communal activities, symbolized by the market, will also cease.

rise up at Perhaps "rise up against," as in Gen 4:8; thus, one would be rebelling against the voice of conscience, perhaps in anger or vengeance.

the sound of a "little bird" *qol ha-tsippor* For the reference here one need look no further than 10:20 above (see nn. there), which introduced the theme of a bird's voice ("a little birdie told me") as a figure of retribution, signifying that whatever evil you do will be reported. Here the traditional theme is refined even further, now signifying the voice of conscience that returns to trouble the dying person. The figure thus continues the theme of judgment in 11:9: "God will call you to account." Here the irony of the response is marked by the repetition of *qol*: Perhaps the sound of the mill will cease, but there is one sound or voice that will only grow louder!

for him all the songbirds will be silenced   K continues along his elegiac way, returning to P's literal sense to stress the cataclysmic results for the individual. Perhaps, too, a more precise sense is intended, since in previous usages in Kohelet the reference was to pleasure ("singers and all human pleasures" in 2:8) and to praise (it is opposed to the sage's reproach in 7:5). "For him" is added in the translation.

12:5   *a higher One   gaboah*   In the same sense as in 5:7 and Ps 113:5: "who sits on high." P returns to the figural plane: there are more serious concerns from "on high" than songbirds!

But there are dangers   we-ḥathatim   Literally, "but there are fears." Perhaps this *waw* is concessive: "Though there are other dangers closer at hand," as they are going to die!

almond tree   shaqed   As in Jer 1:11. Having proved that analogies from inorganic nature are ineffective (chapter 1), P now argues from organic nature. He selects the almond because it is the first to blossom in the Land of Israel.

the locust   Since, for K, all forward motion ends in death, all that blossoms (e.g., the almond tree) will be destroyed, and its destroyer, figured by the locust, will also be unfulfilled because its desire *never* fails.

his eternal dwelling   beit ʿolamo   K insists this dwelling is forever.

and the mourners   In view of K's fears about a decent burial (cf. 6:5, 8:10), P reassures him that, despite the universal silence, the king will still have mourners.

12:6   These four figures of death are for K really figures of disintegration and return of the main elements to their "places," exactly "as they were" before creation (see chapter 1 and the next verse, which summarizes this process according to its two main components).

silver, gold   These elements are not used primarily as figures of speech and much time can be lost in musing over their allegorical equivalents. Recall that K has stated, as an important part of his program, the amassing of silver and gold (2:8). Note also that these material values are often associated with idolatry in the Hebrew Bible: "Do not make for yourselves gods of silver and gods of gold" (Exod 12:44; Deut 7:25, 8:13); indeed, these were the very substances of the idols: "The idols of the nations are silver and gold" (Ps 135:15, also 115:4). The point is that, with the approach of death, idolatrous and unwise desires now recede into the background.

inheritance of silver   Perhaps "inheritance of wealth." This returns to one of K's main worries (cf. 2:18, 5:13). Here *hebel* is synonymous with *nahalah,* with which it is frequently coupled (Deut 32:9 and often). A less likely possibility is to read *hebel* as "pangs," i.e., desires (for wealth and inheritance). Of course, K, followed by the allegorists and most modern readings, understands the words as "cord" (cf. Jos 2:15), which he then reads as being "snapped"; cf. the next n.

    is distant   yeraheq   K rereads this, allegorically, as *yerateq,* "is snapped."

    pot of gold   This translation tries to retain the implication of good fortune implied in the coupling of *hebel* with *goral* in Jos 17:14. The noun *gulat* is important because of its substance, which is gold and therefore a container of precious substances for royalty: if drink is imagined, then the allusion would be to pleasure, whereas oil would suggest reputation. The importance of these values now flees before his sight, along with the loss of royalty (= gold) itself. Parenthetically, there is a punning way to read this distich: "the exile (read *galut* for *gulat*) of gold (as death approaches) will run forth or burst upon you."

    pitcher   kad   Used not only for the transport of water but also for drinking (Gen 24:14), that is to say, whatever is measured out to an individual from a common source.

    fountain   mabu'ah   Drinking easily takes on metaphorical extension. In Prov 5:15 ("Drink water from your own cistern") it means "rejoice in the wife of your youth" (5:18), a sexual metaphor preserved, for example, in the French "je meurs de soif auprès de la fontaine." In Prov 9:5 one is encouraged to drink wisdom (also Abot 1:4: "Drink up their words with thirst"). Here the infrequency of *mabu'ah,* which occurs only in Isa 35:7 and 49:10, coupled with its parallel use with the preposition *'al* in Isa 49:10, suggests a literary allusion. Since the latter passage is addressed as a promise to the returning exiles, the message would now turn from the loss of material desires to the waning of hope: individual death means that the messianic hope will not affect *him*—a sentiment that must have been familiar to anyone who had thought about the death in the desert of the entire generation of the Exodus.

    and the dung descends   we-narots ha-galgal   A punning repetition of the previous *we-taruts gulat.*

    pit   bor   Not "cistern" but rather the more appropriate pit of the grave (Ps 55:24, 69:16). In K's mouth the term is also an ironic pun on P's call to remember the Creator (*bor'eka,* 12:1).

12:7   This verse returns to the issue described in 3:21.

    to the earth   'al ha'arets   It is usually assumed that here *'al* is to be substituted by *'el.* However, man was not created from *'erets* but from *'adamah* (Gen 2:7), and the point here is that the dust that made up the human body returns to its original dwelling place *upon* the earth (and not in or under the ground).

      as it was   Exactly as one would expect. Nothing has been gained and there is no permanent advantage or *yitron*.

      God who gave it   Since it was all a gift, God can expect gratitude.

XIX   (12:8–14)   P's Epilogue and the Ongoing Tradition of Righting

8   **"Vanity of Vanities,"**
said the Cohellector:
"All is Vanity."

9   *In addition, Kohelet was not only himself a sage but also added to wisdom by teaching the people knowledge. He*
10   *listened and pondered, righting many proverbs. Kohelet tried to find pleasing words and writings of uprightness, words of truth, such as:*

11   **"The words of the sages are like goads."**
But like well-fastened nails are the collectors of sayings: They all come from one Shepherd.

12   *But beyond this, my son, be wary, for*
"there is no end to the making of books"
and
"much study is but a weariness of the flesh."

13   *This is the last word, the "all" has been heard. Now fear God and keep His commandments. For this is man's usual*
14   *pursuit: namely, to pass judgment upon every one of God's actions, even all the hidden ones, whether for good or for evil.*

THE SUM OF THE MATTER: YOU HAVE HEARD IT ALL.
NOW FEAR GOD AND KEEP HIS COMMANDMENTS.
FOR THIS IS MAN'S ENTIRE PURSUIT.

Commentary

12:8   *the Cohellector   ha-qohelet*   The use of the article suggests that the proper name is allegorical, a name selected as a reference to a characteristic activity of the person so named.

12:9   *In addition   we-yoter*   This final section (or, as some would have it, final two sections beginning here and in v. 12), harks back pointedly to K's original question of *yitron* (1:3), to the profit or addition that humans can expect from their life under the sun. Through this verbal resonance P stresses the degree of his disagreement and agreement with K: what is left to man is his wisdom, as exemplified by K (!), and beyond this there is nothing. But even when K's negativism is discounted, there still remains the dialogic method.

listened and pondered These are the two essential activities involved in making proverbs (see the next n.): listening to the conclusions of others, whether of sages (v. 11) or of the people (v. 9) and then pondering their truth, separating out their wisdom from their foolishness. The ensuing literary result, therefore, includes what is heard as well as what is added (see Introduction 5b), so that every saying is an intertextual re-creation of preexistent materials, a dialogue with a tradition and with one's own experience as well. Pondering (*ḥiqqer*) also implies research in depth, as when the sage scrutinizes the possible connotations of the received text and finds deeper meanings.

righting The pun is irresistible and allows the sense that the final result belongs to the creator (writing = composing). Nevertheless, the verb *tiqqen* is used elsewhere (7:13) in opposition to "make crooked." The creative activity of the sage is a critical one, involved in "righting" or making straight what is less so. This can be made obvious only if the corrected version also shows the original writing previous to "righting" or re-writing. It is this activity that makes the sage's enterprise truly traditional and intertextual, so that the final result is less an original creation than a critical preservation and correction, a cumulative result and creation.

12:10 *to find mtso'* This seems to have the two basic meanings of the Latin *invenire* and thus to summarize the activity of the sage as set out in the preceding verse: "to find" what others have said, and "to invent" my own. Further, each meaning appears to have its own object; thus, "to invent pleasing words" and "to find writings of uprightness," both of equal worth as summarized by the concluding "words of truth."

writings ktub The singular, where one would expect the plural *ketubei;* but the singular also seems to have the status of a noun, and it may be intended to refer to the present composition, hence the singular.

of uprightness I.e., leading to upright behavior; cf. Prov 2:13, 4:11.

12:11 *the words of the sages* Rashbam (Japhet and Salters 1985) sensed that this saying is inserted here by a presenter, as something that Solomon was in the habit of saying. The verse perhaps also marks the end of the debate in proverbs and the final synthesis, since both the sages' words and their collectors' activities of saving and commenting come from the same Source.

words/goads The English does not adequately render the wordplay *dabar/darbon*. The image seems to be offered as an explanation of the harshness sometimes required to achieve the upright behavior mentioned in the preceding verse. But there is also an allusion to the wider context of the composition of proverbs (cf. 12:9), according to which each saying becomes a "goad" prodding the student and sage to ponder and react. Once this initial "word" has been pondered and set in "pleasant words" (cf. 12:10), then it is worthy to enter the tradition and become "fixed."

sayings   The allusion is to the words of the tradition, as exemplified here by the words of the collectors (note the plural), who come to ponder and "right" the original words.

they all   This refers to the original words of the sages and also to the sayings that arose under their stimulus and are passed down by tradition. This suggests that interpretation is a legitimate, even a necessary, part of traditional wisdom.

12:12   *beyond this*   See 12:9n. *in addition.*

12:13   This difficult verse is best explained dialogically, as it gives closure to K's main arguments by citation: his words of complaint (cf. 1:1, 1:8) and his "All" argument (12:8), both to be evaluated, in P's view, in relation to the fear of God (cf. especially 5:6 and nn., where the themes are related).

the last word   I.e., the last of the many words of reproach announced in 1:1 (cf. n.).

the "all" has been heard   I.e., you have heard as much as language is able to express (but, obviously, not the end of the matter, as language and books can go on indefinitely). This is an injunction not to waste any more time, but rather to proceed to more useful activities such as fearing the Lord, or, as in a parallel passage in Sirach (43:27), praising the Lord.

for this is man's usual pursuit   *ki zeh kol ha-'adam*   "For this is the all of man." "This" (*zeh*) is intended to denigrate, as in Job 14:3: "And dost Thou open thy eyes upon such a one (*zeh*) and bring him into judgment with Thee?" Here it refers to what follows.

12:14   *God's actions*   *'et kol maʿaseh ha-'elohim*   Commentaries have traditionally regarded *'elohim* as the subject, despite the difficulty of the absence of the article after *'et*. It seems more natural to read *maʿaseh* in construct and to continue the subject *'adam* from the previous clause. This would then be an apt summary of a central theme of the entire work, which is not man's deeds but the divine works of creation and how they are to be investigated and explored (1:13) and judged by man (cf. 3:11, 7:13, 7:14 and nn., 8:17, 11:5).

namely   *ki*   Again in its dialogic use of citing an opinion (here K's), with which the speaker disagrees.

for good or for evil   This summarizes the polar movement of the debate, in which K has judged this existence for evil and P for good, much like the debate between the Houses of Hillel and Shammai mentioned at the outset.

THE SUM OF THE MATTER . . .   The usual explanation of MT's repetition of 12:13 at the end of the work is that the author did not want to end on a negative note. It is good to reflect, however, that, as Barthes has said, there is no such thing as a perfect repetition. I propose that whereas 12:13 was directed to giving closure to the dialogue, this concluding repetition is for posterity, a concluding address to the reader, and its words must therefore take on a different reference and tonality.

Part Three

Additional Notes and Remarks

1

*Additional Notes on Kohelet

1:1   *sayings   dibrei*   A better translation of this plural noun may
be "the words and deeds of," as, due to its verbal ambiguity (cf. 1:8),
debarim may designate "things" as well as words, and in the present
work both are appropriate. In 1 Kgs 11:41, for example, it refers to
Solomon's deeds as well as his words, "*all that he did* and his wisdom."
Indeed, in anticipation of the work's autobiographical nature, *dibrei* is
taken by Kimhi as combining these two meanings: words about one's
affairs or things, thus "narrated experiences"; Kimhi cites Kohelet's "I,
Kohelet" (1:12f), Amos 1:1, and also Jeremiah's 1:5f. narrating all the
evil that came upon him as the result of his words of prophesy.

The usual translation, "words of," is perhaps too careful in another
sense as well; although the term can certainly render the prophetic revela-
tions of Amos 1:1 and Jer 1:1, in Prov 31:1 (also 30:1) it refers to a
literary form: "The words (*dibrei*) of Lemuel, king of Massa, *which his
mother taught him,*" thus "sayings." When appended to the name Kohelet
the Collector (see next n.), it is thus possible to understand this term in
context as "the collected sayings." According to this view, the sayings
are not literally of his invention but rather the fruits of his collection.
However, even if the sayings are "his," so to speak, the relation between
personal invention and collecting in wisdom proverbs is inclusive rather
than exclusive, more an accumulation and an appropriation than a personal creation (cf. 12:9n. *listened . . .*).

The Rabbis insisted that *debarim* refer to words of reproach and admonition (see Rashi here and on Deut 1:1). But Whom is Kohelet reproach-
ing for the way the world is made?

Kohelet   It can be argued that this opening verse aims less at
the person of the author of the sayings than at his political role: king, in
Jerusalem (this interpretation is usually rendered by a comma after "David," thus referring the title "king" back to Kohelet). It is to be noted
that a most prominent usage of the root *qhl* in Hebrew Scripture occurs
in such passages as Exod 35:1: "Moses assembled (*wa-yaqhel*) all the
congregation of the people of Israel, and said to them: 'These are the
things that the Lord has commanded you to do.'" This usage may then
be viewed against the historical background of Solomon's (= Kohelet's)

unique achievement in uniting the entire Israelite community as one people, as a single religious and political nation. This achievement is highlighted in 1 Kgs 8:1–2: *yaqhel shlomoh* (parallels in 2 Chr 5:2–3). Given the assertion that all is vanity, the ironic view would be expressed, to be confirmed by later historical developments, that this national unity was fated to end and therefore vanity.

As to the feminine form Kohelet (the masculine would be Kohel), it has been argued that this does not really refer to a woman because in every other case (i.e., here and in 12:10) it is used with a masculine verb. This argument must then account for the difficult case of 7:27, where a feminine verb *is* used: *'amrah Kohelet*. It is explained that this is due to a wrong word division and must therefore be corrected to *'amar ha-Kohelet*, "says the Kohelet," as in 12:8. However, one could as justifiably apply the principle in just the opposite way, retaining 7:27 as it is and explaining 12:8 as incorrect word division, and then postulating that our verse and 12:10 are further instances of denying female authorship. At the very least, there seems to be as good reason to speak of a Lady Kohelet as of a "Lady J" in the Pentateuch, as Harold Bloom (1990) has proposed.

King   The use of a nickname hinting at Solomonic authorship is usually explained apologetically, as a clever way to benefit from Solomon's authority in order to gain easy acceptance into the canon. However, the argument would be more convincing if Solomon were named outright, and one wonders if the argument should not be reversed: Solomon is *not* named precisely in order *not* to abuse authority and thus misrepresent the formation of the canon, which is formed dialogically, as the text will explain in 12:9–11 and nn.

in Jerusalem   According to one midrashic view, this means *only* in Jerusalem, perhaps alluding to the eventual shrinking of David's inheritance because of the sins of his sons or, indeed, his systematic infringement of Deut 17:14–17 in 1 Kgs 9:26–11:49 (Brettler 1991). Also, Jerusalem may be viewed here as the center of learning; cf. 1:16.

1:2   *vanity of vanities*   The placement suggests that these words, this first in a series of "sayings," is Kohelet's motto. It is usually taken as a superlative, much like the Rabbinic reading of "Song of Songs" as the *best* song of all the songs, and thus taken to refer to "everything," since it provokes the astonished question that follows (repeated in 12:8, but as an assertion). It is quite possible, however, that this is not a true superlative (note the absence of the definite article in the second term of the construct) but simply an expression of strong emphasis. Similarly, *'ebed 'abadim* (Gen 9:25, see Ibn Ezra) means "a lowly slave" and not the superlative "lowest of slaves."

1:3   *under the sun*   Two suggestions seem worthy of comment. First, Rashbam (Japhet and Salters 1985) appears to equate the expressions "under the sun" and "under the heavens" by conflation, when he quotes Ps 19:7 6E: "there is nothing hid from its heat," referring, if Rashi is right, to the theme of judgment and "fear of the Lord." The notion could thus be rendered by something like "under the fiery eye of the Judgment of Heaven." Second, Lévinas (1969) has reminded us of the distinction between a totality and an Infinity (cf. Introduction 3d). Whereas the first seeks to be disguised as the second, in fact it is best understood in opposition. In the present context and as the Rabbis insisted, the phrase is actually an exclusion: "*under* the sun, perhaps, but *above* the sun, as it were . . . ?"

For a further midrashic reading of this verse see 5:8n. *is subject to,* where Rashbam takes the second part of the verse as an answer to the first: "What profit does man have?" Answer: "Through all his labor . . ."

1:4–7   On cyclicality, it is admitted that K's concept can also be so described in that he holds to nature's eternal cycle, except that he views it negatively as from birth to death. Conversely, P's perspective is also linear in its movement forward. However, such questions of terminology should not disguise the essential difference between the two views, which is precisely where each sees the beginning and end of each "cycle" (cf. also Introduction 3a). The optimistic view is perfectly typified by Nehama Leibowitz's portrayal (1981, 223) of the sidra *hayyei Sarah,* the weekly Torah reading composed of Gen 23:1–25:18, deliberately phrased as if in opposition to K's perspective: "This sidra features two themes, that of the purchase of the burial plot for Sarah and the bringing of Rebecca to Isaac as his bride—Death and Marriage symbolizing the unchanging cycle of mortal existence. *One generation departs and another takes its place."*

1:4   *the earth*   Two midrashic meanings can also be teased out of this text. Rashi brings down the beautiful reading "the *lowly* earth," referring to the humble or lowly people of the earth (see Introduction 4a and Perry 1987, 84). This will allow K later (5:8) to be ironic about the moralizing tendency of midrash. Alternatively, *ha-'arets* refers to man's magnificent dwelling-place, which was a partner in the original creation of the world (Gen 1:1) and of man: "a mist went up from the earth" (*'arets,* Gen 4:6). In Hebrew Scripture the earth is characterized by its gracious fullness (the serpent crawls upon the *'adamah,* and man's origin is the latter (*'adam/'adamah*). Concerning the possible connection *dor/dur,* Ibn Ezra cites Ps 84:11 10E: "I would rather stand at the threshold of the house of my God than dwell (*dur*) in the tents of wickedness." At least in Rabbinic literature the root is connected to "the land, the earth," whether the land of Israel or the earth in general: "He Who brings light to the earth and to those that dwell therein (*la'arets we-ladarim 'alehah*)," as the Rabbinic prayer read for the Sabbath; or, "a person should always dwell in the Land of Israel (*yadur be'erets Isra'el*)" (BT Ketubot 110).

Such midrashic readings are close to mythical concepts and were exploited in the mystical literature; for the mythical use of Gen 4:6 see Perry (1986), also Introduction 4a.

  endures 'omadet The moralizing resonances of this term should also be noted. There is first of all the association with the important theme of "the fear of God," as in Ps 19:10 E9: "The fear of the Lord is pure, enduring (*'omedet*) forever." Even more suggestive, at least for the moralizing P, is the connection with divine service, since the Priests are said to "*stand* in order to serve"; cf. Deut 18:5; 1 Kgs 8:11; perhaps also 1 Kgs 1:2, where Abishag's "waiting upon the king" (*we-'amdah*) is equated with her service to him (*wa-teshartehu*) in v. 4. This more active sense focuses on the earth not as the end of the cycle of life but rather as its perennial beginning and enduring usefulness.

Alternatively, the end of the verse can refer literally to the earth, as Zola rhapsodized at the end of *La Terre*: "Et la terre seule demeure, l'immortelle, la mère d'où nous sortons et où nous retournons, que nous aimons jusqu'au crime," which seems a creative (though surely unintentional) conflation of Gen 3:19–20.

1:7 *return to their source . . . continue to flow* Literally, "to the place where the rivers go, there they will return (or continue) to go." It is possible to construe the first verb of *shabim lalaket* as an auxiliary + infinitive meaning "to do a thing again" (Barton 1908), thus "continue to flow (in the same direction)." In this reading, "there," meaning "to the place or destination," reads *sham* in the sense of *shammah,* as in 1 Sam 9:6; also Jer 22:27, where the two words are used synonymously, side by side. The order of words is misleading and one would rather expect: "they will return to go there."

However, if the rivers continue, it is implied that they must revert in some way to their source, and this increases the likelihood that *shabim lalaket* is to be construed literally, as "return to go, i.e., return (*from* there rather than *to* there)[1] for the purpose of going forth (again)," with a clause of purpose introduced by *l-*. This allows midrashic readings of this passage to come more clearly into focus. For example, there is a possibility here that the word *shab* elliptically means "to die" (as below 3:20; Job 1:21: "naked I will return there," to the earth or grave). The point is less the rivers' continual frustration than their ever-renewed

---

1. This assumes a haplography, the original *mem* of *mi-sham* having been assimilated by the preceding *mem* of *holkim*. This verse is excellently discussed by Whybray (1989, 42–43).

determination to try again, but this can happen only by their "dying" in the sea and then returning to their source. The point may seem contradictory (when the individual rivers "die" they vanish into the sea), but the view, rather, is that their initial project or desire is to fill the sea and it is this project that is frustrated and dies. Yet—and here is the religious paradox—it is through this dying or return (*shub*) or repentance (*teshubah*, the human extension of that natural movement) that hope is renewed, and this is seen as ultimately the source of universal dynamism. Incidentally, this gives another dimension to the word *sham*, "there," which is a code word for the grave (cf. 3:17n. *in the grave*). At least it gives a different resonance to Rashi's explanation that this refers to the rivers' return to their sources through underground channels.

1:16   *I have greatly added   higdalti we-hosapti*   It is incorrect to appeal to GKC 120d in support of the coordination (actually the subordination) of this pair of verbs, since the cases presented are the reverse and we would require: *hosapti we-higdalti*, meaning "I once again . . ." Rather, wisdom is to be construed as the direct object of both verbs. Thus, *higdalti ḥokmah*, "I made wisdom great" (cf. Isa 9:2 E3), and *hosapti ḥokmah*, "I added wisdom" (1 Kgs 10:7) and thus the implied subordination: "I made wisdom great by adding to it"; see the next n.

          added to the wisdom   hosapti ḥokmah ʿal kol ʾasher hayah   Literally, "I added wisdom to all [the wisdom] that was . . ." Here "all" refers to wisdom and not to sages, since wisdom can be added to wisdom but not to people. However, as the noun is not repeated, the verb *hayah* agrees with *kol*.

     One traditional reading (RSV: "surpassing all who were over Jerusalem before me") is based on construing ʿ*al* as a comparative, but the examples adduced by Barton are unconvincing (1908, 86). Indeed, when later K speaks of being greater than anyone else in worldly riches (2:9, 7), then the preposition used is *min* and not ʿ*al;* moreover, in speaking of comparative superiority in wisdom, Scripture also uses *min* (Job 35:11; Ps 119:98). In brief, there is no point in continuing the attempt to bring our verse into line with the claim that Solomon "was wiser than (*mi*) all other men" (1 Kgs 5:11 4E:31, since the preposition *min* to express the comparative), and that the simple meaning of *lehosip ʿal* in our verse is "to add to," (cf. below 3:14; 2 Chr 28:13).

2:16   On the superiority of sages over fools, there is no stronger expression than that fourteenth-century epigone of Kohelet, Santob de Carrión: "In this world there is no greater superiority—even greater than gold over iron—than that of one man over another. . . . One man can be worth a million others" (*Proverbios morales*, lines 1869–76).

3:1   *an appropriate time*   The pregnant notion of timeliness is recapitulated in the person who performed the vital office of leading out the scapegoat on the Day of Atonement. His title was in fact definitional of man's special characteristic of acting at the appropriate moment: *'ish 'iti,* the "timely man." There seems to be a homiletic usage of the term in 2 Sam 11:1, the incident of David and Bathsheba, which begins by noting that it was the appropriate time (*'et*) when kings go forth to battle, and yet "David remained at Jerusalem." In view of the results of David's dalliance, a more appropriate and timely attention to duties seems strongly hinted.

        under the heavens   Ibn Ezra quotes the opinion of those who see, in the twenty-eight mentions of "time" (*'et*) in the following passage, an allusion to the twenty-eight signs of the Zodiac that the moon traverses each month. This suggestion may help distinguish this phrase from its more common variant "under the sun," with which it is usually regarded as synonymous. The phrase occurs in 1:13 and 2:3. In the first it certainly has the context of universal determinism; in the second, by intimating the same point it adds to K's pessimism and anticipates his answer: "Nothing." In the present context P picks up on the suggestion of universal determinism in K's previous usage and asserts that even "under the heavens" man can choose the right time. One would be hard put to find a more compact statement of the theological paradox of God's total power and man's freedom to choose. The phrase thus places the Book of Kohelet within the traditional theological perspective of reward and punishment of such texts as Deut 29:19, referring to him who refuses the Covenant and walks in the stubbornness of his heart: "God will blot out his name from *under the heavens,*" meaning that he will forfeit both happiness in the here and now and also a name (*zikaron;* see 2:16 below) hereafter.

3:11   *from beginning to end*   Josef Kara's (1881) analysis (eleventh century) of the entire passage culminating in this verse is a welcome antidote to the overintellectualization of Kohelet's skepticism. I quote it here both because it is virtually unknown to modern commentators and because it anticipates my own argument on the binary movements in creation: "Concerning all of these 'times' [listed in Koh 3:1–8] the text cites things that begin in joy and end in sadness, and also things that begin in sadness and end in joy, and then it explains how God conceals things from His creatures so that they cannot know from beginning to end what God has made. For if humans knew what would be in the end, they would not be happy in the hour of happiness, nor would they grieve in the hour of mourning" (ad loc., 13).

5:8   *of all   ba-kol   kol* with the definite article is a loaded word in the Hebrew Bible. It can of course refer to all members of a category, but it has been applied especially to the works of creation (all things in the category of world), and it may be to this level of meaning that K refers when he asserts that ALL is vanity. Thus, referring to the completion of the works of creation: "And the heavens and the earth were finished (*wa-yekullu*) and all (*kol*) their hosts" (Gen 2:1), and God is referred to as the Creator of all things (*ha-kol*, the All, Jer 10:16; 51:19). When preceded by the preposition *b-* it occurs only seven times in all of Hebrew Scripture, the most famous being perhaps the reference to blessings conferred upon Abraham: "And God blessed Abraham with all (good things)" (Gen 24:1). In two other instances it stresses God's superiority over all His creation: "And His kingdom rules over all" (Ps 103:19); "And You rule over all" (1 Chr 29:12). God's continuing responsibility over the whole creation is stressed by David (1 Chr 29:14): "For from You [comes] the all" (RSV: "For all things come from thee"). For an interesting alternative interpretation see Rashbam (Japhet and Salters 1985) in the next n.

    is subject to the soil   Rashbam comments on the first part of the verse as follows: "*and the advantage of the land:* for all men are the same, for they must all till the soil in order to live and make a living from the work of their hands. Even the king must be a farmer *of a cultivated field.* In that he commands his people, compelling them to till the soil for his needs, he is called a farmer [*'obed 'adamah*]" (see Gen 4:2). Here Rashbam (Japhet and Salters 1985) seems to propose a midrashic reading of 1:3: To the question "What is man's advantage?" he reads the sequel as the answer: "[His advantage resides] in all his labor." The reason he does not propose this reading above is that it is midrashic and departs from the plain meaning. His reason for proposing it here is that it strengthens the argument about to unfold concerning the dignity of human labor.

    Rashbam's attractive alternative reading of the first half of the verse reads the preposition of *ba-kol* as "upon," a sense usually reserved to pejorative contexts (e.g., *damaw bo*, "his blood be upon him," Lev 20:9; Ps 7:17 16E: "His mischief returns upon his own head"). Thus: "The advantage of the land is upon all equally; even the king . . ."

    In view of the unusual difficulties of this text, a further midrashic reading can be proposed, here based on a different vocalization: *melek le-shiddah ne'ebad*, "a king enslaved by '*shiddah*'" (v. 2:8). The allusion would therefore be to Solomon's subjugation either to foreign women or to Egyptian instruments of war-making (see 2:8n.).

6:3   For the importance of a proper burial, Boling (1975, 163) observes, with reference to the burial of Gideon in Judg 8:32, that "there was a persistent belief in ancient Israel that the mortal remains of a man, a unitary individual, 'constituted the very essence of that person in death.' " Cf. also such texts as 1 Kgs 21:19f; 2 Kgs 9; 1 Kgs 11:13; 1 Kgs 14:11–13: "Anyone belonging to Jeroboam who dies in the city the dogs will eat; and anyone who dies in the open country the birds of the air will eat. . . . When you set foot in the city, the child will die. And all Israel will mourn for him *and bury him; for he only of Jeroboam shall come to the grave,* because in him there is found something pleasing to the Lord." Such passages may help explain the Israelite's fear at the Red Sea, as they marched out of Egypt: "Was it for lack of graves in Egypt that You have taken us away to die in the wilderness?" (Exod 14:11). In addition to the sign of divine displeasure implied in the lack of a proper burial, the disappearance of all remains (were they not carrying Joseph's bones?) may indicate a diminished portion in the worlds to come. This seems to be one of the points of Abraham's endless haggling with Ephron the Hittite, to acquire an *aḥuzat qeber,* a grave that would become a perpetual possession. The complaint expressed in the Exodus verse is therefore not the death itself but rather the death *"in the wilderness."* This is at least in part the horror felt at the destruction of the Egyptians: "not one of them remained" (Exod 14:28). When the event is recounted in Ps 106 the language is more reminiscent of Kohelet: *eḥad me-hem lo' notar* (v. 11), "they were all destroyed, and completely."

6:6   *a thousand years twice over*   The closest parallel to my knowledge is the midrashic reading of Dame Wisdom's words in Prov 8:30: "I was daily [*yom yom*] His delight, rejoicing before Him always." Since "day" is defined as a thousand years in Ps 90:4 ("For a thousand years in Your sight are like yesterday"), *yom yom* would be equivalent to two thousand years. Such a reading would add a different hint to the present context: Even if a person had the longevity of Wisdom and lived forever, in contrast to Wisdom there would be absolutely no delight.

11:1   The metaphor of food for sexual relations can be traced to the story of the temptation of Joseph: "[his master] left all that he had in Joseph's charge; and having him there he had no concern for anything but the food (*leḥem*) which he ate" (Gen 39:6). Joseph is quite explicit as to what this "food" actually is (39:8–9), as he tells his master's wife: "My master has no concern about anything in the house . . . nor has he kept anything from me except yourself, because you are his wife." In Jewish exegesis this understanding is quite common, as can be seen in Rashi's citation of Gen 39:6 in explanation of Jethro's remark on Exod 2:20: "THAT HE MAY EAT BREAD: Perhaps he [Moses] may wed one of you." This exegetical background may explain why Rashi, on the present verse, cites the example of Jethro: "FOR YOU WILL FIND IT AFTER MANY DAYS: Jethro thought that Moses was an Egyptian and would never see him again. But what did happen in the end? He became his father-in-law . . ."

in the abundance of the waters   be-rob ha-yamim   Traditional criticism has invariably focused on the metaphorical puzzle of the first half of the verse, thus disregarding the perhaps more crucial second half, which it reads temporally, as focusing on some variant of the future, when the good deed will be rewarded: thus, "after many days" (Gordis 1968, Crenshaw 1987), "in the course of time" (Fox 1989). It must be admitted, however, that this temporal usage of the preposition *be-* is peculiar, unless it indicates time when, thus "in the days of harvest" (Zer-Kabod 1973). Any attempt to save the temporality of this difficult expression must resort to Lev 25:16: *le-pi rob ha-shanim,* "according to the number of years . . . ," which retains the definite article but would assume the interchangeability of "days" and "years" (Job 32:7 and frequently) and does not use the preposition *be-*. It is perhaps due to the difficulty of this expression that Kittel (1937, 1226) proposes *be-leb ha-yammim,* "in the heart of the waters." Such a proposal, undoubtedly patterned on Ez 27:4 and Ps 46:3 (*be-leb yammim,* never with the article), has the advantage of the parallelism of "waters" and "oceans"—thus more than mere alliteration, as Crenshaw (1987) has pointed out.

This proposal also enables us to exploit an interesting parallel text. Commentators have often quoted the close parallel from the roughly contemporaneous Egyptian Instruction of Onchsheshonqy (Lichtheim 1980, 174), but without noting its possible relevance:

> Do a good deed and throw it in the water;
> when it dries you will find it."

What this parallel helps determine, or at least imagine, is that the focus is on place rather than time, that a good result is dependent less on the passing of time than on the (place of the) waters, the *location* where the "bread" was cast and will therefore be found. The message would thus forecast the saying two verses later (11:3) which asserts that wherever the seed (alternatively, the tree) falls, you can be confident that that is where it will be, that it will not be out of reach or unattainable or lost. Of course, one would then want to pursue this new image: "for it is in the abundance of the waters that you will find it again," perhaps by recalling P's argument of the fullness of creation (see Introduction 3b) as against K's perception of depletion.

2

Excursus: Dialogue and Its Methods

(2a) Dialogue and Literary Criticism, or "Who Is Speaking?"

In recent literary criticism there is a growing sense of the centrality of dialogue to works of literature in general; indeed, such authors as Bakhtin have viewed literature as dialogic in its essence.[1] This perception includes but goes beyond the generic genres favorable to dialogue such as the drama. It views texts as textures or weavings of various voices, with threads of dialogue that travel in countless directions, at the level of language, narration and genre, tradition, intertextuality, dialogue of discourses, and the like. When students of the Bible study the text as citation and critique of previous texts, they are working with these assumptions. When, for example, critics study the creation story in Genesis as anti-myth, as a deliberate refutation of current ideologies concerning the world's creation, they are viewing the text in one of its dialogic functions.[2] Recent research is beginning to show how proverbs such as those found in Kohelet reveal the presence of an especially intensified level of dialogue, due to their paradigmatic character:

> The dialogue of discourses in the proverb is not of a finalized, emblematic character. It is an ongoing dialogue. The proverb reveals the continuous dialogue between the different discourses that are brought into contact within its framework. Similar to its next of kin, the quotation, the proverb refers constantly to a discourse external to its own occurrence.
>
> (Hasan-Rokem 1990, 106)

1. See Bakhtin (1982); Todorov (1981); Gadamer (1980); Mukarovsky (1977); Bialostosky (1986).

2. I would add that when an earlier generation of critics (Podechard 1912, Barton 1908) tried to deal with Kohelet's contradictions and rapidly shifting argument by imagining multiple sources, they proceeded in the same way, by first distinguishing the multiple voices in the text, by asking "who is speaking?" My suggestion is to avoid extraneous searches, either before or beyond the text, and to conceive of the multiplicity of voices or points of view as inherent in the work's literary structure.

As an example of how a dialogue of discourses can work in a literary text, consider the following description of the Baron's château from the beginning of Voltaire's *Candide* (through the added words in brackets I expand the dialogic possibilities of the text, but without changing its basic nature):

> Monsieur le Baron was one of the most powerful lords of West-phalia [and therefore of the entire world], for his château had a door and windows.

In this single sentence three points of view intersect, for the narrative voice at the start is interrupted twice: by a voice of provincial pride ("and therefore . . ."), and yet again by a more "learned" provincial voice that gives the reason for its greatness ("for it had . . ."). Surely, one may object that it is the same narrative voice from start to finish, uninter-rupted by any of the usual markers of change of voice such as quotation marks. Yet it would be naive to maintain that these two additions ex-press the actual beliefs of the narrator; if the passage is read aloud, then the junctures at which the voice changes would indeed be "marked," perhaps by a slight raising of the voice indicating an ironic distancing. Such a marker is indicative, if not of a change of narrative voice, of something more significant still: a change of perspective, the introduc-tion of a different point of view (with which, of course, the main narra-tor takes an ironic perspective). But one should also note that, despite the absence of quotation marks, the apparently smooth texture of the prose is far from seamless: the shift in voice in each instance is marked, in this case by the marker of conclusion "therefore" and by the marker of cause "for" (*car* in French, *ki* in Hebrew; see below, sec. 2c, Dialogic Markers). Such markers naturally arouse the suspicion of modern read-ers, as a realist or factual narrator does not intrude himself or herself into a narrative with an explanation or a conclusion. This brief text can thus be described as a dialogue of several voices, and from this perspective the main literary problem is to ask, at every juncture, Barthes's crucial question: "Who is speaking?"[3]

---

3. Barthes (1970) focuses on the problem and summarizes the method in one of his asides: "Who is speaking? Is it Sarrasine? The narrator? The author? Balzac the author? Balzac the man? Romanticism? The bourgeoisie? Universal wisdom? The crisscross (*croisement*) of all these origins is what forms literature" (178).

(2b) Dialogue in Ancient Literature and the Hebrew Bible

In a broader sense it would also be possible to sketch out a dialogic view
of reality, to study its emergence into Western culture, and even to
pinpoint the moment when it separated itself from monological and
mythological thinking, when Socratic critical reasoning demurred from
the tribalism of the epic (Havelock 1963). When dialogics erupted upon
the scene of Greek culture in the form of the Platonic dialogue, however,
dialogue as a literary form had long been in existence in lands that came
into closer contact with the Hebrew Bible during the period of its composition. One commonly cites such texts as the Egyptian *Dispute over
Suicide,* or the Babylonian *Dialogue about Human Misery* and *Dialogue of
Pessimism,* which have the literary form of dialogues and also, to an
extent, its spirit.[4] The latter text in particular, the Sumerian *Dialogue of
Pessimism,* is commonly regarded as entirely dialogue and yet displays
none of the usual dialogue markers (Lambert 1960, 139–49; Pritchard
1955, 600–601).

Of course, Hebrew Scripture itself is permeated with dialogue. It is
true that cultic and legal parts of the Torah are typically recorded with no
dissent, but its covenantal theology is based on exchange and dialogue:
Abraham and Moses argue with God, and I–Thou describes the relation
between God and the People from start to finish. In the prophetic writings sharp debate or contestation is a matter of course, and wisdom
literature can be described as contestatory in its essence.[5] Childs (1979,
557) put it nicely:

> The canonical ordering of chs. 10ff. [of the Book of Proverbs]
> . . . has retained the sharp polarities, even flat contradictions, in
> successive proverbs which derive from the earliest collections.
> One hermeneutical implication to be drawn from this shaping is
> that the proverbs continue to function within scripture in their
> original dialogical role.

The implications of this observation for further research should be carefully reflected upon, the possibility that the final dialogic form of such
wisdom texts as Kohelet merely continued and developed earlier forms
of thinking and argumentation. Surely, such a text as Job, which is

---

4. These texts are briefly discussed, with appropriate references, in Scott (1965, xlvi–li).
The topic of ancient dialogue in relation to the Bible deserves its own monograph; for further
reading see Crenshaw (1981), Dijk (1953), Lambert (1960), Lichtheim (1980), Pritchard (1955),
Scott (1970).

5. See especially Perry 1993a, Part Three.

explicitly dialogic and contestatory, would argue in favor of such a likelihood. At any rate, Brueggemann (1970) argues for a return to the dialogic wisdom of the Sages as expressed in wisdom literature, as a way to get beyond the "I-have-all-the-right-answers" attitude that came to dominate theological thinking. What is meant, of course, is dialogue "not as a technique but as a way of life" and a "style of faith" (5); against the polarization of our "salvation" approach, we need "the mood of dialogue where the wise men lived" (7).

Dialogic views of wisdom texts have been expressed by many critics but never formalized into a consistent method of interpretation and translation.[6] A bold step in this direction is Scott's (1965, 175–76) treatment of Prov 30:1–9, which he entitles "Dialogue with a Skeptic":

> The words of Agur ben Yakeh of Massa'.
> The man solemnly affirmed, "There is no
> God! . . . For I am more brute than man,
>   And I am devoid of human understanding.
> I have not learned wisdom,
>   Nor have I knowledge of a divine Being . . .
> What is his name . . . ? Surely you know."
>   (Prov 30:1–4)

Scott senses that the next verses (5–6) are the answer of an orthodox believer to the skeptical challenge of vv. 1–4, according to which "there is no God":

> "Everything God says has stood the test . . . !
> Do not add to his words,
>   Lest he rebuke you and prove you a liar!"
>   (Prov 30:5–6)

This would be, of course, a classic instance of Gordis's (1968) theory of quotation, consisting of the introduction of another point of view. This procedure seems justified in this case by the direct address ("Surely *you*

---

6. The contradictions of Kohelet, though usually taken as referring to content, are typically resolved by critics at the level of structure. Among the views expressed are the following: dialogue (Herder), quotation (Gordis 1968; Fox 1980), diatribe (Lohfink 1980), view/review structure (Ginsberg 1950, 1961), polar structures (Loader 1979), stichoi or twinning (Rousseau), "yes . . . but" reasoning (Müller 1968; Galling 1969 [1940]), one or more redactors (Lauha 1978, who thinks there were two), psychological development (Crenshaw 1987, 48–49), gloss (Crenshaw 1987, 155). Teasingly, Crenshaw (1987, 47) concludes his lengthy synopsis with the question: "Can one detect, then, two voices in dialogue, as Herder thought, as one stating a thesis and the other its antithesis?"

know"), but what makes such a reading attractive is not stylistic but conceptual. Indeed, there are in this text no formal markers indicating change of voice, and one must rely on the perception of abruptly juxtaposed contradictory opinions. It should be added that this example goes beyond a quotation by a dominant and hostile narrator, as this narrator allows the voice of the other to speak in his own words.

Closer to the possible situation behind Kohelet, there is the issue of the representation of Solomon in 1 Kgs in all his complexity. On the one hand, he is portrayed as the wisest of men and legitimate successor of the Davidic line and builder of God's Holy Temple on earth; on the other, there is no attempt to skirt his love of women (like his father) and life of pleasure and forced labor imposed on the population. Scholars are now turning their attention to the attempts in the biblical record itself to deal with these contradictions of character, but there can be little doubt that the text of Kings entertained the various views rather than attempting to bowdlerize the texts and reduce the complexity of character (cf. K. Parker 1988).

(2c) Dialogic Markers

In applying this approach to Kohelet, one of the major problems becomes the identification of levels of dialogue. General theory is fine, but one may still legitimately ask, in the absence of quotation marks,[7] how the reader can recognize changes in voice. At the stylistic level many such markers have been pointed out by critics and include the following:

(a) The alternation between an autobiographical "I" ("I Kohelet") and a voice that speaks of, if not to, that character ("Kohelet was . . ."; see 1:1, 1:2, 1:12, 7:27, 12:9, 12:10).

(b) Within the autobiographical "I" there may also be an internal dialogue, a confrontation of differing points of view ("I spoke with my heart"; cf. 1:13, 1:16).

(c) The "orthodox" presence that contradicts many of the arguments of the book and whose voice may therefore extend throughout the text. Indeed, even conservative critics admit that such an "epilogist" may

---

7. Quotation marks never occur in the Hebrew Bible, but there are convenient substitutes, the most popular being derivatives of 'amar such as va-y'omer, "and he said," and le'emor, "saying." However, it is significant that such markers can be bypassed, as in 1 Sam 20:21: "And behold I will send the lad go find the arrows." In order to clarify the interruption of voice, the RSV is obliged to render as follows: "And behold, I will send the lad, *saying,* 'Go, find the arrows' " (emphasis added).

occasionally appear within the main text and not merely at the fringes.[8] But what is the criterion for recognizing such intrusions except that of argumentative consistency?

(d) Kohelet has the sound of a spoken text, as evidenced by the following:

- Frequent questions (e.g., 1:3, 2:2, 2:12, 2:15, 2:19, 2:22, 3:9, 3:21, 4:8, 4:11, 6:6, 6:8, 6:12, etc.)[9]

- Use of the direct address form "you" (2:1, 4:17, 5:1, 5:4–5, 5:7, 7:16–17, 7:21–22, 9:7, 9:9–10, 11:2, 11:5–6, 11:9, 12:1, also "my son" 12:12)

- The imperative (4:17, 5:6, 7:14, 7:17, 7:21, 8:2, 9:7, 9:9–10, 10:4, 10:20, 11:1, 11:6, 11:10)

- Uses of the formulaic "don't say" (*'al tom'ar:* 5:5, 7:10, 12:1)[10]

There exists also in Kohelet a series of stylistic markers indicating change of speaker or voice:

• *GAM* ("yet")   There is an adversative use of this particle in 2:14 and 4:8 (but see nn.), where it is construed with a preceding *waw;* in 8:17 the *waw* is attached. In 5:18 it is used alone. This particle does not of course always indicate a change of speaker (e.g., 4:14).[11]

• *WAW* ("and" or "but")   The contradictory meaning of this conjunction is especially prevalent in wisdom sayings, and its frequent use in this contradictory function gives rise to what I have called strong reading. Indeed, the multivalent *waw*- connective (Berlin 1985, 6), vague as to the relationship being specified (it can be read as "and, but, since, although, therefore, so that"), often requires a pause and reflection on the precise relation to the preceding, thus again giving rise to the crucial question "who is speaking now?"

• *'ANI* "I" serves not only the purposes of autobiography but also of debate, to set off K's position from that of his interlocutor (cf. 8:2). Similarly, the pleonastic use of the subject pronoun, usually *'ani,* repeated immediately after the verb, is characteristic of Kohelet's style

8. "No satisfactory solution to the problem exists. Because it is almost universally recognized that an epilogist has added the final verses of the book, it is quite possible that the same person inserted 8:12b–13" (Crenshaw 1987, 155).

9. I include here what is usually designated as rhetorical questions, which may be no more than assertions. However, even these gain in pertinence by being related to a dialogic context, by which I mean, of course, not a communication with a reader but rather with another character; cf. 1:3n. *what profit hath.*

10. See Crenshaw (1975, 48–55).

11. See Gordis (1968, 222) and BDB (5).

(e.g., 1:16; 2:24), occurring twenty-two times. Frequently in Kohelet it marks a change of speaker and an objection to what was previously said, as suggested by two texts from Job: "What you know, I also know" (13:2); "Let me have silence, and I will speak" (13:13).

• *KI*   We have observed in the Voltaire text cited above that causatives (*ki* often means "because") are suspect in that they can introduce an extraneous explanation or new idea, be it an ironic one of the narrator. V. 9:4 begins with this particle, which Gordis (1968, on 9:4) calls emphatic and used to introduce a section. Somewhat differently, in Deut 20:19 it is usually taken as the sign of a question, thus synonymous with the Rabbinic expression *we-ki:* "Are the trees in the field men that they should be besieged by you?" Rashi gives the Hebrew equivalent as *dilma',* "perhaps," which introduces a strong hypothesis with which one is invited to disagree.[12] The use of this particle in Kohelet to introduce a refutation invites further reflection on its adversarial uses; cf. 2:21, 25; 8:12, 16, 17; 9:10 (Crenshaw 1975, 49 and nn. 5, 6).

One highly interesting application of the dialogic use of *ki* occurs in the Mishnah (Abodah Zarah 2:5) as a commentary on Cant 1:2: "O that he [RSV: you] would kiss me with the kisses of his [RSV: your] mouth! For (*ki*) your love is better than wine." In spite of the traditional masculine reading *dodeka* ("your love") supported by Rabbi Joshuah, Rabbi Ishmael preferred to read the feminine *dodayik,* thus viewing the second statement *as a reply* by the lover to his beloved:

> Beloved: "Let him kiss me . . ."
> Lover: "Your love is better than wine."

In order for R. Ishmael to propose this, it seems necessary to interpret the *ki* particle no longer as "for" but rather as a particle marking a change of speaker.[13]

The MT preserves several examples of this dialogic use of *ki* as indicating a shift in the narrative voice from the narrator to another party. The pattern is the following:

> . . . and you shall say, "And your servant Jacob is behind us." For he thought [*ki 'amar,* lit. "for he said"], "I may appease him with the present that goes before me . . ." (Gen 32:21)

12. At times questions are simply implied without any markers whatever, as in the heated dialogue between Nathan and the aging King David (1 Kgs 1:24). More frequently, *ki* serves not to explain anything but rather as the simple equivalent of our quotation marks, as in Jos 2:24: "And they said to Joshua, (*ki*) 'the Lord has given . . .' " For the use of *ki* for a question marker, see 7:3n. *Can an angry face.*

13. The suggestion that the statement beginning with *ki* is the reply of the lover seems supported by the Septuagint, which reads *dodim,* "breasts," for *dodeka.*

In order to mark the start of a quotation, other narrative contexts of course used the more explicit part of this pattern:

> Now Adam knew Eve his wife, and she conceived and bore Cain, saying [*wa-t'omer,* "and she said"], "I have gained a man with the help of the Lord." (Gen 4:1)

However, the parallel function of *'amar* and *ki* is demonstrated by the following substitution or variant:

> Joseph named the first-born Manasseh, meaning [*ki*], "God has made me forget completely my hardship and my parental home." (Gen 41:51)[14]

Two further examples bring the discussion full circle and back to a proverb context. Consider the following:

> Then Zebah and Zalmunna said, "Rise yourself and strike us down; for [*ki*] as a man is, so is his strength." (Judg 8:21)

The last statement is in all probability a quotation of a popular proverb, so that a different rendering would be needed:

> "Rise yourself, and strike us down. For [as they say], 'as a man is, so is his strength.' "

Another example of *ki* ("for, as they say"), indicating the rapid introduction of another point of view, is Whybray's (1989) highly interesting—and probably intuitive, since he adduces no further examples—interpretation of Jer 18:18, which would suggest the following punctuation:

> Then they said, "Come, let us make plots against Jeremiah, for [as they say]:
> 'Law shall not perish from priest,
> nor counsel from wise man,
> nor word from prophet.'
> Come, let us smite him with the tongue, and let us not heed any of his words."

14. Trans. NJV; RSV: " 'For,' he said, 'God had made me forget . . .' " Sarna (1989, 39) refers to the quotation in Gen 4:25 as similarly "unintroduced"; I argue that such introduction is performed by *ki*.

Whybray views this as probably "a quotation, introduced by the particle
ki, a quotation which serves the purpose of supporting in some way the
resolve of the speakers to plot against Jeremiah."[15]

As a final, and in my judgment convincing, use of the particle *ki* as a
formal equivalent of a marker opening a quotation, consider the question raised by Abrabanel on 1 Kgs 1:13:[16]

> In verses 13 and 17 it is stated "Didst thou not O lord swear that
> Solomon thy son shall reign after me and that he shall sit upon
> my throne?" Surely it should rather have stated: "that Solomon
> my son shall reign after *thee* and he shall sit upon *thy* throne."

Abrabanel's answer is convincing:

> Because she wanted to recall the oath in the very words in which
> David had spoken them.

In other words, Bathsheba has very good reasons for citing to the king
the very specific words with which he committed himself, and the best
way to do this is through direct quotation. Many translators have tacitly
identified the stylistic problem here, by rendering the oath as direct
quotation. Thus

> Go in at once to King David, and say to him, "Did you not, my
> lord the king, swear to your maidservant, saying [*le'emor ki*],
> 'Solomon your son shall reign after me, and he shall sit upon my
> throne'? Why then is Adoni'jah king?" (RSV, v. 13)

What is recognized here is the use of *le'emor ki* as a citational marker, but
the final step of the process has not been clearly perceived:

> She said to him [Bathsheba to David], "My lord, you swore to
> your maidservant by the Lord your God, saying [*ki*], 'Solomon
> your son . . .' "

15. In a note Whybray (1989) offers the further possibility that the quotation is actually
from Jeremiah's own poetic oracle, thus: ". . . for it is not true that 'Law shall perish from
priest . . .' " Whybray rejects this contradictory use of *ki* on the ground that "there is no
evidence that Jeremiah had in fact spoken these words," by which Whybray means that the
prophet did not speak them as a saying, for the critic already acknowledged that such was in
fact Jeremiah's threat in other passages (27).

16. I quote from Aryeh Newman's translation, in Leibowitz (1981, 255). This function of *ki*
was not noticed in the otherwise excellent study by Schoors (1981).

The virtual juxtaposition of *le'emor ki* and *ki* as equivalent expressions makes it easier to view the compression of the longer formula into the shorter one and to explain how *ki* came to function as the equivalent of our marker introducing a quotation.[17]

• *RE'EH* "look, consider"   Often indicates a change of point of view (see 1:10 and n.).

Repetitions are extremely frequent in dialogue, as when one speaker takes up the words of another for ironic or sarcastic purposes. In a sequence such as 7:13–14, for example, the second speaker repeats the *RE'EH* ("enjoy," also "consider") of the first, as if to say: "Now *you* consider." In 7:27–29 the technique is even more pronounced: "Look, I have found this," which is mimicked in the reply: "And *I* have found *this*."

Repetitions are thus an important element of refutation and emphasis. In Kohelet this frequently takes the form of irony and wordplay, so that one should be on guard when words and sound patterns are repeated in close proximity.[18]

Ultimately, however, the main criterion for deciding change of voice is consistency of argument, based on the coherent points of view with which the text is woven. In order to get a clearer view of the workings of debate and dialogue in this work, it is therefore necessary to see what exactly the issues are and how they conflict. Then it is important to ask, as we did at the end of the Introduction, why it was necessary to repre-

17. As a further example consider two parallel texts:

> And Gad came that day to David, and said to him, "Go up, rear an altar to the Lord on the threshing floor of Araunah the Jebusite." (2 Sam 24:18)

This direct quotation is later rendered as follows:

> The angel of the Lord commanded Gad to say to David that David should go up and rear an altar . . . [*le'emor le-Dawid ki Dawid ya'aleh*]. (1 Chr 21:18)

What is interesting about this example is that the usual quotation marker *le'emor* is preempted by the Lord's speech to Gad, so that another marker (here *ki*) is needed. Thus, another rendering seems possible:

> The angel of the Lord commanded Gad to say to David: "Let David go up and rear an altar . . ."

Schoors (1981) has a different explanation here (255).

As another example consider the following, notable for the indecision of the translator:

> The Lord God has sworn by his holiness that, behold [*ki hinneh*], the days are coming upon you . . . (Amos 4:2)

Schoors (1981, 249) insists on the clumsiness of this version and rightly prefers the omission of "that" but neglects to insert the implied quotation marks:

> The Lord God has sworn by his holiness: "behold, the days are coming upon you . . ."

18. See notes to 2:15, 4:1, 4:3, 8:9, 9:5, 10:9.

sent *both* sides of the debate, why contradictions are not incidental but rather essential to Kohelet's spirituality.[19]

(2d) Debates in Proverbs

Debates in proverbs are well known to folklorists as well as students of literature. Recall, for example, those Renaissance collections entitled "The Crossing of Proverbs," which strip away all contextual settings and set one proverb against another (Taylor 1965, 7). From the use of such techniques in African law cases and disputes (Messenger 1959), it is possible to infer their popularity and antiquity. As observed—or perhaps reconstructed—by Jean Paulhan (Andriantsilaniarivo 1982), here is an excerpt of a conversation between two tribesmen of Madagascar:

IBOALA: This time you will mend your ways, I trust. You lost fifty francs in one evening!

BELELAO: Now is the time to gamble and get them back.

IBOALA: Remember the proverb: *"We don't get what we hope, we lose what we have."*

BELELAO: Forget that. When one has patience, the moment always arrives that proves that *"when the calf is born in autumn, there is both joy and wealth."*

Important in such contexts is the highly allusive and generalizing nature of proverbs, their ability to be applied to widely different situations. But even more crucial than their semantic adaptability is their social flexibility, as proverbs may be a "particularly suitable form of communication in situations and relationships of potential or latent conflict" (Finnegan 1981, 31). In Kohelet the debate is in fact dangerous, as the power balance is heavily weighted:

> Kohelet versus the Creator
> The Presenter-Adviser versus Kohelet the King
> The student and commentator (Presenter) versus
>   Kohelet the Sage

In consequence, advice and especially criticism has to resort constantly to a language of indirection, of stating the truth while leaving a way

---

19. As a point of contrast, the creation story in Genesis, although certainly written to dispute certain theological claims, "is spoken quietly, without polemic or debate" (Cassuto 1969, 1).

out.[20] Fortunately, the omnipresence of irony and sarcasm assures us that humor is never far off.[21]

Such techniques often occur in strings, and there are numerous examples in our text: 1:1–11, 3:1–8, 3:14, 4:5–6, 5:9, 7:1, 8:3, 9:11, 10:8–11, 11:1–6.[22]

20. For further uses of the language of indirection in our text, cf. 1:8n. *cannot speak;* 1:9n. *what will be . . . ;* 5:1n.; 8:3n. *don't remain;* 10:5n.; 10:8–11.
21. Because "proverbs tend to take themselves very seriously" (A. Parker 1981, 268), they are thus good candidates for debunking.
22. In Perry 1993a I discuss the string phenomenon, with specific reference to Kohelet 7:1–8 and 4:2–12.

Selected Bibliography

Alter, Robert
  1989   *The Pleasures of Reading in an Ideological Age.* New York: Simon and Schuster.
Amichai, Yehuda
  1991   "Poems, Prayers and Psalms. Interview." *Jerusalem Post International Edition.* August 10:12.
Andriantsilaniarivo, E.
  1982   "Hain-teny." In *Cahiers Jean Paulhan,* 2:274–85. Paris: Gallimard.
Babylonian Talmud
  1935–48   Edited by I. Epstein. London: Soncino.
Bakhtin, M.
  1982   *The Dialogic Imagination.* Edited by Michael Holquist. Translated by Caryl Emerson and Michael Holquist. Austin: University of Texas Press.
Barthes, Roland
  1970   *S/Z.* Paris: Seuil.
Barton, George A.
  1908   *The Book of Ecclesiastes.* International Critical Commentary. Edinburgh: T. & T. Clark.
Bergant, Dianne
  1984   *What Are They Saying about Wisdom?* New York: Paulist Press.
Berlin, Adele
  1985   *The Dynamics of Biblical Parallelism.* Bloomington: Indiana University Press.
Bialostosky, Don
  1986   "Dialogics as an Art of Discourse in Literary Criticism." *PMLA* 101:788–97.
Bloom, Harold
  1990   *The Book of "J."* New Haven: Yale University Press.
Boling, Robert G. (translator)
  1975   Judges. Anchor Bible, 6A. New York: Doubleday.
Brettler, Marc
  1991   "The Structure of 1 Kings 1–11." *JSOT* 49:87–97.
Brisman, Leslie
  1990   *The Voice of Jacob.* Bloomington: Indiana University Press.
Brown, Francis, S. R. Driver, and C. A. Briggs
  1907   *A Hebrew and English Lexicon of the Old Testament, with an Appendix Containing the Biblical Aramaic.* Oxford: Clarendon Press.
Brueggemann, Walter
  1970   "Scripture and an Ecumenical Life-Style." *Interpretation* 24:3–19.
  1990   *First and Second Samuel.* Interpretation. Louisville, Ky.: John Knox.
Buccellati, G.
  1972   "Tre Saggi sulla Sapienza Mesopotamica—II Dialogo del pessimismo: La Scienza degli Opposti come Ideali Sapienzale." *Oriens Antiquus* 11:81–100.
Camus, Albert
  1942   *Le Mythe de Sisyphe.* Paris: Gallimard.
Cassuto, U.
  1969   *Commentary on the Book of Genesis.* 5th ed. [in Hebrew]. Jerusalem: Magnes.

Childs, Brevard S.
1979 *Introduction to the Old Testament as Scripture*. Philadelphia: Fortress.
Crenshaw, James L.
1975 "The Problem of Theodicy in Sirach: On Human Bondage." *Journal of Biblical Literature* 94:47–65.
1976 (editor) *Studies in Ancient Israelite Wisdom*. New York: KTAV.
1981 *Old Testament Wisdom*. Atlanta, Ga.: John Knox.
1987 *Ecclesiastes: A Commentary*. Old Testament Library. Philadelphia: Westminster.
Dijk, J. J. A. van
1953 *La Sagesse Suméro-Accadienne*. Leiden: Brill.
Falk, Marcia (translator)
1977 *The Song of Songs: Love Poems from the Bible*. New York and London: Harcourt Brace Jovanovich.
Finkielkraut, Alain
1984 *La Sagesse de l'amour*. Paris: Gallimard.
Finnegan, Ruth
1981 "Proverbs in Africa." In Mieder and Dundes 1981:10–42.
Fishbane, Michael
1979 *Text and Texture*. New York: Schocken.
Fox, Michael V.
1980 "The Identification of Quotations in Biblical Literature." *ZAW* 92:416–31.
1989 *Qohelet and His Contradictions*. Bible and Literature Series No. 18. *JSOT* Supplement Series No. 71. Sheffield: Almond.
Gadamer, Hans-Georg
1980 *Dialogue and Dialectic*. Translated by P. Christopher Smith. New Haven: Yale University Press.
Galling, Kurt
1969 (1940). *Der Prediger*. Handbuch zum Alten Testament 18. Tübingen: J. C. B. Mohr.
Gesenius, F. W.
1910 *Hebrew Grammar*. 2d English ed. Revised by E. Kautzsch. Edited and translated by A. E. Cowley. Oxford: Oxford University Press.
Gilman, Neil
1990 *Sacred Fragments: Recovering Theology for the Modern Jew*. Philadelphia: Jewish Publication Society.
Ginsberg, H. Lewis
1950 *Studies in Kohelet*. New York.
1961 *Kohelet* [in Hebrew]. Jerusalem.
Gordis, Robert
1939–40 "Quotations in Wisdom Literature." *Jewish Quarterly Review* 30:123–47. Reprinted in Crenshaw 1976:220–44.
1968 *Kohelet—The Man and His World: A Study of Ecclesiastes*. 3d ed. New York: Schocken.
1981 "Virtual Quotations in Job, Sumer and Qumran." *VT* 31:410–27.
Greenberg, Moshe (translator)
1983 *Ezekiel 1–20*. Anchor Bible, 22. New York: Doubleday.
Hammer, Reuven (translator)
1986 *Sifre: A Tannaitic Commentary on the Book of Deuteronomy*. New Haven: Yale University Press.
Hamon, Philippe
1981 *Introduction à l'analyse du descriptif*. Paris: Hachette.

Hasan-Rokem, Galit
  1990   "The Esthetics of the Proverb: Dialogue of Discourses from Genesis to
         Glasnost." *Proverbium* 7:105–16.
Havelock, Eric A.
  1963   *Preface to Plato*. Cambridge: Harvard University Press.
Japhet, Sara, and Robert B. Salters
  1985   *The Commentary of R. Samuel Ben Meir Rashbam on Qoheleth*. Jerusalem:
         Magnes.
Jarick, John
  1990   *Gregory Thaumaturgos' Paraphrase of Ecclesiastes*. Society of Biblical Litera-
         ture Septuagint and Cognate Studies Series No. 29. Atlanta, Ga.: Scholars
         Press.
Jastrow, Marcus
  1919   *The Gentle Cynic*. Philadelphia: Lippincott.
  1950   *A Dictionary of the Targumim, the Talmud Babli and Yerushalmi, and the Mid-
         rashic Literature*. New York: Judaica Press.
Jobling, David
  1986   *The Sense of Biblical Narrative*, vol. 2. *JSOT* Supplement Series No. 39.
         Sheffield: Sheffield Academic Press.
Kara, Josef
  1881   *Commentary on Kohelet* [in Hebrew]. Edited by B. Einstein. Berlin: Ad.
         Mamp.
Keil, Yehudah
  1983   *The Book of Proverbs* [in Hebrew]. Jerusalem: Mossad Harav Kook.
Kirshenblatt-Gimblet, Barbara
  1973   "Towards a Theory of Proverb Meaning." *Proverbium* 22:821–27. Re-
         printed in Mieder and Dundes 1981:111–21.
Kittel, Rudolf
  1937   *Biblia Hebraica*. 4th ed. Edited by A. Alt and O. Eissfeldt. MT annotated by
         P. Kahle. Kohelet edited by F. Horst. Stuttgart: Württembergische Bibelanstalt.
Kolakowski, Leszak
  1989   *The Presence of Myth*. Translated by Adam Czerniawski. Chicago: Univer-
         sity of Chicago Press.
Kugel, James
  1981   *The Idea of Biblical Poetry: Parallelism and Its History*. New Haven: Yale
         University Press.
Kuusi, Matti
  1972   *Towards an International Type-System of Proverbs*. Helsinki: *FF Communica-
         tions* 211. Reprinted in *Proverbium* 19:699–735.
Lambert, W. S.
  1960   *Babylonian Wisdom Literature*. Oxford: Clarendon Press.
Lamm, Norman
  1987   "Responsibility and Leadership." *L'Eylah* 23:7–12.
Lauha, Aarre
  1978   *Kohelet*. Biblischer Kommentar Altes Testament 19. Neukirchen: Neu-
         kirchener Verlag.
Leibowitz, Nehama
  1981   *Studies in Bereshit (Genesis)*. 4th rev. ed. Translated by Aryeh Newman.
         Jerusalem: World Zionist Organization.
Lévinas, Emmanuel
  1969   *Totality and Infinity*. Translated by Alfonso Lingis. Pittsburgh: Duquesne
         University Press.

1976 [1963]   *Difficile liberté*. 3d rev. ed. Paris: Albin Michel.
Lichtheim, Miriam
   1980   *Ancient Egyptian Literature,* vol. 3. Berkeley and Los Angeles: University of
       California Press.
Loader, J. A.
   1969   "Qohelet 3:2–8—A 'Sonnet' in the Old Testament." *ZAW* 81:240–42.
   1979   *Polar Structures in the Book of Qohelet. Beihefte zur ZAW* 152. Berlin: de
       Gruyter.
   1986   *Ecclesiastes: A Practical Commentary.* Grand Rapids, Mich.: Eerdmans.
Lohfink, Norbert
   1980   *Kohelet.* Stuttgart: Echter.
McKane, William
   1970   *Proverbs: A New Approach.* Old Testament Library. London: SCM Press.
Menachem ha-Meiri
   1969   *Commentary on the Book of Proverbs* [in Hebrew]. Edited by Menachem
       Mendel Zahav. Jerusalem: Otsar ha-Poskim.
Messenger, J. C.
   1959   "The Role of Proverbs in a Nigerian Judicial System." *Southwestern Journal
       of Anthropology* 15:64–73.
Mieder, Wolfgang, and Alan Dundes (editors)
   1981   *The Wisdom of Many: Essays on the Proverb.* New York: Garland.
Mishnah
   1932   Edited and translated by Herbert Danby. Oxford: Clarendon.
   1988   Edited and translated by Jacob Neusner. New Haven: Yale University
       Press.
Mukarovsky, Jan
   1977   *The Word and Verbal Art.* Translated by John Burbank and Peter Steiner.
       New Haven: Yale University Press.
Müller, Hans-Peter
   1968   "Wie sprach Qohälät von Gott?" *VT* 18:507–21.
Murphy, Roland E.
   1981   *Wisdom Literature. The Forms of Old Testament Literature,* vol. 13. Grand
       Rapids, Mich.: Eerdmans.
   1990a   "On Kohelet's Theology." Paper presented at the SBL Conference, New
       Orleans.
   1990b   "The Sage in Ecclesiastes and Qohelet the Sage." In *The Sage in Israel and
       the Ancient Near East,* edited by John G. Gammie and Leo G. Perdue, Winona
       Lake: Eisenbrauns, 263–71.
Néher, André
   1951   *Notes sur Qohelet.* Paris.
Neusner, Jacob. *See* Mishnah 1988.
The New Oxford Annotated Bible: Revised Standard Version
   1977   New York: Oxford University Press.
Ogden, Graham S.
   1984   "The Mathematics of Wisdom: Qoheleth IV 1–12." *VT* 34:446–53.
   1987   *Qohelet.* Sheffield: JSOT Press.
Parker, Alexander A.
   1968   *The Allegorical Drama of Calderón: An Introduction to the Autos Sacramentales.*
       Oxford: Dolphin.
   1981   "The Humor of Spanish Proverbs." In Mieder and Dundes 1981:257–74.
Parker, Kim Ian
   1988   "Repetition as a Structuring Device in 1 Kings 1–11." *JSOT* 42:19–27.

Paulhan, Jean
1970 *Le Repas et l'amour chez les Mérinas*. Paris: Fata Morgana.
Perry, T. A.
1986 "Metaphors of Sacrifice in the Zohar." *Studies in Comparative Religion* 16:188–97.
1987 *The Moral Proverbs of Santob de Carrión*. Princeton: Princeton University Press.
1990 "Dialogues with Kohelet: Towards a New Translation of Ecclesiastes." *LIT* 1, vol. 3:191–98, Gordon and Breach, Science Publishers.
1993a *Wisdom Literature and the Structure of Proverbs*. University Park: Penn State Press.
1993b "Just Say No: Montaigne's Negative Ethics." In *Approaches to Teaching Montaigne's Essays,* edited by Patrick Henry. New York: Modern Language Association of America.
Pirkei Abot [Ethics of the Fathers]. In Mishnah 1932:446–61.
Podechard, E.
1912 *L'Écclésiaste*. Paris: Lecoffre.
Pritchard, S. B. (editor)
1955 *Ancient Near-Eastern Texts Related to the Old Testament*. 2d ed. Princeton: Princeton University Press.
Rad, Gerhard von
1972a *Genesis, A Commentary*. Rev. ed. Philadelphia: Westminster.
1972b *Wisdom in Israel*. Nashville: Abingdon.
Rashbam (Samuel ben Meir). *See* Japhet and Salters 1985.
Revised Standard Version (Bible). *See* New Oxford Bible 1977.
Rousseau, François
1981 "Structure de Qohelet I:4–11 et plan du livre." *VT* 31:200–217.
Russo, Joseph
1983 "The Poetics of the Ancient Greek Proverb." *Journal of Folklore Research* 20:121–30.
Sarna, Nahum M.
1989 *The JPS Torah Commentary: Genesis*. Philadelphia: Jewish Publication Society.
Savran, George S.
1988 *Telling and Retelling: Quotation in Biblical Narrative*. Bloomington: Indiana University Press.
Schoors, A.
1981 "The Particle *ki*." *Oudtestamentische Studiën* 21:240–76.
Scott, Robert B. Y.
1965 (translator) Proverbs, Ecclesiastes. Anchor Bible, 18. New York: Doubleday.
1970 "The Study of Wisdom Literature." *Interpretation* 24:24–45.
Skehan, Patrick W. (translator)
1987 *The Wisdom of Ben Sira*. Commentary by Alexander A. DiLella. Anchor Bible, 39. New York: Doubleday.
Sternberg, Meir
1985 *The Poetics of Biblical Narrative*. Bloomington: Indiana University Press.
Tanakh: The Holy Scriptures.
1988 The New JPS Translation According to the Traditional Hebrew Text. Philadelphia: Jewish Publication Society.
Taylor, Archer
1965 "The Study of Proverbs." *Proverbium* 1:7.

Thompson, John Mark
 1974 *The Form and Function of Proverbs in Ancient Israel*. The Hague: Mouton.
Todorov, Tzvetan
 1981 *Mikhaïl Bakhtine: le principe dialogique*. Paris: Seuil.
Verheij, Arian
 1991 "Paradise Retried: On Qohelet 2.4–6." *JSOT* 50:113–15.
Whybray, R. N.
 1974 *The Intellectual Tradition in the Old Testament*. Berlin: de Gruyter.
 1982 "Qohelet, Preacher of Joy." *JSOT* 23:87–98.
 1988 "Ecclesiastes I:5–7 and the Wonders of Nature." *JSOT* 44:105–12.
 1989 Ecclesiastes. New Century Bible Commentary. Grand Rapids, Mich.: Eerd-mans.
Williams, James G.
 1976 "What Does It Profit a Man?: The Wisdom of Kohelet." In Crenshaw 1976:375–89.
 1981 *Those Who Ponder Proverbs: Aphoristic Thinking and Biblical Literature*. Bible and Literature Series No. 2. Sheffield: Almond.
Zer-Kabod, Mordechai.
 1973 *Commentary on Kohelet* [in Hebrew]. Jerusalem: Mossad Harav Kook.
Zimmerli, Walther.
 1933 "Zur Struktur der alttestamentlichen Weisheit." *Zeitschrift für die alttestamentliche Wissenschaft* 10:177–204. Reprinted as "Concerning the Structure of Old Testament Wisdom," in Crenshaw 1976:175–207.
 1962 *Das Buch des Predigers Salomo*. Das Alte Testament Deutsch 16. Göttingen: Vandenhoeck & Ruprecht.

Index

Index of Biblical References

Index of Postbiblical Jewish Texts